The
ANAGRAM
Dictionary

Michael Curl is a computer software specialist who also contributes crosswords and puzzles to a number of journals including the *Guardian* and *Financial Times*. His other publications include *The Yorkshire Puzzle Book*. He is married with three children and lives in Leeds.

The
ANAGRAM
Dictionary

MICHAEL CURL

ROBERT HALE • LONDON

ISBN 0 7090 5864 0

Robert Hale Limited
Clerkenwell House
Clerkenwell Green
London EC1R 0HT

3   5   7   9   10   8   6   4

Printed in Great Britain by
St Edmundsbury Press, Bury St Edmunds, Suffolk.
Bound by WBC Book Manufacturers Ltd,
Bridgend, Mid-Glamorgan

Thy genius calls thee not to purchase fame
In keen iambics, but mild anagram:
Leave writing plays, and choose for thy command
Some peaceful province in Acrostic Land.
Where thou mayest wings display and altars raise
And torture one poor word ten thousand ways.

Dryden

Contents

Ars Magna—The Great Art

A Brief History of Anagrams

According to some historians, anagrams originated in the fourth century B.C. with the Greek poet Lycophron, who found favour with the rich and mighty by devising flattering anagrams of their names. Other sources claim that anagrams date further back to the sixth century B.C. when they were used by Pythagoras and his disciples, who found philosophical meanings therein.

It was believed at this time that anagrams had a mystical significance, and they were at times used in prophecy. Alexander the Great, during the siege of Tyre, dreamed one night of a satyr dancing in the woods. His soothsayers, when they were called on to interpret the dream, revealed that the letters of the word 'satyr' could be transposed to spell 'Tyre is thine'. On the following day the city of Tyre fell to Alexander, thus justifying the soothsayers' faith in anagrams.

Anagrams were also known to the Romans, though most surviving example of Roman anagrams are imperfect. An anagrammatic significance has been attached to the most famous example of Roman word play, the so-called SATOR word square. This word square was first discovered during excavation of the site of the Roman city at Cirencester. It was found inscribed on a wall, and reads as follows:

```
R O T A S
O P E R A
T E N E T
A R E P O
S A T O R
```

This can be translated as 'Arepo the sower guides the wheels at work' or more freely as 'God controls the universe'. The word square was for many years believed to be of early Christian origin, and it was pointed out by one scholar that the letters could be arranged like this:

```
                A
                P
                A
                T
                E
                R
A P A T E R N O S T E R O
                O
                S
                T
                E
                R
                O
```

The A and the O were said to stand for Alpha and Omega—the beginning and the end. This theory lent weight to the view that the SATOR word square was used—as was the pictorial symbol of a fish—in early Christian communities, fearful of persecution, as a cryptic affirmation of the faith.

Various other anagrams were proposed, such as RETRO SATANA TOTO OPERE ASPER (Begone, Satan, cruel in all thy works). Such speculations, however, were ended when another example of the word square was found at Pompeii, the dating of which proved that the square was definitely of pre-Christian origin. So the AREPO word square remains a mystery. Is it merely a piece of clever popular wordplay—the Roman equivalent of our crossword puzzles—or does it have some deeper significance?

After the Greeks and Romans, anagrams did not appear again to any extent until the thirteenth century. They were then used by the Jewish Cabbalists, who again found mystical significance in them.

The popularity of anagrams spread rapidly among the learned of Europe in the Middle Ages. They were especially popular in France, where one Thomas Billon was appointed Royal Anagrammatist to King Louis XIII. King Charles IX of France was also fond of anagrams and delighted in the fact that the name of his mistress Marie Touchet could be transposed to JE CHARME TOUT (the letters I and J at that time being interchangable, as were U and V).

Also in France, a certain André Pujon, discovering that his name could be transposed to PENDU A RION, and having great faith in the mystical nature of anagrams, committed a murder in the town of Rion so that he could be hanged there, thus fulfilling the anagrammatic prophecy.

The principal activity of anagrammatists in the Middle Ages, however, was in forming anagrams on religious texts. One of the most popular texts for this exercise was the Angel's Salutation in Mark's gospel: AVE MARIA, GRATIA PLENA, DOMINUS TECUM (Hail Mary, full of grace, the Lord is with thee). Devoted anagrammatists found literally thousands of different anagrams of this phrase, as, for example: VIRGO SERENA, PIA, MUNDA ET IMMACULATA (Virgin serene, holy, pure and immaculate). It is said that one man alone produced over 3,000 different anagrams from this phrase.

One of the most famous mediaeval anagrams was that based on Pilate's question at the trial of Jesus—QUID EST VERITAS? (What is truth?)—to form the reply VIR EST QUI ADEST (It is the man before thee).

Many authors used pseudonyms based on anagrams. François Rabelais used the name Alcofribas Nasier and Calvinus was the pen-name of Alcuinus. Voltaire was the pseudonym of Arouet 1.j. (Arouet le jeune or Arouet the younger). Honoré de Balzac used the pseudonym Lord Rhoone for some of his earlier works.

In the seventeenth century it was also common practice for scientists to record the results of their research in anagram form if further verification was needed before the discoveries could be published openly. Galileo, Huygens and Robert Hooke, among others, used this system, the purpose being to stake their claim to the discovery and to prevent anyone else from claiming the credit.

In the nineteenth century there was a vogue for forming anagrams from the names of prominent people. Usually these were rather unsophisticated by today's standards—for example, TEAR IT, MEN, I ATONE from MARIE ANTOI-NETTE. Occasionally, however, there were examples which have never been bettered, as, for example, FLIT ON, CHEERING ANGEL for FLORENCE NIGHTINGALE or I LEAD, SIR for DISRAELI. These two anagrams, incidentally, are both the creations of Lewis Carroll, who also challenged his readers to form one word from the letters in NEW DOOR—the answer being, of course, ONE WORD.

The Victorian era was the heyday of the cognate anagram—transposing the letters of a common word or phrase to form another word or phrase with some relevance to the original—turning ASTRONOMER into MOON STARER, for example. Many of the cognate anagrams listed in the appendix originated in this period.

Today the anagram lives on mainly within the confines of the crossword puzzle, where one may discover such little gems as these:

Tree producing fir cone (7)	CONIFER
New Orleans in Italy (7)	SALERNO
Supersonic instruments (10)	PERCUSSION
Soldiers armed with guns? (9)	GUARDSMEN
Noiseless wild animals (9)	LIONESSES
The raffia-weaving business (6)	AFFAIR
They are used for duplicating clients' letters (8)	
	STENCILS

And finally:

INDICATORY ANAGRAM BOOK (10)	DICTIONARY

A

Aaronic ocarina
aba baa
abaca Caaba
abactor acrobat
abactors acrobats
abas baas; Saab; Saba
abash Sabah
abates sea-bat
abba baba
abbas babas
abbé babe
abbés babes
ABC cab
Abdera abrade
abed bade; bead
Abel able; albe; bael; bale; blae;
  Elba; Labe
abele Albee
abet bate; beat; beta
abetment batement
abets baste; bates; beast; beats;
  besat; Sebat; tabes
abhorrent earthborn
abides biased
ablaut tabula
able Abel; albe; bael; bale; blae;
  Elba; Labe
abled baled; blade
abler baler; blare; blear
ables bales; Basel; Basle; blaes;
  blasé; sable
ablest ablets; bleats; stable; tables
ablet blate; bleat; table
ablets ablest; bleats; stable; tables
abling baling
ablution Abutilon
ably blay
Abo boa
aboard abroad; Baroda
abode adobe
abord board; broad
aborded boarded
abording boarding
abords adsorb; boards; broads
abort boart; Rabot; tabor
aborted borated; tabored
aborting borating; taboring
aborts boarts; Strabo; tabors
Abos boas
about U-boat

abrade Abdera
abridge brigade
abridged brigaded
abridges brigades
abridging brigading
abrin bairn; brain; Brian
abroad aboard; Baroda
absit baits
absorber reabsorb
absorbers reabsorbs
abstain Tsabian
abstains Tsabians
abuser bursae
abusers surbase
abut buat; tabu; tuba
Abutilon ablution
abuts buats; tabus; tubas
aby bay
abysmal balsamy
acarian Acarina
acaridan Arcadian
Acarina acarian
acates sea-cat
accidents desiccant
accoil calico
accompt compact
accompts compacts
accourted accoutred
accourting accoutring
accoustrement accoutrements
accoutred accourted
accoutrements accoustrement
accoutres coruscate; court case
accoutring accourting
accoyld cacodyl
accretions Cestracion
accrued cardecu
accrues accurse; accuser
accurate carucate
accurse accrues; accuser
accursed cardecus
accurses accusers
accused succade
accuser accrues; accurse
accusers accurses
acer acre; care; race
acerb brace; caber; cabré
acerous carouse
acers acres; cares; carse; races;
  scare; scrae; sérac

13

aces aesc; case
ache each
achenes enchase
aches chase
acid cadi
acids asdic; cadis
acid test dictates
aciform Formica
acme came; mace
acmes maces
acmite micate
acne ance; Caen; cane
acnode canoed; deacon
acnodes deacons
acol coal; cola
aconites canoeist
acre acer; care; race
acred arced; cadre; cared; cedar;
 raced
acres acers; cares; carse; races;
 scare; scrae; sérac
acrid caird; daric; Dirac
acrobat abactor
acrobats abactors
acrolein Caroline; Cornelia;
 creolian
across Oscars
acrostic Socratic
acroter creator; reactor
acroters creators; reactors
act cat
acted cadet
actinal alicant
actinide indicate
actinides indicates
action atonic; cation
actioning incognita
actions cations; Scotian
active Cavite
acton canto; cotan; octan
actons cantos; Octans
actor Crato; Croat; taroc
actors castor; Castro; Croats; scrota;
 tarocs
actress casters; Castres; recasts
acts cast; cats; scat
acture curate
acute Ceuta
acutes cuesta
ad da
Adamites diastema
Adar Arad
add dad

adder aredd; dared; dread
adders dreads; sadder
addle dedal; laded
addles saddle
addresser readdress
adds dads
adeem Medea
adeems seamed
Adeline aliened; delaine
Aden Dane; dean; Edna
Adeni Andie; Denia; Diane; Edina
Adenis Sendai
adept pated; taped
adepts pasted
adermin Amerind; inarmed
ad finem infamed
adhere header; hedera
adhered redhead
adherent neatherd
adherents neatherds
adherer reheard
adheres headers; sheared
adios aidos
adit dita
adits ditas; staid
adjuster readjust
adjusters readjusts
Adler alder
Adlestrop Portslade
ad lib Blida
adminicle medicinal
administer mistrained
admire Mérida
admirer married
admires misread
admonition domination
admonitive dominative
admonitor dominator
admonitors dominators
adobe abode
adore oared; oread
adored deodar
adorer roared
adorers Drosera
adores oreads; soared
adoring Gordian; gradino; roading
adorn Donar
adorned road-end
adown downa
adpress spreads
ad rem armed; derma; dream
adret dater; rated; tared; trade;
 tread

adrets   daters; stared; trades; treads
Adrian   Andria; radian
adroitly   dilatory; idolatry
adroitness   intradoses
adry   dray; yard
ads   das; sad
adsorb   abords; boards; broads
adoum   Dumaoj maudo
adult   dault
adults   daults
adverb   braved
adverts   starved
advise   Davies; visaed
adze   daze
adzes   dazes
ae   ea
aerometer   areometer
aerometers   areometers
aerometric   areometric
aerometry   areometry
aery   Ayer; eyra; yare; year
aesc   aces; case
aesir   Aries; arise; raise; Riesa; serai;
   Seria
aestival   salivate
aether   heater; hereat; reheat
afar   Afra
affair   raffia
affirmer   reaffirm
affirmers   reaffirms
afield   failed
afire   feria
Afra   afar
afreets   feaster; sea-fret
afro   faro
aft   fat
afters   faster; strafe
agar   Agra; raga
age   gae
aged   egad; gade; gaed
ageless   sea-legs
agelong   Legnago
Agen   gane; gean; gena
age-old   gaoled; old age
ages   gaes; sage
agger   eggar
aggers   eggars; sagger; seggar
aggress   saggers; seggars
agin   Agni; gain; Gina
agist   gaits
agister   gaiters; sea-girt; stagier;
   strigae; triages
agnail   Anglia; Ilagan

agname   manage
agnamed   managed
agnames   manages; Mesagna
Agnes   geans; genas; Senga
Agni   agin; gain; Gina
agnise   easing
agnostic   coasting; coatings
ago   Coa
agone   Genoa; Onega
agonised   diagnose; San Diego
Agra   agar; raga
agree   eager; eagre
agreed   dragée; geared
agrees   eagres; grease
agrin   garni; grain
ah   ha
ahem   hame; Mahé
aid   Dai; Ida
Aidan   Diana; naiad
aide   idea
aided   idea'd
aider   aired; irade; redia
aiders   irades; raised
aides   aside; ideas; Sadie
Aidin   India
aidos   adios
aids   dais; Dias; Sadi; said; Sida
aiglet   ligate; taigle
aiglets   ligates; taigles
ail   Ali
ailed   Delia; ideal
aileron   alerion; alienor
ailerons   alerions; alienors; Rosaline
ailing   nilgai
ailment   aliment
ailments   aliments; manliest;
   salt-mine
ails   Isla; Lias; Lisa; sail; sial
aim   Mia
aimed   amide; media
aimless   Melissa; mesails; samiels;
   seismal
aims   Amis; Mais; Siam; sima
ain't   Tain; Tina
Aintree   retinae; trainee
air   Ira; ria
air-beds   braised; darbies; sea-bird
aired   aider; irade; redia
airers   raiser; Sérrai; sierra
airless   sailers; serails; serials
airman   Marian; marina
airmen   marine; Marnie; remain
airn   Iran; Nair; rain; rani

15

airs Asir; Isar; rias; sair;
sari
airt rait
airted raited; tirade
airts astir; raits; sitar; Sitra; stair;
stria; tarsi; Trias
airy Iyar
aisle Elias
aisled deasil; ideals; ladies;
sailed
aisles eassil; laisse; lassie
Aisne anise; Siena
ait ita; tai
aits Asti; itas; sati; sita
ajar raja
Akron Koran; krona
Ala Dagh Galahad
Alan anal; lana; nala
Alaric racial
alarm malar; ramal
alarming marginal
alarmingly marginally
alarmist alastrim
alas Sala
Alastrim alarmist
alb lab
Alba Baal; Bala
Alban banal; Laban
albe Abel; able; bael; bale; blae;
Elba; Labe
Albee abele
albeit albite
albert labret; tabler
Alberta ratable
Alberti librate; triable
alberts blaster; labrets; stabler;
tablers
Albi bail; Bali
albino Albion; Alboin
Albion albino; Alboin
albite albeit
Alboin albino; Albion
albs labs; slab
alburnum laburnum
alchemic chemical
alchemist St. Michael
Alcinoüs unsocial
alcove coeval; Levoca
alcoves coevals
Alcuin Lucian; Lucina; uncial
alder Adler
aldern darnel; enlard; lander
alders sardel

Aldine alined; Daniel; Delian;
denial; lead-in; nailed
Aldis dalis; dials; slaid
Aldred ladder; larded; raddle
Aldus lauds; udals
ale e-la; lea
Alec Clea; lace
alecost lactose; locates; scatole;
talcose
Alecto locate
aleft fetal
alegar laager
alerce cereal
alerion aileron; alienor
alerions ailerons; alienors; Rosaline
alert alter; artel; later; ratel; taler
alerted altered; related; treadle
alerting altering; integral; relating;
triangle
alerts alters; artels; laster; ratels;
salter; slater; staler; stelar; tarsel
ales Elsa; leas; sale; seal; slae
alevin alvine; venial
alexin xenial
alfa fa-la
al fine finale
Alfred fardel; flared
alga gala
algae galea
Algenib Belgian; Bengali
Algeria regalia
Algerian regalian
Algerines releasing
Algernon non-glare
Algiers lea-rigs
algin align
algor argol; goral; largo
algum almug; glaum; mulga
Ali ail
alibility liability
alible Belial; Biella; labile; liable
alicant actinal
Alice Celia; ileac
alien aline; anile; Elian; liane
alienation alineation
alienator rationale
alienators senatorial
aliened Adeline; delaine
alienism Milesian
alienist Latinise; litanies
alienists Latinises
alienor aileron; alerion
alienors ailerons; alerions; Rosaline

aliens alines; lianes; saline; Selina; silane
align algin
aligned dealing; leading
aligner engrail; learing; nargile; realign; reginal
aligners engrails; realigns; Salinger; sanglier; seal-ring
alignment lamenting
aligns signal
aliment ailment
aliments ailments; manliest; salt-mine
aline alien; anile; Elian; liane
alineation alienation
alined Aldine; Daniel; Delian; denial; lead-in; nailed
alines aliens; lianes; saline; Selina; silane
alining nailing
aliped elapid; paidle; Pleiad
alipeds elapids; lapides; paidles; palsied; Pleiads
Alister realist; retails; saltier; saltire; slatier
alit Atli; Lita; tail; tali
Allan nalla
allées sallee
allegorist legislator
allegorists legislators
allergies galleries
allergy gallery; largely; regally
alliance canaille
all in Lalin
allonge galleon
allonges galleons
allot atoll
allots atolls
allows sallow
alloy loyal
allude aludel
alludes aludels
allure laurel
allured udaller
allures laurels
ally y'all
alma lama
almah halma; hamal
almas lamas
alme Elam; Elma; lame; leam; Lema; male; meal
Almeric Carmiel; claimer; miracle; reclaim

almes lames; leams; males; meals; Salem; samel; Selma
almond dolman; old man
almonds dolmans
almoner nemoral
alms lams; slam
alms-fee females
almug algum; glaum; mulga
alnage Angela; anlage; galena; lagena
alod load; odal
alods loads; odals
aloetics societal
aloft float; flota
alone Olean
along Golan; Logan; longa; NALGO
alp lap; pal
alpine Epinal; penial; pineal
alpines spaniel
alpinist pintails
alps laps; pals; salp; slap
als sal
Alsager laagers
Al Sirat lariats
also Laos; sola
Altair atrial; lariat; latria
altar ratal; talar
altars astral; talars; tarsal
alter alert; artel; later; ratel; taler
alterant alternat
altered alerted; related; treadle
altering alerting; integral; relating; triangle
altern antler; learnt; rental; ternal
alternat alterant
alters alerts; artels; laster; ratels; salter; slater; staler; stelar; tarsal
Althing halting; lathing
altitude latitude
altitudes latitudes
altitudinal latitudinal
altitudinarian latitudinarian
altitudinarians latitudinarians
altitudinous latitudinous
alto lota; tola
altos Salto; Talos; tolas
altruism ultraism
altruist ultraist
altruistic ultraistic
atruists ultraists
aludel allude
aludels alludes

alum   maul; Mula
alumna   manual
Alva   aval; lava; Vaal
Alvin   anvil; nival; Vilna
alvine   alevin; venial
Alvis   salvi; silva; vails; valis; vials
alyssum   asylums
am   ma
amain   amnia; anima; mania
amarant   Maranta
amass   Assam; massa
amassing   siamangs
amateurs   Satu-Mare
amber   bream; embar
ambers   breams; embars; Sambre
amble   blame; Mabel; Melba
ambled   balmed; bedlam; beldam;
   blamed; lambed
ambler   blamer; marble; ramble
amblers   blamers; marbles; rambles
ambles   blames
ambling   balming; blaming;
   lambing
ambo   boma; M'Bao; Moab
ambones   bemoans
ambos   bomas; Sambo
Ambridge   game-bird
ameers   Mersea; seamer
amelcorn   cornmeal
amen   mane; mean; Mena; name
amenable   nameable
amend   maned; Medan; menad;
   named
amende   amened; demean
amender   enarmed; meander;
   renamed
amenders   meanders
amendes   demeans
amends   desman; menads
amened   amende; demean
amening   meaning
amenity   any time
amens   manes; manse; means;
   Mensa; names; samen
ament   Manet; meant
amentia   animate
aments   mantes; stamen
amerce   raceme
amerced   creamed; racemed
amerces   racemes
amercing   creaming; Germanic;
   Mérignac
American   Cinerama; in camera

Americas   mesaraic
Amerind   adermin; inarmed
amherst   hamster
amhersts   hamsters
amic   mica
amices   camise
amid   maid
amide   aimed; media
amides   mid-sea
Amiens   amines; inseam; mesian
Amin   main; mina
amine   animé, en ami; Maine;
   Menai; minae
amines   Amiens; inseam; mesian
amir   Mari; Mira; rami; rima
Amis   aims; Mais; Siam; sima
amiss   missa
ammeter   metamer
ammeters   metamers
amnesties   meatiness; seminates
amnia   amain; anima; mania
Amon   moan; mona; Oman
among   mango
amorets   maestro
amortise   atomiser; Timor Sea
amortises   atomisers
Amos   moas; soma
amount   moutan
amounts   moutans
amoves   vamose
Amoy   Mayo
amp   map; pam
ample   maple; pelma
ampler   Marple; palmer
amply   palmy
amps   maps; pams; samp; spam
amused   Medusa
amuser   Maseru; mauser
amusers   Erasmus; masseur;
   mausers
amuses   assume; Seamus
Amy   may; Mya; yam
an   na
anacreontic   canceration
anadem   maenad
anadems   maenads
anal   Alan; lana; nala
analog   Angola
analogist   nostalgia
anan   anna; nana
anapest   peasant
anapests   peasants
ance   acne; Caen; cane

ancestor enactors; Escatrón
ancestral Lancaster
Anchises inchases
anchor archon; Charon; rancho
anchored rondache
anchorites chain-store
anchors archons; ranchos
anchovies schiavone
ancients canniest; instance
ancile Celina; inlace
ancon Conan
ancones sonance
and dan
andante at an end; Dantean
Andersen ensnared
Andes Danes; deans; Desna;
  sedan; snead
Andie Adeni; Denia; Diane; Edina
Andrew Darwen; dawner; wander;
  warden; warned
Andria Adrian; radian
Androcles colanders
ane ean; Ena; nae
anear arena
aneath Athena
aneled leaden; leaned; nealed
aneling eanling; leaning; nealing
anemic cinema; iceman
anemograph phanerogam
anerly nearly
Aneto atone; oaten; Onate
anew Ewan; wane; wean
angel angle; Galen; genal; glean
Angela alnage; anlage; galena;
  lagena
angelic anglice; Galenic
angelical Galenical
angels angles; gleans
Angelus lagunes
anger range; Regan; renga
angered derange; en garde;
  enraged; grandee; grenade
angering enraging
angers ranges; Sanger; serang
angina Nagina
angle angel; Galen; genal; glean
angled dangle; Glenda
angler regnal
angles angels; gleans
Anglet tangle
Anglia agnail; Ilagan
Anglic lacing
anglice angelic; Galenic

anglist lasting; salting; slating;
  staling
Angola analog
angora Aragon
angostura Argonauts
angrier earring; grainer; rearing
angriest astringe; ganister;
  gantries; granites; ingrates; inert
  gas; reasting
angriness ranginess
angry rangy
angst gants; gnats; stang; tangs
ani Ian
anil lain; nail
anile alien; aline; Elian; liane
anima amain; amnia; mania
animal lamina; manila
animals laminas
animas Maasin; manias; Manisa;
  Samian
animate amentia
animated diamante
animé amine; en ami; Maine;
  Menai; minae
anis Isna; Nias; Nisa; sain; Sian
anise Aisne; Siena
anker Karen; naker; nerka
ankers Karens; nakers
ankh hank; Kahn; khan
ankhs hanks; khans; shank
ankled Kendal
anklets asklent
anlage alnage; Angela; galena;
  lagena
Ann Nan
anna anan; nana
annalist santalin
Annam manna
annas nanas
Anne Enna
Annie inane
annoyed anodyne
annuities insinuate
anodyne annoyed
anoint nation
anointed antinode
anoints nations; onanist
Anselm lemans; mensal
answer awners
answers rawness
ant Nat; tan
antagonist stagnation
ant-bears ratsbane

ante   Aten; etna; neat; Tean
anted   Dante
antedate   edentata
anteing   antigen
antes   etnas; nates; Nesta; Senta;
  stane; stean; Teans
anthem   hetman
anthems   hetmans
anther   Tehran; thenar
anthers   thenars
anthesis   shanties
anthropophagus   phonautographs
anticor   carotin; Cortina
antigen   anteing
Antigone   negation
Antilope   antipole
antimonial   antinomial; lamination
antimonic   antinomic
antimony   antinomy
antinode   anointed
antinomial   antimonial; lamination
antinomic   antimonic
antinomy   antimony
antipole   Antilope
antipyretic   pertinacity
antique   quinate
antiques   quantise
antiseptic   psittacine
antitrade   attainder
antler   altern; learnt; rental; ternal
antlers   rentals; saltern; sternal
antra   ratan
antres   astern; sterna
Antirm   martin
antrum   Truman
ants   Stan; tans
anvil   Alvin; nival; Vilna
anvils   silvan
any   nay
any time   amenity
aorist   satori
ape   pea
apert   pater; peart; Petra; prate;
  taper; trape
apertly   pteryla
apertures   repasture
apery   payer; Peary; repay
apes   apse; peas; spae
apheresis   Pharisees
aphetic   hepatic
aphis   apish; spahi
apices   spicae
Apis   pais; Pias; Pisa

apish   aphis; spahi
aplite   Pilate
apodes   soaped
appal   papal
apparent   trappean
appealing   lagniappe
appel   apple; pepla
appels   apples
append   napped
appends   snapped
appertains   satin-paper
apple   appel; pepla
apples   appels
applies   lappies
appraised   disappear
appress   sappers
apricots   piscator
April   Pilar; prial
aprons   parson; Prosna
apse   apes; peas; spae
apses   passé; spaes
apso   soap
apsos   psoas; soaps
apt   pat; tap
aptly   patly
aptness   patness
aptote   teapot
aptotes   teapots
ar   Ra
Arab   arba; Raab
arable   Arbela
Arabs   arbas; Basra; sabra
Arad   Adar
Aragon   angora
Aram   mara; Rama
Aramaic   cariama
Aran   Nara; rana
Aras   Saar; Sara
Arawaks   Sarawak
arba   Arab; Raab
arbas   Arabs; Basra; sabra
Arbela   arable
arbiter   rarebit
arbiters   rarebits
arbute   Tauber
arc   car
Arcadian   acaridan
arcading   cardigan
arcadings   cardigans
arced   acred; cadre; cared; cedar;
  raced
arch   char; rach
archaism   charisma; machairs

arched   chared
archeress   searchers
arches   chares; chaser; eschar;
  raches; search
Archie   cahier
arching   chagrin; charing
archon   anchor; Charon; rancho
archons   anchors; ranchos
Archy   chary
arcing   caring; racing
arcked   carked; dacker; racked
arcking   carking; racking
arco   Cora; Orca; Roca
arcs   cars; scar
Ardea   aread
ardeb   Bader; bared; beard; bread;
  Breda; debar
ardebs   beards; breads; debars;
  sabred; serdab
Ardèche   reached
Arden   dearn; Derna
ardent   endart; ranted; red ant
are   ear; era
aread   Ardea
areca   Ceará
ared   dare; dear; eard; rade; read
aredd   adder; dared; dread
arede   deare; eared; Reade
aredes   deares; erased; Red Sea;
  reseda; seared
areding   dearing; deraign; gradine;
  grained; reading
arefies   faeries; freesia; sea-fire
arefy   faery; Freya
arena   anear
areometer   aerometer
areometers   aerometers
areometric   aerometric
areometry   aerometry
ares   arse; ears; eras; rase; sear;
  sera
aret   rate; tare; tear
arête   eater; reate; Taree
arêtes   easter; eaters; reates; reseat;
  saeter; teaser; Teresa
arets   aster; astre; earst; rates; reast;
  resat; stare; strae; tares; tears; teras
arett   tater; tetra; treat
aretted   treated
aretting   treating
aretts   stater; taster; taters; tetras;
  treats
argent   garnet

argentic   catering; citrange;
  creating; reacting
Argentine   tangerine
arghan   hangar
argil   grail; Lairg
Argive   garvie; rivage
Argives   garvies; rivages
argol   algor; goral; largo
argon   groan; Ongar; orang; organ
Argonauts   angostura
Argonne   Garonne
Argos   sargo
argot   groat
argots   groats
argue   auger
argues   augers; sauger; Segura;
  usager
Argus   gaurs; sugar
Arician   Icarian
arid   dari; raid
aridness   sardines
Aries   aesir; arise; raise; Riesa; serai;
  Seria
ariette   iterate
ariettes   iterates; treaties; treatise
aright   graith
aril   lair; liar; lira; rail; rial
ariot   ratio
arise   aesir; Aries; raise; Riesa; serai;
  Seria
arisen   arsine; Resina
arises   raises; serais
arish   hairs; Shari
arising   raising
arista   tarsia; tiaras
aristae   Astaire; asteria; atresia
arked   daker; drake; raked
arking   raking
arkose   soaker
arks   Kars; sark
Arlberg   garbler
arles   earls; lares; laser; lears; reals;
  seral
Arlon   loran; Lorna
arm   mar; ram
Armagh   Graham
armaments   men-at-arms
armed   ad rem; derma; dream
Armenian   Marianne
armet   mater; tamer; trema
armets   master; maters; stream;
  tamers
armful   fulmar

armfuls fulmars
armies maires
arming ingram; margin
armlet martel
armlets martels
armpit impart
armpits imparts
armrest smarter
arms mars; rams
Armstrong strongarm
army Mary; Myra
Arne earn; nare; near; Rena
Arnhem Herman
arnica carina; crania
Arno Nora; Oran; roan; Rona
Arnold Landor; lardon; Roland; Ronald
aroid radio
aroids radios
aroint ration
aroints rations
arose soare
aroynt notary
Arp par; rap
arpent enrapt; entrap; panter; parent; trepan
arpents entraps; panters; parents; trepans
arrect carter; crater; tracer
arrest arrêts; raster; raters; Sartre; starer; terras
arrester rearrest
arresters rearrests
arresting astringer
arrests rasters; starers
arrêt rater; terra
arrêts arrest; raster; raters; Sartre; starer; terras
arride raider
arrides raiders
arrish Harris; shirra; sirrah
arrive Rivera; varier
arrives variers
arrowy yarrow
arse ares; ears; eras; rase; sear; sera
arsenate serenata
arsenide nearside
arsenite stearine
arses rases; rasse; sears
arsine arisen; Resina
arsis saris
arson roans; sonar
art rat; tar

artel alert; alter; later; ratel; taler
artels alerts; alters; laster; ratels; salter; slater; staler; stelar; tarsel
Artemis imarets; maestri; maister; misrate; semitar; St. Marie
artesian Erastian; resinata
Arteveld traveled
article recital
articles recitals; sterical
artisan tsarina
artisans tsarinas
artist sittar; strait; strati; traits
artiste attires; striate; tastier
artists sittars; straits; tsarist
artless lasters; salters; slaters; tarsels
Artois ratios
arts rats; star; tars; tsar
artsman Mansart; mantras
artsmen martens; sarment; smarten
arty tray
arums ramus; rusma; Sarum
Arun raun
Arundel launder; lurdane; rundale
arval larva; lavra
Arve aver; rave; vare; Vera
ary Ayr; ray
aryl Lyra; ryal
aryls ryals
Asben banes; beans
ascend dances
ascender reascend
ascenders reascends
ascension canonises
ascent enacts; secant; stance
ascents secants; stances
ascertain Cartesian; sectarian
ascertains Cartesians; sectarians
Ascot coast; coats; costa; Tosca
ascribe Brescia
ascription crispation
asdic acids; cadis
ash has
ash-bin banish
ashen Hanse; Shane
ashet haste; hates; heats
ashets hastes; tashes
ashler lasher
ashlers lashers
ashore hoarse
ashy hays; shay

Asians Niassa
aside aides; ideas; Sadie
asides dassie
Asir airs; Isar; rias; sair; sari
Aske kaes; keas; sake
asked kades
asker kesar; rakes; reaks; saker;
  skear
askers kesars; sakers; skears
askew wakes; wekas
asklent anklets
asleep elapse; please; sapele
asp pas; sap; spa
aspen napes; neaps; panes; peans;
  sneap; spane; spean
aspens sneaps; spanes; speans
asper pares; parse; pears; prase;
  presa; rapes; reaps; spaer; spare;
  spear
asperge presage
asperged presaged
asperger presager
aspergers presagers
asperges presages
aspergill pillagers
asperging presaging
aspers parses; passer; repass;
  spaers; spares; sparse; spears
asperse Parsees
aspersed repassed
asperses Passeres; repasses
aspersing repassing
asphalt taplash
asphodel pholades
aspic Capis; picas; spica
aspirant partisan
aspirants partisans
aspirate parasite; septaria
aspirates parasites; satrapies
aspire paries; Persia; praise
aspired despair; diapers; praised
aspires paresis; praises; Serapis
aspiring praising
asport pastor; portas; sap-rot
asports pastors
aspread parades
asps pass; saps; spas
Assam amass; massa
assaying gainsays
assemble beamless
assent sanest; snaste; stanes;
  steans
assenter earnests; sarsenet

assentor senators; star-nose;
  treasons
assentors star-noses
assents snastes
assert asters; astres; reasts; stares;
  Stresa
asserter reassert; serrates
asserters reasserts
assertion Señoritas
assertor oratress; roasters
asses sasse
asset sates; seats; tasse; Tessa
assets tasses
assignor Signoras
assist stasis
assistant Satanists
assort roasts
assot oasts; stoas; Tasso
assuage sausage
assuages sausages
assume amuses; Seamus
Astaire aristae; asteria; atresia
asteism Matisse; samites; tamises
astelic Castile; elastic; laciest;
  latices
aster arets; astre; earst; rates; reast;
  resat; stare; strae; tares; tears; teras
asteria aristae; Astaire; atresia
asterid astride; diaster; disrate;
  staired; tirades
asterids diasters; disaster; disrates
asterism maisters; misrates;
  semitars
astern antres; sterna
asters assert; astres; reasts; stares;
  Stresa
asthenics Caithness
Asti aits; itas; sati; sita
astilbe bestial; stabile
astir airts; raits; sitar; Sitra; stair;
  stria; tarsi; Trias
Astor roast; rotas; Sarto; taros;
  Troas
astral altars; talars; tarsa;
astray satyra; tayras
astre arets; aster; earst; rates; reast;
  resat; stare; strae; tares; tears; teras
astres assert; asters; reasts; stares;
  Stresa
astrex extras; taxers
Astrid triads
astride asterid; diaster; disrate;
  staired; tirades

astringe angriest; ganister; gantries; granites; inert gas; ingrates; reasting
astringer arresting
astute statue
aswim swami
aswing sawing
asylums alyssum
asyndetic syndicate
at ta
atabal balata
atabeg tea-bag
atabegs tea-bags
at an end andante; Dantean
ate eat; eta; tae; tea
ateliers earliest
Aten ante; etna; neat; Tean
atheism Hamites
atheist staithe
atheists staithes
Athena aneath
Athens hasten; snathe; sneath; thanes
a'thing hating
athirst tartish
Athlone ethanol
Athos hoast; hosta; oaths; shoat
atingle elating; gelatin; genital
atlas Salta
Atli alit; Lita; tail; tali
atoc Cato; coat
atoll allot
attolls allotts
atom moat
atomies atomise; osmiate
atomise atomies; osmiate
atomiser amortise; Timor Sea
atomisers amortises
atomises osmiates
atomists somatist
atoms moats; stoma
atonal Latona
at once octane
atone Aneto; oaten; Onate
atoned donate; nodate
atoner ornate
atones Easton; Seaton
atonic action; cation
atresia aristae; Astaire; asteria
Atreus Auster; Seurat
atrial Altair; lariat; latria
atrip parti; tapir
atrocity citatory

Ats sat
attainder antitrade
attar Tatar
attempered temperated
attempering temperating
attended dentated
attentive tentative
attic tacit
attics static
attire ratite; Tiaret
attires artiste; striate; tastier
attrite tattier; titrate
attrition titration
attune Tetuán
attuned taunted
attunes tetanus
attuning taunting
auction caution
auctionary cautionary
auctioned cautioned; education
auctioning cautioning
auctions cautions
auger argue
augers argues; sauger; Segura; usager
auks skua
auld dual; laud; udal
aumbry bay rum
aunt tuan; tuna
aunter nature; Neutra; tea-urn
aunters natures; saunter; tea-urns
auntie uniate
aunties sinuate
aunts tunas
aural Laura
auric curia
auricled radicule
Auster Atreus; Seurat
Australian saturnalia
authoress share-outs
avails saliva; salvia; Valais
aval Alva; lava; Vaal
Avalon Avlona; Valona
avarice caviare
ave Eva; vae
avenge geneva
avenger engrave
avengers engraves
avens Evans; naves; Sevan; vanes
aver Arve; rave; vare; Vera
Averno Verona
avers raves; saver; vares
averse reaves; Varese

avert   taver; trave
averted   tavered
avertible   veritable
averting   tavering; vintager
averts   starve; tavers; traves; vaster
Aves   save; vaes; vase
avid   diva; Vida
Aviles   Leavis; valise
avine   Neiva
Avis   siva; visa
avital   Latvia
Avlona   Avalon; Valona
avocations   Nova Scotia
avocet   octave
avocets   octaves
Avon   nova
avoset   ovates
avulse   values
awe   wae
a-weather   wheatear
awed   wade
aweless   weasels
awes   wase

awesome   waesome
awing   Wigan
awl   law
awls   laws; slaw
awn   wan
awned   dewan; waned
awner   Narew
awners   answer
awning   waning
awns   sawn; swan
awry   wary
Axel   axle
axes   Saxe
axle   Axel
axle-pin   explain
axle-pins   explains
axons   Naxos; Saxon
aye   yea
Ayer   aery; eyra; yare; year
Ayr   ary; ray
azin   Nazi
azym   mazy

B

baa   aba
Baal   Alba; Bala
Baalite   labiate
Baalites   labiates; satiable
baas   abas; Saab; Saba
baba   abba
babas   abbas
babbled   blabbed
babbler   blabber; brabble
babblers   blabbers; brabbles
babbling   blabbing
babe   abbé
babes   abbés
backer   reback
backers   rebacks
backets   backset; setback
backfire   fire-back
backfires   fire-backs
back-rest   brackets
backset   backets; setback
backsets   setbacks
backside   dies back
backward   drawback
backwards   drawbacks
bacco   caboc
bacon   banco; Coban

bacterial   calibrate
baculites   bisulcate
bad   dab
bade   abed; bead
Bader   ardeb; bared; beard; bread;
   Breda; debar
badge   begad
badger   barged; garbed
badly   baldy
bael   Abel; able; albe; bale; blae;
   Elba; Labe
bag   gab
bagarre   barrage
bagarres   barrages
bagel   belga; gable
bagels   belgas; gables
bagnio   gabion
bagnios   gabions
bags   gabs
Bahai   Bahia
Bahia   Bahai
baht   bath
bahts   baths
bail   Albi; Bali
bailer   librae
bails   basil; labis

Baird braid; rabid
bairn abrin; brain; Brian
bairns brains
baiter barite; terbia
baits absit
bake beak
baker brake; break
bakers basker; brakes; breaks
bakes beaks
baking ink-bag
Bala Alba; Baal
balancer barnacle
balancers barnacles
balas balsa; basal; Sabal
balata atabal
bald blad
balder bedral; blared
baldies disable
baldy badly
bale Abel; able; albe; bael; blae;
 Elba; Labe
baled abled; blade
baleen enable
baler abler; blare; blear
balers blares; blears
bales ables; Basel; Basle; blaes;
 blasé; sable
Bali Albi; bail
baling abling
ballast ballats
ballats ballast
balm lamb
balmed ambled; bedlam; beldam;
 blamed; lambed
balmier Mirabel; mirable; remblai
balmiest timbales
balming ambling; blaming;
 lambing
balms lambs
balsa balas; basal; Sabal
balsamic cabalism
balsamy abysmal
Balt blat
Balts blast; blats
baluster rustable
bam Mab
ban nab
banal Alban; Laban
banalities insatiable
banco bacon; Coban
bander Brenda
banderol Oberland
banderole bandoleer

banderoles bandoleers; endorsable
bandoleer banderole
bandoleers banderoles; endorsable
bandore broaden
bandores broadens
bane bean
banes Asben; beans
banger graben
bangers grabens
bangle Bengal
Bangor barong; brogan
banish ash-bin
banishes banshies
bank nabk
banker barken
bankers barkens
banks nabks
bans nabs; snab
banshies banishes
bantam batman
bantams batsman
banter Barnet
banterings string-bean
banzai Zabian
bar bra; Rab
barbed dabber
barbel rabble
barbels rabbles; slabber
barbet rabbet
barbets rabbets; stabber
bard brad; drab
bards brads; drabs
bardy Darby
bare bear; brae
bared ardeb; Bader; beard; bread;
 Breda; debar
barege bargee
Bareilly reliably
barely barley; bleary
bares baser; bears; braes; saber;
 sabre
barest baster; bestar; breast; Tarbes
bargained gabardine
barge begar; Berga; garbe
barged badger; garbed
bargee barege
barge in bearing
barges garbes
barges in bearings
barging garbing
Bari rabi
baric Carib; rabic
barite baiter; terbia

baritone   obtainer
baritones   obtainers
barium   Umbria
barked   braked; debark
barken   banker
barkens   bankers
barking   braking
Barkis   Biskra
barley   barely; bleary
barn   bran
barnacle   balancer
barnacles   balancers
Barnet   banter
barney   Bayern; Bernay
Barnsley   blarneys
Baroda   aboard; abroad
barong   Bangor; brogan
barongs   brogans
barony   baryon
barque   Braque
barracan   barranca
barrage   bagarre
barrages   bagarres
barranca   barracan
barret   barter
barrets   barters
Barrie   Ribera
bars   bras
Barsac   scarab; Scarba
Barsacs   scarabs
Bart   brat
barter   barret
barters   barrets
Barts   brast; brats
baryon   barony
barytes   betrays
basal   balas; balsa; Sabal
basaltic   cabalist
based   beads
Basel   ables; bales; Basle; blaes;
   blasé; sable
basely   belays
baser   bares; bears; braes; saber;
   sabre
bases   basse
basest   basset; bastes; beasts
bashed   bedash
basil   bails; labis
basin   sabin
basinet   Antibes; besaint; bestain
basinets   bassinet; besaints;
   bestains
basins   sabins

basis   bassi
basker   bakers; brakes; breaks
basketwork   work-basket
basking   ink-bags
Basle   ables; bales; Basel; blaes;
   blasé; sable
Basra   Arabs; arbas; sabra
basse   bases
Bassein   sabines
basset   basest; bastes; beasts
bassi   basis
bassinet   basinets; besaints;
   bestains
bast   bats; stab; tabs
bastard   tabards
baste   abets; bates; beast; beats;
   besat; Sebat; tabes
baster   barest; bestar; breast; Tarbes
basters   bestars; breasts
bastes   basest; basset; beasts
bastion   obtains
basto   boast; boats; sabot; Sobat
Basuto   U-boats
bat   tab
bate   abet; beat; beta
batement   abetment
bates   abets; baste; beast; beats;
   besat; Sebat; tabes
bath   baht
bather   bertha; breath
bathers   berthas; breaths
bathes   Shebat
bathos   boshta
baths   bahts
batman   bantam
bats   bast; stab; tabs
batsman   bantams
battels   battles; tablets
battens   test-ban
batter   tabret
batters   tabrets
battier   biretta; ratbite
battle   tablet
battler   blatter; brattle
battlers   blatters; brattles
battles   battels; tablets
baud   daub
baulk   Kabul
bawble   wabble
bawbles   wabbles
bawler   warble
bawlers   warbles
bay   aby

bayed   beady
Bayern   barney; Bernay
bayou   boyau
bay rum   aumbry
bazar   zabra
bazars   zabras
bead   abed; bade
beadiest   diabetes
beads   based
beadsmen   beam-ends; bedesman
beady   bayed
beak   bake
beaks   bakes
be-all   Bella; label
beam   bema; Emba
beam-ends   beadsmen; bedesman
beamers   besmear
beamless   assemble
beamy   embay; maybe
bean   bane
beans   Asben; banes
bean soup   subpoena
bean tree   Tenebrae
bear   bare; brae
bear-cat   cabaret
bear-cats   cabarets
beard   ardeb; Bader; bared; bread;
  Breda; debar
bearded   breaded
bearding   breading
beards   ardebs; breads; debars;
  sabred; serdab
bearing   barge in
bearings   barges in
bears   bares; baser; braes; saber;
  sabre
bearskin   breaks in; inbreaks
beast   abets; baste; bates; beats;
  besat; Sebat; tabes
beasts   basest; basset; bastes
beat   abet; bate; beta
beater   berate; rebate
beaters   berates; rebates
Beatles   belates
beats   abets; baste; bates; beast;
  besat; Sebat; tabes
beaut   Butea; taube; tubea
beauts   taubes
beavered   bereaved
becalms   scamble
Béchar   breach; Rechab
becharm   brecham; chamber;
  chambré

becharmed   chambered
becharming   chambering
becharms   brechams; chambers
becked   bedeck
bed   deb
bedash   bashed
bedaub   daubed
bedeck   becked
bedel   bleed
bedell   belled
bedels   bleeds
bedesman   beadsmen; beam-ends
bedim   imbed
bedims   imbeds
bedlam   ambled; balmed; beldam;
  blamed; lambed
bedlams   beldams
bedless   blessed
bedrail   ridable
bedral   balder; blared
bedrid   bidder; birded; brided
bedroom   boredom; broomed
bedrop   probed
beds   debs
bed-sit   bidets; debits
bedsore   sobered
beduck   bucked
bedung   bunged
bedust   bestud; busted; debuts
bedusts   bestuds
beeches   beseech
beech-fern   free-bench
beefier   freebie
bee-fly   feebly
been   bene
beer   bere; bree
beers   beres; brees
beet   bete
beetroot   boot-tree
beets   beset; betes
beflum   fumble
beflums   fumbles
begad   badge
begar   barge; Berga; garbe
begild   bilged
begin   being; binge
begins   beings; besing; binges
begird   bridge
begirds   bridges
begrudge   buggered; debugger
begrudges   debuggers
behest   Thebes
bein   Beni; bien; bine

being   begin; binge
beings   begins; besing; binges
Beira   Beria; Eibar
belated   bleated
belates   Beatles
belating   bleating; tangible
belays   basely
beldam   ambled; balmed; bedlam; blamed; lambed
beldame   bemedal
beldames   bemedals
beldams   bedlams
belga   bagel; gable
belgas   bagels; gables
Belgian   Algenib; Bengali
Belgians   Bengalis; singable
Belial   alible; Biella; labile; liable
belied   debile; edible
Bella   be-all; label
belled   bedell
bellied   delible
bellows   Boswell
belonged   englobed
belonging   englobing
below   bowel; elbow
belt   blet
Beltane   tenable
belts   blest; blets
beluga   blague
bema   beam; Emba
bemean   bename
bemeans   benames
bemete   beteem
bemetes   beteems
bemire   bireme
bemires   biremes
bemoans   ambones
bemoil   emboil; emboli; mobile
bemoiled   emboiled
bemoiling   emboiling
bemoils   emboils; mobiles
ben   neb
bename   bemean
benames   bemeans
bendier   inbreed
bends   S-bend
bendy   by-end
bene   been
Bengal   bangle
Bengali   Algenib; Belgian
Bengalis   Belgians; singable
Beni   bein; bien; bine
Benoni   bonnie

bens   nebs; sneb
berate   beater; rebate
berated   betread; debater; rebated
berates   beaters; rebates
berating   rebating
bere   beer; bree
bereaved   beavered
beres   beers; brees
Berga   barge; begar; garbe
Beria   Beira; Eibar
Bernard   brander
Bernay   barney; Bayern
berried   briered
bertha   bather; breath
berthas   bathers; breaths
berthing   brighten
besaint   Antibes; basinet; bestain
besainted   bestained
besainting   bestaining
besaints   basinets; bassinet; bestains
besat   abets; baste; bates; beast; beats; Sebat; tabes
beseech   beeches
beset   beets; betes
besing   begins; beings; binges
besings   bigness
besit   bites
besmear   beamers
besom   mebos
besotted   obtested
besotting   obtesting
best   bets
bestain   Antibes; basinet; besaint
bestained   besainted
bestaining   besainting
bestains   basinets; bassinet; besaints
bestar   barest; baster; breast; Tarbes
bestarred   redbreast
bestars   basters; breasts
bestead   debates
bestial   astilbe; stabile
bestiary   sybarite
bestill   billets
bestir   bister; bistre; biters; tribes
bestrew   webster
bestrews   websters
bestuck   buckets
bestud   bedust; busted; debuts
bestuds   bedusts
beta   abet; bate; beat
bete   beet

beteem   bemete
beteems   bemetes
betes   beets; beset
betid   bidet; debit
betided   debited
betiding   debiting
betrays   barytes
betread   berated; debater; rebated
betreads   breasted; debaters
betrim   timber; timbre
betrims   timbers; timbres
betrod   debtor
bets   best
Betsy   bytes
Bette   Tebet
Betti   Tibet
bever   breve
bevers   breves
Bevis   vibes
bey   bye
beys   byes
bheesti   bhistee
bhistee   bheesti
biased   abides
bicorn   bicron
bicron   bicorn
bid   dib
bidder   bedrid; birded; brided
bide   dieb
bidet   betid; debit
bidets   bed-sit; debits
bids   dibs
Biel   bile
Biella   alible; Belial; labile; liable
bien   bein; Beni; bine
bier   Brie; Ribe
biers   birse; Ribes
big   gib
Big Ben   ebbing
big end   binged
biggin   gibing
bigness   besings
bigoted   dog-bite
Bikaner   break in; inbreak
bike   kibe
bikes   kibes
bilboes   lobbies
bile   Biel
bilged   begild
billets   bestill
bilobed   lobbied
biltong   bolting
bin   nib

binary   brainy
binder   brined; inbred; rebind
binders   rebinds
bind over   ovenbird
binds over   ovenbirds
bine   bein; Beni; bien
binge   begin; being
binged   big end
binges   begins; beings; besing
bins   nibs; snib
biogeny   obeying
bionic   niobic
bird   drib
bird-call   call-bird
bird-calls   call-birds
birded   bedrid; bidder; brided
birdie   Bridie
birding   briding
bird-like   Kilbride
birds   dribs
bireme   bemire
biremes   bemires
biretta   battier; ratbite
birettas   ratbites
birled   bridle
birles   birsle
biros   Boris
birse   biers; Ribes
birsle   birles
birsled   bridles
birsles   ribless
bis   sib
Biskra   Barkis
bister   bestir; bistre; biters; tribes
bistre   bestir; bister; biters; tribes
bistro   orbits
bisulcate   baculites
bit   Tib
biter   rebit; Tiber; tribe
biters   bestir; bister; bistre;
   tribes
bites   besit
bito   obit
bittern   Britten
bizarre   brazier
blabbed   babbled
blabber   babbler; brabble
blabbers   babblers; brabbles
blabbing   babbling
black earth   blackheart
blackheart   black earth
blad   bald
blade   abled; baled

blae   Abel; able; albe; bael; bale;
   Elba; Labe
blaes   ables; bales; Basel; Basle;
   blasé; sable
blague   beluga
Blake   bleak
blame   amble; Mabel; Melba
blamed   ambled; balmed; bedlam;
   beldam; lambed
blamer   ambler; marble; ramble
blamers   amblers; marbles; rambles
blames   ambles
blaming   ambling; balming;
   lambing
blare   abler; baler; blear
blared   balder; bedral
blares   balers; blears
blarneys   Barnsley
blasé   ables; bales; Basel; Basle;
   blaes; sable
blast   Balts; blats
blasted   stabled
blastema   lambaste
blaster   alberts; labrets; stabler;
   tablers
blasters   stablers
blasting   stabling
blat   Balt
blate   ablet; bleat; table
blats   Balts; blast
blatter   battler; brattle
blatters   battlers; brattles
blay   ably
bleak   Blake
blear   abler; baler; blare
blears   balers; blares
bleary   barely; barley
bleat   ablet; blate; table
bleated   belated
bleating   belating; tangible
bleats   ablest; ablets; stable; tables
bleed   bedel
bleeds   bedels
blessed   bedless
blessing   glibness
blest   belts; blets
blet   belt
blets   belts; blest
Blida   ad lib
blinder   brindle
blinders   brindles
blister   bristle
blisters   bristles

blithe   thible
bloated   lobated
bloater   Latrobe
bloaters   sortable; storable
bloating   bog-Latin; obligant
bloats   oblast
Blois   boils
blonde   bolden; Döbeln
blondes   boldens
bloods   'sblood
bloomer   rebloom
bloomers   reblooms
blore   borel
blot   bolt
blots   bolts
blotted   bottled
blotter   bottler
blotters   bottlers
blotting   bottling
blouse   boules; obelus
bloused   doubles
blow   bowl
blowed   bowled
blower   bowler
blowers   bowlers
blowing   bowling
blows   bowls
blude   blued
bludge   bugled; bulged
bludger   burgled
blue   Lebu
blued   blude
bluenose   nebulose
bluenotes   bluestone
bluer   ruble
blue-rot   boulter; trouble
blues   bulse
bluest   bustle; sublet; subtle
bluestone   bluenotes
blunge   bungle
blunged   bungled
blunger   bungler
blungers   bunglers
blunges   bungles
blunging   bungling
blur   burl
blurs   burls; slurb
blushes   bushels
bluster   bustler; butlers; subtler
blusters   bustlers
bo   ob
boa   Abo
boar   bora

31

board abord; broad	**boles** lobes
boarded aborded	**bolide** boiled
boarder broader	**Bols** lobs; slob
boarding abording	**bolster** bolters; lobster
boardings signboard	**bolsters** lobsters
boardroom Broadmoor	**bolt** blot
boards abords; adsorb; broads	**bolters** bolster; lobster
boars boras	**bolting** biltong
boart abort; Rabot; tabor	**bolts** blots
boarts aborts; Strabo; tabors	**bolus** lobus
boas Abos	**boma** ambo; M'Bao; Moab
boast basto; boats; sabot; Sobat	**bomas** ambos; Sambo
boaster boaters; borates	**bombed** mobbed
boasters Botsares	**bombing** mobbing
boasting bostangi	**bon** nob
boasts sabots	**bondage** dogbane
boater borate	**bone** ebon
boaters boaster; borates	**boned** Boden
boat-hook book-oath	**boneless** noblesse
boat-hooks book-oaths	**boner** borne
boathouse houseboat	**bongo** boong
boathouses houseboats	**bongos** boongs
boats basto; boast; sabot; Sobat	**boning** Ningbo
bobac cabob	**bonnie** Benoni
bobak kabob	**bonsai** Bosnia
boches bosche	**bonus** bosun; bouns
bode Obed	**bonzer** bronze
Boden boned	**booby** yobbo
Boer bore; Ebro; robe	**booh** hobo
Boers bores; brose; robes; sober	**book** boko; Obok
bog gob	**bookcase** casebook
bogeys goes by	**bookcases** casebooks
bog-Latin bloating; obligant	**bookies** booksie
bogle globe	**book-oath** boat-hook
bogles globes	**book-oaths** boat-hooks
Bogota Tobago	**books** bokos
bogs gobs	**booksie** bookies
bogy boyg; go by	**booms** bosom
boh hob	**boong** bongo
boil lobi	**boongs** bongos
boiled bolide	**boons** boson
boiler reboil	**boor** broo
boilers reboils	**boors** broos
boils Blois	**boose** oboes
bok kob	**boost** boots
boko book; Obok	**boot-jack** jackboot
bokos books	**boot-jacks** jackboots
boks bosk; kobs	**boots** boost
Bolbec cobble	**boot-tree** beetroot
bolden blonde; Döbeln	**bor** orb; rob
boldens blondes	**bora** boar
bolder bordel	**boracic** braccio
bole lobe; Loeb	**boras** boars

borate boater	**bourgs** Burgos
borated aborted; tabored	**bourn** Bornu
borates boaster; boaters	**bourne** unrobe
borating aborting; taboring	**bournes** unrobes
bordel bolder	**bourns** suborn
bordello doorbell	**Bowdler** lowbred
bordellos doorbells	**bowel** below; elbow
bore Boer; Ebro; robe	**bowels** elbows
bored orbed; robed	**bowers** bowser; browse
boredom bedroom; broomed	**bowery** bowyer
borel blore	**bow-hands** show band
bores Boers; brose; robes; sober	**bowl** blow
boring orbing; robing	**bowled** blowed
Boris biros	**bowler** blower
born Brno; Bron	**bowlers** blowers
borne boner	**bowling** blowing
Borneo Oberon	**bowls** blows
Bornu bourn	**bows** swob
bosche boches	**bowser** bowers; browse
bosh hobs	**bowsers** browses
boshta bathos	**bowyer** bowery
boshter bothers	**boy** yob
bosk boks; kobs	**boyau** bayou
bos'n nobs; snob	**boyg** bogy; go by
Bosnia bonsai	**boys** sybo; yobs
bos'ns snobs	**bra** bar; Rab
bosom booms	**brabble** babbler; blabber
boson boons	**brabbles** babblers; blabbers
boss sobs	**Brac** crab
bosses obsess	**braccio** boracic
bossing obsigns	**brace** acerb; caber; cabré
bostangi boasting	**braced** decarb
bosun bonus; bouns	**braces** cabers
Boswell bellows	**brackets** back-rest
bothering night-robe	**brad** bard; drab
bothers boshter	**brads** bards; drabs
bots stob	**brae** bare; bear
Botsares boasters	**braes** bares; baser; bears; saber;
bottled blotted	sabre
bottler blotter	**brag** garb; grab
bottlers blotters	**brags** garbs; grabs
bottling blotting	**Brahmi** mihrab
boules blouse; obelus	**braid** Baird; rabid
boult U-bolt	**braids** disbar
boulter blue-rot; trouble	**brail** libra
boulters troubles	**Braille** liberal
boults U-bolts	**brails** libras
bounced buncoed	**brain** abrin; bairn; Brian
bouncing buncoing	**brains** bairns
bounder rebound; unrobed	**brainy** binary
bounders rebounds; suborned	**braise** rabies; Serbia
bounding unboding	**braised** air-beds; darbies; sea-bird
bouns bonus; bosun	**braises** brassie

braize zeriba
brake baker; break
braked barked; debark
brakes bakers; basker; breaks
braking barking
bran barn
Brandeis brandies
brander Bernard
brandies Brandeis
Braque barque
bras bars
brasserie brassiere
brasseries brassieres
brassie braises
brassiere brasserie
brassieres brasseries
brast Barts; brats
brat Bart
brats Barts; brast
brattle battler; blatter
brattles battlers; blatters
braved adverb
brawled warbled
brawler warbler
brawlers warblers
brawling warbling
brawly byrlaw
brayed Red Bay
braze zebra
brazes zebras
brazier bizarre
breach Béchar; Rechab
bread ardeb; Bader; bared; beard;
  Breda; debar
bread-corn corn-bread
breaded bearded
breading bearding
breadnut turbaned
breads ardebs; beards; debars;
  sabred; serdab
break baker; brake
break in Bikaner; inbreak
breaking out outbreaking
break out outbreak
breaks bakers; basker; brakes
breaks in bearskin; inbreaks
breaks out outbreaks
break-up upbreak
break-wind wind-break
bream amber; embar
breams ambers; embars; Sambre
breast barest; baster; bestar; Tarbes
breasted betreads; debaters

breasts basters; bestars
breath bather; bertha
breathes Hartbees
breaths bathers; berthas
brecham becharm; chamber;
  chambré
brechams becharms; chambers
Breda ardeb; Bader; bared; beard;
  bread; debar
brede breed
bredes breeds
bree beer; bere
breed brede
breeds bredes
brees beers; beres
brehon Hebron
Brenda bander
Brescia ascribe
breve bever
breves bevers
Brian abrin; bairn; brain
bribed dibber; ribbed
bribing ribbing
bricole corbeil
bricoles corbeils
bridal labrid; ribald
bride Diber; rebid
brided bedrid; bidder; birded
brides debris; rebids
bridge begird
bridges begirds
Bridgeton Tonbridge
Bridie birdie
briding birding
bridle birled
bridles birsled
Brie bier; Ribe
brief fiber; fibre
briefed debrief
briefless fibreless
briefs fibers; fibres
briered berried
brigade abridge
brigaded abridged
brigades abridges
brigading abridging
brighten berthing
brindle blinder
brindles blinders
brined binder; inbred; rebind
brines nebris
brining inbring
brisance carbines

bristle	blister
bristled	driblets
bristles	blisters
brisure	bruiser; buriers
brisures	bruisers
Britten	bittern
Brno	born; Bron
broachers	shore crab
broad	abord; board
broadcaster	rebroadcast
broadcasters	rebroadcasts
broaden	bandore
broadens	bandores
broader	boarder
Broadmoor	boardroom
broads	abords; adsorb; boards
broadside	sideboard
broadsides	sideboards
broadway	wayboard
broadways	wayboards
brogan	Bangor; barong
brogans	barongs
broke out	outbroke
brome	ombre
Bron	born; Brno
bronze	bonzer
broo	boor
brooked	red-book
broomed	bedroom; boredom
brooms	Sombor
broomy	byroom
broos	boors
brose	Boers; bores; robes; sober
broth	throb
broths	throbs
browse	bowers; bowser
browses	bowsers
bruckle	buckler
Brue	Bure
Brugge	bugger
bruin	burin
bruins	burins
bruise	buries; busier; rubies
bruised	burdies; bus-ride
bruiser	brisure; buriers
bruisers	brisures
bruit	Tibur
brumal	labrum; lumbar; umbral
brume	umber; umbre
Brunei	rubine
brunet	bunter; burnet
brunets	bunters; burnets; bursten
brunt	burnt

Brusa	bursa
brush	shrub
brute	rebut; tuber
brutes	buster; rebuts; tubers
buat	abut; tabu; tuba
buats	abuts; tabus; tubas
bucked	beduck
buckets	bostuck
buckle	Lubeck
buckler	bruckle
bud	dub
budder	redbud
budders	redbuds
budge	debug
budges	debugs
buds	dubs
buffer	rebuff
buffered	rebuffed
buffering	rebuffing
buffers	rebuffs
bugger	Brugge
bugle	bulge
bugled	bludge; bulged
bugler	bulger; burgle
buglers	bulgers; burgles
bugles	bulges
bugling	bulging
builder	rebuild
builders	rebuilds
bulge	bugle
bulged	bludge; bugled
bulger	bugler; burgle
bulgers	buglers; burgles
bulges	bugles
bulging	bugling
bulse	blues
bummle	mumble
bummled	mumbled
bummles	mumbles
bummling	mumbling
bun	nub
buncoed	bounced
buncoing	bouncing
bunged	bedung
bungle	blunge
bungled	blunged
bungler	blunger
bunglers	blungers
bungles	blunges
bungling	blunging
bunk	knub
bunked	debunk
bunks	knubs

buns   nubs; snub
bunted   but-end
bunter   brunet; burnet
bunters   brunets; burnets; bursten
bur   rub
buran   unbar; urban
burans   unbars
burble   lubber; rubble
burbles   lubbers; slubber
burd   drub
burden   burned; unbred
burdie   buried; rubied
burdies   bruised; bus-ride
burds   drubs
Bure   Brue
burg   grub
burgee   Gueber; Guebre
burgees   Guebers; Guebres
burgle   bugler; bulger
burgled   bludger
burgles   buglers; bulgers
Burgos   bourgs
burgs   grubs
buried   burdie; rubied
buriers   brisure; bruiser
buries   bruise; busier; rubies
burin   bruin
burins   bruins
burl   blur
burletta   rebuttal
burls   blurs; slurb
Burma   rumba; umbra
Burmese   embrues
burned   burden; unbred
burnet   brunet; bunter
burnets   brunets; bunters; bursten
Burnley   Leyburn
burnt   brunt
burs   rubs
bursa   Brusa
bursae   abuser
burse   rebus; suber
Burslem   lumbers; rumbles;
   slumber

bursten   brunets; bunters; burnets
bury   ruby
bus   sub
bush   hubs
bushels   blushes
bushier   Bushire
Bushire   bushier
busier   bruise; buries; rubies
busman   subman
bus-ride   bruised; burdies
bus-rides   disburse
buss   subs
bus station   substation
bus stations   substations
bust   buts; stub; tubs
busted   bedust; bestud; debuts
buster   brutes; rebuts; tubers
bustle   bluest; sublet; subtle
bustler   bluster; butlers; subtler
bustlers   blusters
busts   stubs
busy   buys
but   tub
butchers   Schubert
Bute   tube
Butea   beaut; taube; tubae
but-end   bunted
butlers   bluster; bustler; subtler
buts   bust; stub; tubs
buttered   rebutted
buttering   rebutting
buyer   Ebury
buys   busy
bwana   nawab
bwanas   nawabs
by-blow   wobbly
bye   bey
by-end   bendy
byes   beys
by-form   Formby
byrlaw   brawly
byroom   broomy
byte   ybet
bytes   Betsy

C

Caaba   abaca
cab   ABC
cabalism   balsamic
cabalist   basaltic
cabaret   bear-cat

cabarets   bear-cats
caber   acerb; brace; cabré
cabers   braces
cable   Caleb
cabob   bobac

caboc   bacco
cabré   acerb; brace; caber
cabs   scab
cachets   catches
cackled   clacked
cackler   clacker; crackle
cacklers   clackers; crackles
cackling   clacking
cacodyl   accoyld
caddie   Eddaic
cade   dace
cadent   canted; decant
cades   cased
cadet   acted
cadets   casted
cadge   caged
cadger   graced
cadi   acid
cadis   acids; asdic
cadre   acred; arced; cared; cedar;
   raced
cadres   cedars; sacred; scared
cads   scad
caduceus   caucused
Caen   acne; ance; cane
caestus   cuestas
cafe   face
cafes   faces
caged   cadge
Caher   chare; rache; reach
cahier   Archie
cahiers   cashier
Cahors   orachs
caiman   maniac
caimans   maniacs
Cain   Inca
caird   acrid; daric; Dirac
caisson   casinos; cassino
Caithness   asthenics
calamint   claimant
calamints   claimants
calcines   scenical
Calder   cradle; credal
Caleb   cable
Caledon   celadon
calendar   landrace
calendars   landraces
calender   encradle
calenders   encradles
calends   candles
calenture   crenulate
caliber   calibre
calibers   calibres

calibrate   bacterial
calibre   caliber
calibres   calibers
caliche   chalice
calico   accoil
califs   fiscal
caliper   replica
calipers   replicas; spiracle
caliphate   hepatical
caliver   clavier
calivers   claviers; visceral
calk   lack
calked   lacked
calker   lacker
calkers   lackers; slacker
calking   lacking
calks   lacks; slack
call-bird   bird-call
call-birds   bird-calls
caller   cellar; recall
callers   cellars; recalls; scleral
calligraphy   graphically
callosity   stoically
calls   scall
callus   sulcal
calm   clam
calmed   macled
calmer   Carmel; marcel
calmest   camlets
calms   clams
Calne   clean; lance
calories   Escorial
caloyers   coarsely
calp   clap
calque   claque
calques   claques
calumets   muscatel
calumnies   masculine
Calvary   cavalry
calve   cavel; clave
calver   carvel; claver
calvers   carvels; clavers
calves   cavels; claves; sclave
cam   mac
camber   cembra
cambered   embraced
cambering   embracing
cambers   cembras
cambrel   clamber
cambrels   clambers; scramble
came   acme; mace
camel   macle
camels   macles; mascle; mescal

camerated   demarcate; macerated
cameration   maceration
Cameron   Cremona; Menorca;
   romance
camion   manioc
camise   amices
camlets   calmest
camped   decamp
campers   scamper
campled   clamped
campling   clamping
camps   scamp
cams   macs
camus   caums; Musca; sumac
canaille   alliance
canaries   Cesarian
canaster   caterans
canceration   anacreontic
cancroid   draconic
Candia   Dacian
Candide   candied
candied   Candide
candies   incased
candle   lanced
candles   calends
cane   acne; ance; Caen
cane-chairs   saccharine
caned   dance
caneh   nache
canehs   naches
canephor   Cape Horn; chaperon
canephore   chaperone
canephores   chaperones
canephors   chaperons
canes   scena
cangue   uncage
cangues   uncages
canis   Incas; Sican
canister   scantier
canisters   scenarist
canker   Neckar
canners   scanner
canniest   ancients; instance
cannot   canton
canny   Nancy
canoe   ocean
canoed   acnode; deacon
canoeist   aconites
canoeists   cessation
canoes   oceans
canoness   sonances
canonises   ascension
canonist   contains; sanction

canonists   sanctions
canopies   caponise
cans   scan
canst   cants; scant
canted   cadent; decant
canter   carnet; creant; Cretan;
   nectar; recant; tanrec; trance
cantered   crenated; decanter;
   nectared; recanted
cantering   recanting
canters   carnets; Cretans; recants;
   tanrecs; trances
canthus   chaunts; staunch
canticles   lac insect
cantle   cental; lancet
cantles   centals; lancets
canto   acton; cotan; octan
canton   cannot
cantor   Carnot; carton; contra
cantors   cartons; contras
cantos   actons; Octans
cants   canst; scant
cantus   Tuscan
Canute   uncate
capable   pacable
cape   pace
caped   paced
Cape Horn   canephor; chaperon
capelin   panicle; pelican
capelins   panicles; pelicans
caper   crape; pacer; recap
capers   Casper; crapes; escarp;
   pacers; parsec; recaps; scrape;
   spacer
capes   Caspe; paces; scape; space
capillarity   piratically
caping   pacing
Capis   aspic; picas; spica
capitan   captain
capitans   captains
Capitol   coal-pit; optical; pit-coal;
   topical
caple   place
caples   places
capon   Copàn
caponise   canopies
Capote   toecap
Caprese   escaper; percase
Capri   carpi
capsular   scapular
capsulary   scapulary
capsule   specula
captain   capitan

captains capitans
caption paction; Pontiac
captioned pactioned
captioning pactioning
captions pactions
capuchin china cup
capuchins china cups
car arc
carat carta
carats cartas
carbines brisance
carbon corban
carbonise escribano
carbonises escribanos
carcinoma macaronic
cardecu accrued
cardecus accursed
carder Redcar
carders scarred
cardigan arcading
cardigans arcadings
care acer; acre; race
cared acred; arced; cadre; cedar;
  raced
careen enrace
careens caserne; enraces
cares acers; acres; carse; races;
  scare; scrae; sérac
caress carses; crases; scares; scraes;
  séracs
caret carte; cater; crate; react; recta;
  trace
carets cartes; caster; caters; crates;
  Cresta; reacts; recast; traces
cargoes corsage; socager
Carib baric; rabic
carina arnica; crania
carinate craniate
caring arcing; racing
cark rack
carked arcked; dacker; racked
carking arcking; racking
carks racks
carline en clair; Linacre
Carlist St. Clair
Carlos carols; claros; corals
Carluke caulker
Carmel calmer; marcel
Carmiel Almeric; claimer; miracle;
  reclaim
carmine Crimean; Mercian
carnage cranage
carneous nacreous

carnet canter; creant; Cretan;
  nectar; recant; tanrec; trance
carnets canters; Cretans; recants;
  tanrecs; trances
Carnot cantor; carton
Carnoustie cautioners
carob coarb; Cobar; cobra
carobs coarbs; cobras
caroche coacher
caroches coachers
carol claro; coral; Lorca
Carole coaler; oracle
caroli lorica
Carolina conarial
Caroline acrolein; Cornelia;
  creolian
carolled collared
carolling collaring
carols Carlos; claros; corals
caroms Marcos
carotin anticor; Cortina
carouse acerous
carp crap
carped craped; redcap
carpel parcel; placer
carpels clasper; parcels; placers;
  scalper
carpets precast; spectra
carpi Capri
carping craping
carps craps; scarp; scrap
carries scarier
carrot trocar
carrots trocars
cars arcs; scar
carse acers; acres; cares; races;
  scare; scrae; sérac
carses caress; crases; scares; scraes;
  séracs
carta carat
cartas carats
carte caret; cater; crate; react; recta;
  trace
carted crated; Dectra; redact; traced
cartel claret; rectal; tarcel
cartels clarets; scarlet; tarcels
carter arrect; crater; tracer
carters craters; tracers
cartes carets; caster; caters; crates;
  Cresta; reacts; recast; traces
Cartesian ascertain; sectarian
Cartesians ascertains; sectarians
cart-horse orchestra

cart-horses orchestras
Cartier cirrate; erratic
carting tracing
carton cantor; Carnot; contra
cartons cantors; contras
cartoon coranto; Cortona
cartoons corantos; ostracon
carts scart; scrat
carucate accurate
carucates Crustacea
carve caver; crave; varec
carved craved
carvel calver; claver
carvels calvers; clavers
carven cavern; craven
carver craver
carvers cravers
carves cavers; craves
carving craving
carvings cravings
Cary racy
case aces; aesc
casebook bookcase
casebooks bookcases
cased cades
casein incase
casern cranes; rances
caserne careens; enraces
cash Chas.
cashed chased
cashed in inchased
Cashel chelas; laches
cashes chases; chasse
cashier cahiers
cash in chains
cashing chasing
cashmere marchese
casing Signac
casinos caisson; cassino
cask sack
casked sacked
casking sacking
casks sacks
Caspe capes; paces; scape; space
Casper capers; crapes; escarp;
pacers; parsec; recaps; scrape;
spacer
casque sacque
casques sacques
Cassel scales
cassette test-case
cassettes test-cases
cassia Isaacs

cassino caisson; casinos
cassock Cossack
cassocks Cossacks
cast acts; cats; scat
Castalian Satanical
caste cates; sceat
casted cadets
caster carets; cartes; caters; crates;
Cresta; reacts; recaşt; traces
casters actress; Castres; recasts
Castile astelic; elastic; laciest;
latices
cast-iron Nicastro
castle cleats; sclate
castles sclates
castling catlings
castor actors; Castro; Croats; scrota;
tarocs
cast out outcast
castrated Tadcaster
Castres actress; casters; recasts
Castro actors; castor; Croats; scrota;
tarocs
casts scats
casts out outcasts
casual causal
casually causally
cat act
catalogue coagulate
catalogued coagulated
catalogues coagulates
cataloguing coagulating
catchers cratches
catches cachets
catechism schematic
categories categorise
categorise categories
category grey-coat
cater caret; carte; crate; react; recta;
trace
caterans canaster
catered cedrate; created; reacted
caterer retrace; terrace
caterers retraces; terraces
cateress Cerastes
catering argentic; citrange;
creating; reacting
caters carets; cartes; caster; crates;
Cresta; reacts; recast; traces
cates caste; sceat
Cath chat; tach
Cathy yacht
Catilines inelastic; sciential

cation   action; atonic
cations   actions; Scotian
catkins   catskin
catlings   castling
Cato   atoc; coat
Catrine   ceratin; certain; crinate; nacrite
cats   acts; cast; scat
cat-silver   verticals
catskin   catkins
cat's-tail   statical
catsup   upcast
catsups   upcasts
cattier   citrate
caucused   caduceus
caudle   cedula; Claude
cauld   Claud; ducal
caulker   Carluke
cauls   Lucas
caums   camus; Musca; sumac
causal   casual
causally   casually
cause   sauce
caused   sauced
causer   cesura; Creúsa; saucer
causers   cesuras; saucers; sucrase
causes   sauces
causing   saucing
caution   auction
cautionary   auctionary
cautioned   auctioned; education
cautioner   Cointreau
cautioners   Carnoustie
cautioning   auctioning
cautions   auctions
cavalry   Calvary
caveat   vacate
caveats   vacates
cavel   calve; clave
cavels   calves; claves; sclave
caver   carve; crave; varec
cavern   carven; craven
cavers   carves; craves
caviare   avarice
cavils   clavis; Slavic
Cavite   active
cavitied   vaticide
caws   scaw
Ceará   areca
ceasing   incages
Cebu   cube
Cebus   cubes

cedar   acred; arced; cadre; cared; raced
cedarn   craned; dancer; ranced
cedars   cadres; sacred; scared
cedi   dice; iced
cedis   dices
cedrate   catered; created; reacted
Cedrela   cleared; creedal; declare
Cedros   coders; credos; scored
cedula   caudle; Claude
ceil   ciel; lice
ceiled   cieled
ceiling   cieling; Lignice
ceilinged   diligence
ceils   ciels; Leics.; Sicel; slice
celadon   Caledon
celebrate   erectable
Celia   Alice; ileac
Celina   ancile; inlace
cellar   caller; recall
cellared   recalled
cellaring   recalling
cellars   callers; recalls; scleral
Celsius   sluices
cembra   camber
cembras   cambers
cementer   cerement
cementers   cerements
Cenis   since
cense   scene
censed   scened
censer   screen; secern
censers   screens; secerns
censes   scenes
censing   scening
censor   crones; oncers
censorial   Creolians
censual   launces; unlaces; unscale
cental   cantle; lancet
centals   cantles; lancets
centaur   untrace
centaurs   Etruscan; recusant; untraces
center   centre; recent; tenrec
centering   centreing
centerings   centreings
centers   centres; tenrecs
centiare   creatine; increate; iterance
centigram   cremating
cento   conte; Notec
centos   contes
centralise   interlaces
centre   center; recent; tenrec

centred   credent; red cent
centreing   centering
centreings   centerings
centres   centers; tenrecs
centroid   Crediton; doctrine
centroids   doctrines
cents   scent
centurion   continuer
centurions   continuers
cephalometric   petrochemical
Ceram   crame; cream; Crema; macer; Merca
ceramet   cremate; meercat
ceramets   cremates; meercats
ceramist   matrices
Cerastes   cateress
cerate   create; ecarté
cerates   creates; secreta
ceratin   Catrine; certain; crinate; nacrite
Ceratodus   croustade; educators
cercus   cruces
cere   cree
cereal   alerce
cereals   rescale
cered   creed
cerement   cementer
cerements   cementers
ceres   crees; scree
ceresin   sincere
Cereus   ceruse; Creuse; recuse; rescue; secure
ceria   Erica
cering   cringe
ceriph   cipher
ceriphs   ciphers; spheric
cerite   recite; tierce
cero   core
ceros   cores; corse; score
cerous   course; crouse; Crusoe; source
cerris   criers
certain   Catrine; ceratin; crinate; nacrite
certes   erects; resect; secret
certifiable   rectifiable
certification   rectification
certified   rectified
certifier   rectifier
certifiers   rectifiers
certifies   rectifies
certify   rectify
certifying   rectifying

certitude   rectitude
certs   crest
ceruse   Cereus; Creuse; recuse; rescue; secure
cervices   crescive
Cesarian   canaries
Cesena   encase; seance; Seneca
cessation   canoeists
cession   cosines; Oscines
Cestoda   coasted
cestodes   cosseted
Cestracion   accretions
Ceti   cite; tice
Ceuta   acute
chaco   coach
Chagres   charges; creaghs
chagrin   arching; charing
chain   Chian; china
chained   echidna
chainlet   ethnical
chainman   Chinaman
chainmen   Chinamen
chains   cash in
chain-store   anchorites
chairs   Charis; rachis
Chaldee   Cheadle; leached
chalet   thecal; Thecla
chalets   latches; satchel
chalice   caliche
cham   mach
chamber   becharm; brecham; chambré
chambered   becharmed
chambering   becharming
chambers   becharms; brechams
chambré   becharm; brecham; chamber
changed   ganched
changes   ganches
changing   ganching
chant   natch
chanter   tranche
chanters   snatcher; stancher; tranches
chants   snatch; stanch
Chanute   unteach
chape   cheap; peach
chapel   pleach
chaperon   canephor; Cape Horn
chaperone   canephore
chaperones   canephores
chaperons   canephors

chapiter patchier; phreatic
chaps Pasch
chapter patcher
chapters patchers
char arch; rach
characterless clear-starches
chare Caher; rache; reach
chared arched
chares arches; chaser; eschar;
  raches; search
charge creagh
charges Chagres; creaghs
charing arching; chagrin
chariot haricot
chariots haricots
Charis chairs; rachis
charisma archaism; machairs
Charles larches
charm march
charmed marched
charmer marcher
charmers marchers
charming marching
Charon anchor; archon; rancho
charpoy Corypha
chars crash
chart ratch
charters Chartres; starcher
Chartres charters; starcher
charts scarth; starch
chary Archy
Chas. cash
chase aches
chased cashed
chaser arches; chares; eschar;
  raches; search
chasers crashes; eschars
chases cashes; chasse
chasing cashing
chasse cashes; chases
chaste cheats; sachet; scathe; taches
chasten natches
chat Cath; tach
chattel latchet
chattels latchets
chatter ratchet
chatters ratchets
chaunt nautch
chaunters stauncher
chaunts canthus; staunch
chawing chinwag
chaws schwa
Cheadle Chaldee; leached

cheap chape; peach
cheat tache; teach; theca
cheater hectare; teacher
cheaters hectares; teachers
cheating teaching
cheats chaste; sachet; scathe; taches
check-in chicken
check-ins chickens
cheeps peches; speech
cheer reech
cheerly lechery
cheero choree; cohere; echoer;
  re-echo
cheers creesh
cheery reechy
cheiropterans terpsichorean
chela leach
chelas Cashel; laches
Chelsea leaches
chemical alchemic
chenar enarch
chenars ranches
chenille Hellenic
Cheops epochs
chesil chiels; chiles; chisel; elchis;
  Schlei
chest techs
Chester etchers; retches
chesty scythe
chetahs hatches
Chian chain; china
chicken check-in
chickens check-ins
chicle cliche
chider herdic
chiders herdics
chiel chile; elchi
chiels chesil; chiles; chisel; elchis;
  Schlei
Chiem chime; miche
childer chirled
chile chiel; elchi
Chilean Lachine
chiles chesil; chiels; chisel; elchis;
  Schlei
chillies ice-hills
chime Chiem; miche
chimed miched
chimes miches
chiming miching
chin inch
china chain; Chian
china cup capuchin

china cups   capuchins
Chinaman   chainman
Chinamen   chainmen
chine   niche
chined   inched; niched
chines   chinse; inches; niches
chining   inching; niching
chinrest   christen; citherns
chinrests   christens
chinse   chines; inches; niches
chinwag   chawing
chirled   childer
chirre   richer
chirt   crith
chirted   ditcher
chirts   Christ; criths
chisel   chesil; chiels; chiles; elchis; Schlei
chit   itch
chits   stich
chitters   stitcher
chivy   Vichy
chlorite   clothier
choice   echoic
choir   ichor
choirman   harmonic
choirs   orchis
choked   hocked
choker   hocker
chokers   hockers; shocker
choking   hocking
cholera   chorale
Cholet   clothe
choline   helicon
choltries   clothiers
choose   cohoes
chooser   soroche
chopin   phonic
chopines   Echinops
chopins   phonics
choral   lorcha
chorale   cholera
chore   ochre
chorea   Horace; ochrea; orache
choree   cheero; cohere; echoer; re-echo
chorees   coheres; echoers
chores   cosher; ochres
chorist   ostrich
chose   Soche
chou   ouch
chouse   ouches
choused   douches; hocused

chousing   hocusing
chout   couth; touch
chowder   cowherd
chrism   smirch
Christ   chirts; criths
christen   chinrest; citherns
christens   chinrests
chromates   stomacher
chrysolite   chrysotile
chrysotile   chrysolite
chum   much
churl   lurch
churn   runch
cider   cried; dicer; riced
cider-and   riddance
ciders   dicers; scried
cidery   dry ice
ci-devant   Vedantic
ciel   ceil; lice
cieled   ceiled
cieling   ceiling; Lignice
ciels   ceils; Leics; Sicel; slice
cigar   craig
cigars   craigs
cilia   iliac
Cilla   lilac
cinder   crined
cinders   discern; rescind
cinema   anemic; iceman
cineol   Nicole
Cinerama   American; in camera
cinereal   reliance
Cinna   Incan
cinque   quince
Cinto   tonic
cipher   ceriph
ciphers   ceriphs; spheric
circle   cleric
circles   clerics
ciré   eric; icer; rice
cirrate   Cartier; erratic
cirrose   corries; crosier
ciseleur   ciselure
ciselure   ciseleur
cist   cits; tics
cisted   edicts
cistern   cretins
cit   tic
citadel   deltaic; dialect; edictal
citadels   dialects
citatory   atrocity
cite   ceti; tice
cited   edict

cites   tices
cither   thrice
citherns   chinrest; christen
citrange   argentic; catering; creating; reacting
citranges   recasting
citrate   cattier
citrates   cristate; scattier
citreous   cries out; outcries
citric   critic
citrin   nitric
citrine   crinite; inciter
Citroen   noticer
citrus   rustic
cits   cist; tics
cive   vice
cives   vices
civet   evict
civets   evicts
clacked   cackled
clacker   cackler; crackle
clackers   cacklers; crackles
clacking   cackling
claes   laces; scale
claim   malic
claimant   calamint
claimants   calamints
claimed   decimal; declaim; medical
claimer   Almeric; Carmiel; miracle; reclaim
claimers   miracles; reclaims
Claire   éclair; lacier
Clairton   contrail
clam   calm
clamber   cambrel
clambers   cambrels; scramble
clamped   campled
clamping   campling
clams   calms
clanged   glanced
clanging   glancing
clans   Lancs.
clap   calp
claps   clasp; scalp
claque   calque
claques   calques
Clare   clear
Clares   clears; scaler; sclera
claret   cartel; rectal; tarcel
clarets   cartels; scarlet; tarcels
clarino   clarion; Locrian
clarinos   clarions; Locrians

clarion   clarino; Locrian
clarionet   crotaline
clarions   clarinos; Locrians
claro   carol; coral; Lorca
claros   Carlos; carols; corals
clasp   claps; scalp
clasped   scalped
clasper   carpels; parcels; placers; scalper
claspers   scalpers
clasping   scalping
clasps   scalps
classed   declass
clat   talc
clatters   scrattle
Claud   cauld; ducal
Claude   caudle; cedula
clave   calve; cavel
claver   calver; carvel
clavers   calvers; carvels
claves   calves; cavels; sclave
clavier   caliver
claviers   calivers; visceral
clavis   cavils; Slavic
clay   lacy
clayed   lac-dye
clay-marl   lacrymal
claymores   lacrymose
clay-pit   typical
clays   scaly
Clea   Alec; lace
clean   Calne; lance
cleaned   elanced; enlaced
cleaners   cleanser
cleaning   elancing; enlacing
cleans   lances; Senlac
cleanse   elances; enlaces; scalene
cleanser   cleaners
cleansers   clearness
clear   Clare
cleared   Cedrela; creedal; declare
clearest   treacles
clearness   cleansers
clear out   colature
clears   Clares; scaler; sclera
clear-starches   characterless
cleat   éclat; lacet
cleats   castle; sclate
cleeks   seckel
cleep   clepe
cleeps   clepes
clematis   climates
clement   Tlemcen

Cleo cole
Cleon clone; Colne
clepe cleep
clepes cleeps
cleric circle
clerics circles
cliché chicle
clientage genetical
clients stencil
climates clematis
climaxes exclaims
clime melic
clinker crinkle
clinkers crinkles
Clio coil; loci
clipes splice
clipper cripple
clippers cripples
clobber cobbler
clobbers cobblers
clocked cockled
clocking cockling
clod cold
clodly coldly
clodpoles scolloped
clods colds; scold
clogged coggled
clogging coggling
cloister coistrel; cortiles; costlier
cloisters coistrels
cloke Locke
cloked locked
cloking locking
clone Cleon; Colne
close coles; socle
closed dolces
closer cresol
closes socles
closest closets
closet clotes
closets closest
close-up couples; opuscle; upclose
close-ups Scopelus; upcloses
closure colures
clot colt
clotes closet
clothe Cholet
clothier chlorite
clothiers choltries
clots colts
clotter crottle
cloud could
clouding Dulcigno

clous locus
clouts locust
Clovis Volsci
clow cowl
clows cowls; scowl
cloy coly
clue luce
clues cluse; luces
clumber crumble
clumbers crumbles
Clunes uncles
cluse clues; luces
cluster culters; custrel; cutlers; relucts
clusters custrels
clutch cultch
clutched declutch
Cnut cunt
coach chaco
coacher caroche
coachers caroches
coachmen Comanche
co-agent cognate
co-agents cognates
coagulate catalogue
coagulated catalogued
coagulates catalogues
coagulating cataloguing
coal Acol; cola
coaler Carole; oracle
coalers escolar; oracles; solacer
coalitionist solicitation
coalitionists solicitations
coal-pit Capitol; optical; pit-coal; topical
coals colas
coarb carob; Cobar; cobra
coarbs carobs; cobras
coarsely caloyers
coarsest coasters; Socrates
coast Ascot; coats; costa; Tosca
coasted Cestoda
coasters coarsest; Socrates
coasting agnostic; coatings
coastline sectional
coat atoc; Cato
coating cotinga
coatings agnostic; coasting
coats Ascot; coast; costa; Tosca
coax coxa
Coban bacon; banco
Cobar carob; coarb; cobra
cobble Bolbec

cobbler   clobber
cobblers   clobbers
cobra   carob; coarb; Cobar
cobras   carobs; coarbs
cocaine   oceanic
cockled   clocked
cockling   clocking
cod   doc
code   coed; Doce
codein   coined; no dice
coder   cored; credo; decor
coders   Cedros; credos; scored
codes   coeds
codex   coxed
codille   collide; collied
codlings   scolding
coed   code; Doce
coeds   codes
coeternal   tolerance
coeval   alcove; Levoca
coevals   alcoves
co-exist   exotics
coffers   scoffer
coffs   scott
coggled   clogged
coggling   clogging
cognate   co-agent
cognates   co-agents
cognation   contagion
cognise   coignes
cognition   incognito
cogs   scog
co-heir   heroic
co-heirs   heroics
cohere   cheero; choree; echoer;
   re-echo
coheres   chorees; echoers
cohoes   choose
coif   fico; foci
coign   incog
coignes   cognise
coil   Clio; loci
coiled   docile
coin   icon
coined   codein; no dice
coiner   orcein; orcine
coiners   crinose; cronies; sericon
coins   icons; scion; sonic
Cointreau   cautioner
coistrel   cloister; cortiles; costlier
coistrels   cloisters
cola   Acol; coal
colanders   Androcles

colas   coals
colation   location
colature   clear out
cold   clod
coldly   clodly
colds   clods; scold
cold tea   located
cole   Cleo
Colenso   console
coles   close; socle
Colin   Nicol
colitis   solicit
collapse   escallop
collapsed   scalloped
collapses   escallops
collapsing   scalloping
collared   carolled
collaring   carolling
collide   codille; collied
collie   ocelli
collied   codille; collide
collier   Corelli
colliers   orsellic
collinear   coralline
collops   scollop
collusive   colluvies
colluvies   collusive
Colne   Cleón; clone
colonialist   oscillation
colonialists   oscillations
colonies   colonise
colonise   colonies
coloured   decolour
colt   clot
colters   corslet; costrel
colts   clots
colures   closure
coly   cloy
Comanche   coachmen
comarb   crambo
combat   tombac
combers   Scomber
combo   coomb
combos   coombs
comedian   daemonic; demoniac
come out   outcome
comer   crome
comers   cromes
comes out   outcomes
comet   Comte
comforter   recomfort
comforters   recomforts
comics   cosmic

Comines incomes; mesonic
coming gnomic
comities semiotic
comity myotic
commercialist microclimates
commits Comtism
Como coom
compact accompt
compacts accompts
companied compendia
compare compear
compares compears; mesocarp
compear compare
compears compares; mesocarp
compeer compère
compeers compères
compendia companied
compère compeer
compères compeers
compile polemic
compiled complied
compiler complier
compilers compliers
compiles complies; polemics
complaint compliant
complexed decomplex
compliant complaint
complied compiled
complier compiler
compliers compilers
complies compiles; polemics
compounded decompound
compressed decompress
comsat mascot
comsats mascots
Comte comet
Comtism commits
Conan ancon
conarial Carolina
concerted concreted
concerti necrotic
concerting concreting
concertino concretion
concertinos concretions
concetti tectonic
concreates consecrate
concreted concerted
concreting concerting
concretion concertino
concretions concertinos
conder corned
conders corsned; scorned
conditioner recondition

conditioners reconditions
condoles consoled
condor cordon
condors cordons
conduits discount
condyles secondly
condylomatous monodactylous
cone once
cones Cosne; scone; sonce
conflate falconet
conflates falconets
confrère enforcer
confrères enforcers
confrérie reinforce
confréries reinforces
congas Gascon
congeries recognise
congested decongest
Congreve converge
congruity crying out; outcrying
conical laconic
conies cosine; oscine
conifer fir cone; inforce
conifers fir cones; forensic;
 forinsec; inforces
conine Connie
Coniston scontion
conk nock
conked nocked
conker reckon
conkers reckons
conking nocking
conks nocks
Connie conine
Conrad Dacron
consecrate concreates
conservant conversant
conservation conversation
conservational conversational
conservationist conversationist
conservationists conversationists
conservative conversative
conserve converse
conserved conversed
conserves converses
conserving conversing
Consett contest
considerate desecration
consigned seconding
consist tocsins
consolate stone-coal
console Colenso
consoled condoles

consoles coolness
consolidates disconsolate
consort crotons
conster cornets; cronets
constipate costean-pit
constipates costean-pits
constrainers contrariness
construe cornutes; counters; recounts; trounces
consume muscone
consumed mud-cones
contadine contained
contagion cognation
contained contadine
container crenation
containerised inconsiderate
containers crenations
contains canonist; sanction
conte cento; Notec
contenting contingent
contes centos
contest Consett
contingent contenting
continued unnoticed
continuer centurion
continuers centurions
contour cornuto; crouton
contours cornutos; croutons
contra cantor; Carnot; carton
contrail Clairton
contrariness constrainers
contras cantors; cartons
contravene covenanter
contravenes covenanters
contuses countess
converge Congreve
conversant conservant
conversation conservation
conversational conservational
conversationist conservationist
conversationists conservationists
conversative conservative
converse conserve
conversed conserved
converses conserves
conversing conserving
converter reconvert
converters reconverts
conveyer reconvey
conveyers reconveys
cool loco
cooled locoed
coolers creosol

coolest ocelots
cooling locoing
coolness consoles
cools locos
coom Como
coomb combo
coombs combos
cooms Cosmo
coop poco
coopers scooper
coops scoop
co-ordinate decoration
co-ordinates decorations
coost coots; scoot
coot toco
coots coost; scoot
Copàn capon
copartner procreant
copers corpse
copes copse; Pecos; scope
copied epodic
copiers persico
copse copes; Pecos; scope
copses scopes
copula cupola
copular cupolar
copulated cupolated
cor orc; roc
Cora arco; Orca; Roca
coral carol; claro; Lorca
coralline collinear
corals Carlos; carols; claros
coral-tree correlate
coral-trees correlates
coranto cartoon; Cortona
corantos cartoons; ostracon
corban carbon
corbeil bricole
corbeils bricoles
cordate redcoat
cordon condor
cordons condors
cords scrod
core cero
corea ocrea
cored coder; credo; decor
coreless recloses; sclerose
Corelli collier
corer crore
corers crores; scorer
cores ceros; corse; score
cork rock
corked docker; rocked

corker   rocker
corkers   rockers
corkier   rockier
corkiest   rockiest; stockier
corking   rocking
corks   rocks
cork-tree   rocketer
cork-trees   rocketers
corky   rocky
corn-bread   bread-corn
corned   conder
Cornelia   acrolein; Caroline; creolian
Cornelius   reclusion
corners   scorner
cornet   cronet
cornets   conster; cronets
corniche   enchoric
corniness   incensors
cornmeal   amelcorn
corns   scorn
cornus   Cronus
cornute   counter; recount; trounce
cornuted   trounced
cornutes   construe; counters; recounts; trounces
cornuting   trouncing
cornuto   contour; crouton
cornutos   contours; croutons
corny   crony
corona   racoon
coronal   Locarno
coronas   racoons
coroner   crooner
coroners   crooners
coronet   Cotrone
corps   crops
corpse   copers
corpses   process
corpus   croups
correlate   coral-tree
correlates   coral-trees
corries   cirrose; crosier
cors   orcs; rocs
corsage   cargoes; socager
corsages   socagers
corse   ceros; cores; score
corselet   electors; selector
corselets   selectors
corses   scores; scorse
corset   Cortes; coster; escort; scoter; sector; Tresco
corseted   escorted

corseting   escorting
corsets   costers; escorts; scoters; sectors
corslet   colters; costrel
corslets   costrels; crosslet
corsned   conders; scorned
Cortes   corset; coster; escort; scoter; sector; Tresco
cortiles   cloister; coistrel; costlier
Cortina   anticor; carotin
Cortona   cartoon; coranto
coruscate   accoutres; court case
coruscates   court cases
corves   covers
corvet   covert; vector
corvets   coverts; vectors
Corvinae   Veronica
Corydon   Croydon
Corypha   charpoy
cos   soc
cosec   secco
cosher   chores; ochres
cosine   conies; oscine
cosines   cession; Oscines
cosmic   comics
Cosmo   cooms
Cosne   cones; scone; sonce
Cossack   cassock
Cossacks   cassocks
cosset   estocs
cosseted   cestodes
cost   cots; scot
costa   Ascot; coast; coats; Tosca
costean   octanes
costean-pit   constipate
costean-pits   constipates
coster   corset; Cortes; escort; scoter; sector; Tresco
costers   corsets; escorts; scoters; sectors
cost-free   scot-free
costing   gnostic
costlier   cloister; coistrel; cortiles
costrel   colters; corslet
costrels   corslets; crosslet
costs   scots
cotan   acton; canto; Octan
coteries   esoteric
cotillion   octillion
cotillions   octillions
cotinga   coating
cotlands   Scotland
Cotrone   coronet

cots   cost; scot
coudé   douce
could   cloud
counsel   unclose
counsels   uncloses
counter   cornute; recount; trounce
countercharm   countermarch
countered   recounted
countering   recounting
countermarch   countercharm
counter-paled   counterplead
counterplead   counter-paled
counters   construe; cornutes;
  recounts; trounces
countess   contuses
countries   cretinous
counts   Tucson
couper   croupe; cuerpo; recoup
coupers   croupes; recoups
couples   close-up; opuscle; upclose
couplet   octuple
couplets   octuples
coupures   cupreous
course   cerous; crouse; Crusoe;
  source
coursed   scoured
courser   scourer
coursers   cursores; scourers
courses   Croesus; sources; sucrose
coursing   scouring
court   Turco
court case   accoutres; coruscate
court cases   coruscates
courted   eductor
courtesan   nectarous; outrances
courtiers   scrutoire
courts   scruto; Turcos
cousins   Socinus
couth   chout; touch
covenanter   contravene
covenanters   contravenes
covers   corves
covert   corvet; vector
coverts   corvets; vectors
coveting   Viet-Cong
cowers   escrow
cowherd   chowder
cowl   clow
cowls   clows; scowl
cowries   scowrie
cows   scow
coxa   coax
coxed   codex

crab   Brac
crabs   scrab
crackle   cackler; clacker
crackles   cacklers; clackers
cradle   Calder; credal
craft   fract
crafts   fracts
crags   scrag
craig   cigar
craigs   cigars
crake   creak
crakes   creaks; sacker; screak
cram   marc
crambo   comarb
crame   Ceram; cream; Crema;
  macer; Merca
crames   creams; macers; scream
crampit   ptarmic
crampits   ptarmics
crams   scram
cranage   carnage
crane   crena; nacre; rance
craned   cedarn; dancer; ranced
cranes   casern; rances
crania   arnica; carina
craniate   carinate
craning   rancing
crans   scran
Cranston   Scranton
crap   carp
crape   caper; pacer; recap
craped   carped; redcap
crapes   capers; Casper; escarp;
  pacers; parsec; recaps; scrape;
  spacer
craping   carping
craps   carps; scarp; scrap
crare   racer
crares   racers
crases   caress; carses; scares; scraes;
  séracs
crash   chars
crashes   chaser; eschars
crass   scars
cratches   catchers
crate   caret; carte; cater; react; recta;
  trace
crated   carted; Dectra; redact; traced
crater   arrect; carter; tracer
craters   carters; tracers
crates   carets; cartes; caster; caters;
  Cresta; reacts; recast; traces
Crato   actor; Croat; taroc

cravat Vratca
crave carve; caver; varec
craved carved
craven carven; cavern
craver carver
cravers carvers
craves carves; cavers
craving carving
cravings carvings
crawlers scrawler
crawls scrawl
craws scraw
crayoned deaconry
creagh charge
creaghs Chagres; charges
creak crake
creaks crakes; sacker; screak
cream Ceram; crame; Crema;
   macer; Merca
creamed amerced; racemed
creamers screamer
creaming amercing; Germanic;
   Mérignac
creams crames; macers; scream
creant canter; carnet; Cretan;
   nectar; recant; tanrec; trance
crease searce
creased searced
creases searces
creasing Grecians; searcing
creatable traceable
create cerate; ecarté
created catered; cedrate; reacted
creates cerates; secreta
creatine centiare; increate; iterance
creating argentic; catering;
   citrange; reacting
creation reaction
creational laceration
creations reactions
creative reactive
creatively reactively
creativity reactivity
creator acroter; reactor
creators acroters; reactors
crêches screech
credal Calder; cradle
credent centred; red cent
credit direct; triced
credited directed
crediting directing
Crediton centroid; doctrine
creditor director

creditors directors
credits directs
credo coder; cored; decor
credos Cedros; coders; scored
cree cere
creed cered
creedal Cedrela; cleared; declare
creeds screed
creep crêpe
creeps crepes
crees ceres; scree
creesh cheers
Creil relic
Crema Ceram; crame; cream;
   macer; Merca
cremate ceramet; meercat
cremates ceramets; meercats
cremating centigram
cremation manticore
cremator Mercator
Cremona Cameron; Menorca;
   romance
crena crane; nacre; rance
crenated cantered; decanter;
   nectared; recanted
crenation container
crenations containers
crenulate calenture
creolian acrolein; Caroline;
   Cornelia
Creolians censorial
Creon crone; oncer
creosol coolers
crêpe creep
crêpes creeps
crescive cervices
cresol closer
Crespin pincers; princes
cresset resects; secrets
Cressida sidecars
crest certs
Cresta carets; cartes; caster; caters;
   crates; reacts; recast; traces
Cretan canter; carnet; creant;
   nectar; recant; tanrec; trance
Cretans canters; carnets; recants;
   tanrecs; trances
Crete erect; terce
cretinoid direction
cretinous countries
cretins cistern
cretism metrics
Creüsa causer; cesura; saucer

Creuse   Cereus; ceruse; recuse; rescue; secure
crews   screw
cribbles   scribble
cried   cider; dicer; riced
cried out   outcried
criers   cerris
cries   erics; icers; seric
cries out   citreous; outcries
Crimea   Mercia
Crimean   carmine; Mercian
crimeful   merciful
crimeless   merciless
criminate   metrician
criminates   metricians
crimps   scrimp
crinate   Catrine; ceratin; certain; nacrite
crinated   Dicentra
crine   nicer
crined   cinder
cringe   cering
crinite   citrine; inciter
crinites   inciters
crinkle   clinker
crinkles   clinkers
crinose   coiners; cronies; sericon
cripes   Persic; precis; prices; spicer
cripple   clipper
cripples   clippers
crises   scries
crisp   scrip
crispate   picrates; practise
crispated   practised
crispation   ascription
crisps   scrips
cristate   citrates; scattier
crith   chirt
criths   chirts; Christ
critic   citric
critters   restrict; stricter
Croat   actor; Crato; taroc
Croats   actors; castor; Castro; scrota; tarocs
crochets   crotches
crocus   succor
Croesus   courses; sources; sucrose
crome   comer
cromes   comers
crone   Creon; oncer
crones   censor; oncers
cronet   cornet
cronets   conster; cornets

cronies   coiners; crinose; sericon
Cronos   croons
Cronus   cornus
crony   corny
crooner   coroner
crooners   coroners
croons   Cronos
crops   corps
croquet   rocquet
crore   corer
crores   corers; scorer
crosier   cirrose; corries
crossed   scorsed
crosser   recross
crosses   scorses
crossing   scorsing
crosslet   corslets; costrels
crotaline   clarionet
crotals   scrotal
crotches   crochets
crotons   consort
crottle   clotter
croupe   couper; cuerpo; recoup
crouped   produce
crouper   procure
croupers   procures
croupes   coupers; recoups
croups   corpus
crouse   cerous; course; Crusoe; source
croustade   Ceratodus; educators
crouton   contour; cornuto
croutons   contours; cornutos
crowned   decrown
crows   scrow
Croydon   Corydon
cru   cur; ruc
cruces   cercus
crud   curd
cruddle   curdled
crude   cured
cruds   curds
cruel   lucre; ulcer
cruells   cullers; sculler
cruels   ulcers
cruelty   cutlery
cruet   cuter; eruct; truce
cruets   cruset; Custer; eructs; rectus; truces
cruise   crusie; curies
cruiser   curries
cruisers   scurries
cruises   crusies; cuisser

cruives cursive
crumble clumber
crumbles clumbers
crumpets spectrum
crunodes unscored
crus curs; rucs; scur
crusades used cars
cruse cures; curse; sucre
cruses curses; cusser
cruset cruets; Custer; eructs;
  rectus; truces
crusie cruise; curies
crusies cruises; cuisser
Crusoe cerous; course; crouse;
  source
crust curst
Crustacea carucates
crustae curates
crustal curtals
crustier recruits
crusty curtsy
crutches scutcher
cruve curve
cruves curves
crying out congruity;
  outcrying
cry out outcry
Ctesiphon phonetics
cube Cebu
cubes Cebus
cubist cubits
cubits cubist
cuddles scuddle
cuds scud
cue écu
cued duce
cueist cuties
cuerpo couper; croupe; recoup
cues écus
cuesta acutes
cuestas caestus
cuffs scuff
cuisser cruises; crusies
Culdees seclude
Culebra curable
Culion uncoil
Cullera cure-all
cullers cruells; sculler
cullings sculling
cullions scullion
culls scull
cultch clutch
culter cutler; reluct

culters cluster; custrel; cutlers;
  relucts
cumbers scumber
cuneal launce; Lucena; unlace
Cuneo ounce
cunt Cnut
cupid pudic
cupidity pudicity
cupids cuspid; Sidcup
cupola copula
cupolar copular
cupolated copulated
cuppers scupper
cupreous coupures
cuprite picture
cups cusp; scup
cur cru; ruc
curable Culebra
curaçao curaçoa
curaçoa curaçao
curate acture
curates crustae
curbs scrub
curd crud
curdle curled
curdled cruddle
curdles scudler
curds cruds
cure ecru
cure-all Cullera
cured crude
cureless recluses
curer recur
curers curser; recurs
cures cruse; curse; sucre
curia auric
curial uracil; Uralic
curies cruise; crusie
curled curdle
curries cruiser
curs crus; rucs; scur
curse cruse; cures; sucre
curser curers; recurs
curses cruses; cusser
cursive cruives
cursores coursers; scourers
curst crust
curtail trucial
curtain turacin
curtals crustal
curtness encrusts
curtsy crusty
curve cruve**

curves cruves
Cush such
cusk suck
cusks sucks
cusp cups; scup
cuspate teacups
cuspid cupids; Sidcup
cusser cruses; curses
Custer cruets; cruset; eructs; rectus; truces
custos scouts
custrel cluster; culters; cutlers; relucts
custrels clusters
cuter cruet; eruct; truce
cuties cueist
cut in incut; tunic

cutler culter; reluct
cutlers cluster; culters; custrel; relucts
cutlery cruelty
cutlet cuttle
cutlets cuttles; scuttle
cuts scut
cuts in tunics
cutters scutter
cuttings tungstic
cuttle cutlet
cuttles cutlets; scuttle
cyders descry
cylindrite indirectly
cylix xylic
Cyril lyric

D

da ad
dab bad
dabber barbed
dabbler rabbled
dabbles slabbed
dace cade
Dacian Candia
Dacians scandia
dacker arcked; carked; racked
Dacron Conrad
dad add
daddles saddled
dado Odda
dads adds
daemon Menado; moaned; Modane; Modena; nomade
daemonic comedian; demoniac
daemons monades; nomades
Daf fad
dafter farted; rafted
dag gad
dagger ragged
daggle lagged
daggles slagged
dago goad
dagoes dosage; sea-dog; sea-god
Dagon donga; gonad; Gonda
dagos gadso; goads
dags gads
dah had
dahs dash; shad
Dai aid; Ida

daidle laddie
daidles laddies
daiker raiked
Dail dali; dial; laid
dailies sedilia
daily Lydia
daimen Damien; demain; maiden; median; Medina
daimon domain
daimons domains; Madison
daintiest dittanies
Dairen Darien; rained; randie
dairies diaries
dairy diary
dairyman mainyard
dais aids; Dias; Sadi; said; Sida
Dakar Kadar
daker arked; drake; raked
dakers drakes
dal lad
dale deal; lade; lead; Leda
dales deals; lades; leads; slade
dalesman leadsman
dalesmen leadsmen
dali Dail; dial; laid
dalis Aldis; dials; slaid
Dallas sallad
dalle Della; ladle
dalles ladles
dallied dialled
dallier dialler; rallied
dalliers diallers

dallies sallied
dals lads
dam mad
dame Edam; made; mead
dames meads
Damien daimen; demain; maiden;
  median; Medina
damnatory mandatory
damned demand; madden
Damon monad; nomad
damper ramped
dampish phasmid
dams mads
damsel medals
damson monads; nomads
dan and
dance caned
dancer cedarn; craned; ranced
dances ascend
dander darned; narded
dandle landed
Dane Aden; dean; Edna
Danes Andes; deans; Desna;
  sedan; snead
danger gander; garden; ranged
dangers ganders; gardens
dangle angled; Glenda
dangled gladden
dangler gnarled
danglers glanders
dangles slanged
Daniel Aldine; alined; Delian;
  denial; lead-in; nailed
Danish sandhi
Danite detain; Taiden
Danites detains; instead; sainted;
  stained
danker darken; narked; ranked
dans sand
Dante anted
Dantean andante; at an end
dap pad
dapper rapped
dapple lapped; palped
dapples slapped
daps pads
darbies air-beds; braised; seabird
Darby bardy
dare ared; dear; eard; rade; read
dared adder; aredd; dread
dares dears; rased; reads
darg drag; Gard
darga Garda

dargs drags
dari arid; raid
daric acrid; caird; Dirac
Darien Dairen; rained; randie
daring gradin
Darius radius
darken danker; narked; ranked
darkle larked
darling larding
darn nard; rand
darned dander; narded
darnel aldern; enlard; lander
darner errand; Renard
darners errands; Randers
darning narding
darns nards; rands
dart drat; trad
darted traded
darter dartre; retard; tarred; trader
darters retards; starred; traders
darting trading
dartre darter; retard; tarred; trader
darts drats; strad
Darwen Andrew; dawner; wander;
  warden; warned
Darwin draw in; inward
das ads; sad
dash dahs; shad
dashed shaded
dasher shared
dashes sashed; shades
dashing shading
dassie asides
Datel dealt; delta; lated
date-line entailed; lineated
date-palm palmated
dater adret; rated; tared; trade;
  tread
daters adrets; stared; trades; treads
dates sated; stade; stead
date-sugar graduates
dato toad
datos toads
Datsun daunts
daturine indurate; ruinated;
  urinated
daub baud
daubed bedaub
dault adult
daults adults
daunted undated
daunts Datsun
Dave deva; vade; Veda

Davies advise; visaed
daw wad
dawd wadd
dawded wadded
dawdle waddle
dawdled waddled
dawdler drawled; waddler
dawdlers swaddler; waddlers
dawdles swaddle; waddles
dawdling waddling
Dawley yawled
dawn wand
dawner Andrew; Darwen; wander; warden; warned
dawnered wandered
dawnering wandering
dawners wanders; wardens
dawns wands
daws swad; wads
dawtie waited
dawties waisted
daze adze
dazes adzes
deacon acnode; canoed
deaconry crayoned
deacons acnodes
dead Edda
deadlier derailed
deadlock deck-load
deadlocks deck-loads
dead-set sedated; steaded
deaf fade
deafer feared
deafest defeats; feasted
deafly flayed
deal dale; lade; lead; Leda
dealed leaded
dealer leader
dealers leaders
dealing aligned; leading
dealings leadings
deals dales; lades; leads; slade
dealt Datel; delta; lated
dean Aden; Dane; Edna
deaner Dearne; earned; endear; neared
deaners endears
deanery renayed; yearned
deans Andes; Danes; Desna; sedan; snead
dear ared; dare; eard; rade; read
deare arede; eared; Reade
dearer reader; reared; reread

deares aredes; erased; Red Sea; reseda; seared
dearest derates; estrade; reasted
dearies readies
dearing areding; deraign; gradine; grained; reading
dearn Arden; Derna
Dearne deaner; earned; endear; neared
dears dares; rased; reads
dearth hatred; red-hat; thread
dearths hardest; hatreds; red-hats; threads; trashed
deary deray; rayed; ready; yeard
deasil aisled; ideals; ladies; sailed
death hated
deaths hasted; 'sdeath; tashed
deave evade
deaved evaded
deaves evades
deaving evading
deb bed
debar ardeb; Bader; bared; beard; bread; Breda
debark barked; braked
debars ardebs; beards; breads; sabred; serdab
debase sea-bed
debater berated; betread; rebated
debaters betreads; breasted
debates bestead
debating Nebit-Dag
debile belied; edible
debit betid; bidet
debited betided
debiting betiding
debitor orbited
debits bed-sit; bidets
debrief briefed
debris brides; rebids
debs beds
debtor betrod
debug budge
debugger begrudge; buggered
debuggers begrudges
debugs budges
debunk bunked
debut tubed
debuts bedust; bestud; busted
decal laced
decals scaled
decamp camped
decamps scamped

decant   cadent; canted
decanter   cantered; crenated; nectared; recanted
decants   descant; scanted
decarb   braced
decastere   desecrate
decasteres   desecrates
Decatur   traduce
deceiver   received
decide   de-iced
decider   decried
deciders   descried
decigram   grimaced
decimal   claimed; declaim; medical
decimally   medically
decimals   declaims; medicals
decimate   medicate
decimated   medicated
decimates   medicates
decimating   medicating
decimation   medication
decker   recked
deck-load   deadlock
deck-loads   deadlocks
declaim   claimed; decimal; medical
declaimer   reclaimed
declaims   decimals; medicals
declare   Cedrela; cleared; creedal
declares   rescaled
declass   classed
declines   licensed; silenced
declutch   clutched
decollate   ocellated
decolour   coloured
decomplex   complexed
decompound   compounded
decompress   compressed
decongest   congested
decor   coder; cored; credo
decoration   co-ordinate
decorations   co-ordinates
decree   recede
decreed   receded
decrees   recedes; seceder
decrepit   depicter
decrial   radicel; radicle
decried   decider
decries   de-icers
decrown   crowned
Dectra   carted; crated; redact; traced
dedal   addle; laded
dedans   sadden; sanded
dedimus   muddies

deduce   deuced; educed
deduces   seduced
Dee   Ede
deem   deme; Mede; meed
deems   demes; Medes; meeds
deep   peed
deepen   peened
deeper   De Pere; peered
deepest   steeped
deeps   speed
deer   dere; dree; rede; reed
default   faulted
defeats   deafest; feasted
defend   fended
defer   freed
deferment   fermented
defiant   fainted
de fide   defied
defied   de fide
defiled   fielded
defiler   fielder
defilers   fielders
defiling   fielding
deflex   flexed
deflorate   floreated
deflower   flowered; reflowed
deforces   frescoed
deforest   forested; fostered
deform   formed
deformer   reformed
defoul   fouled
defray   frayed
defrock   frocked
defrost   frosted
degarnish   garnished
Degas   gades
degust   gusted
dehorn   horned
dehort   red-hot
dehorts   shorted
de-iced   decide
de-icers   decries
deification   edification
deified   edified
deifies   edifies
deify   edify
deifying   edifying
deign   Nigde
deigns   design; sdeign; signed; singed
deil   eild; idle; lied
deils   idles; sidle; slide
Deirdre   derider; ridered

deism dimes
deist diets; dites; edits; id est; sited; St. Dié; stied; tides
deistic diciest
deists desist; sisted
delaine Adeline; aliened
delapse elapsed; pleased
delate elated
Delaware Weardale
delay leady
delayer layered; relayed
deles Edsel; Leeds; seled
deletes sleeted; steeled
deletion entoiled
delf fled
Delia ailed; ideal
Delian Aldine; alined; Daniel; denial; lead-in; nailed
delible bellied
delicateness delicatessen
delicatessen delicateness
deligation intaglioed
delight lighted
delights slighted
delimit limited
deliver livered; relived; reviled
deliverer redeliver
deliverers redelivers
delivers desilver; silvered; slivered
Della dalle; ladle
Delorme remodel
Delos doles; lodes; soled
Del Rio roiled
delta Datel; dealt; lated
deltaic citadel; dialect; edictal
deltas desalt; lasted; salted; slated; staled
delude eluded
deluding indulged; ungilded
delusion insouled; unsoiled
demain daimen; Damien; maiden; median; Medina
demains maidens; medians; sideman
demand damned; madden
demanded maddened
demander remanded
demanding maddening
demands maddens
demarcate camerated; macerated
deme deem; Mede; meed
demean amende; amened
demeanour enamoured

demeans amendes
demerge emerged
demerit dimeter; Edremit; merited
demerits dimeters
demersal emeralds
demerse emersed; redeems
demes deems; Medes; meeds
demesnes seedsmen
demi-god Megiddo
demi-lance endemical
demireps premised; simpered
demise Medise
demised Medised; misdeed
demises Medises
demising Medising
demit timed
demits misted; stimed
demo dome; Edom; mode
demoniac comedian; daemonic
demos domes; modes
demote emoted
demount mounted
demounts mudstone
demur mured
demurred murdered
demurrer murderer
demurrers murderers
demurring murdering
den end; Ned
denarius Eridanus; unraised
denary yarned
denatures sauntered
dene Eden; need
denes dense; needs
Denia Adeni; Andie; Diane; Edina
denial Aldine; alined; Daniel; Delian; lead-in; nailed
denials lead-ins; snailed
denied indeed
denier nereid; reined
deniers nereids
denies seined
denim mined
Denis dines; snide
Denison ondines
Dennis sinned
denominate emendation
denotes Tenedos
denounce enounced
dens ends; send; sned
dense denes; needs
denser sender
densimeter determines

density   destiny
dent   tend
dentated   attended
dentation   intonated
dented   tended
dentex   extend
denting   tending
dentist   stinted
Denton   tendon
dents   stend; tends
dentures   sederunt; underset;
  undesert
denude   dudeen; Dundee
denudes   dudeens
denunciate   enunciated
Denver   nerved; vender; Verden
deny   dyne
Deo   doe; ode
deodar   adored
depart   parted; prated; petard;
  traped
departs   petards
depasture   depurates
depend   pended
De Pere   deeper; peered
depicter   decrepit
depilate   epilated; pileated
depletes   steepled
depone   opened
depones   spondee
deport   de trop; ported
deports   sported
depose   epodes; speedo
deposes   speedos
deposit   dopiest; posited; topside
depositor   droopiest
deposits   side-post; topsides
depot   opted; poted; toped
depots   despot; posted; stoped
deprave   pervade
depraved   pervaded
depraves   pervades
depraving   pervading
depress   pressed; spersed
depurates   depasture
deraign   areding; dearing; gradine;
  grained; reading
deraigns   gradines; readings
derail   laired; Lérida; railed; relaid
derailed   deadlier
derails   sideral
derange   angered; en garde;
  enraged; grandee; grenade

deranged   gardened
deranges   grandees; grenades
deranging   gardening
derates   dearest; estrade; reasted
derating   gradient; red giant;
  treading
deration   ordinate; rationed;
  Rodentia
deray   deary; rayed; ready; yeard
derayed   yearded
deraying   readying; yearding
derays   yeards
dere   deer; dree; rede; reed
dered   dreed
deres   drees; redes; reeds; Seder
Derg   dreg
derham   harmed
derider   Deirdre; ridered
derides   desired; resided
dering   dinger; engird; girned;
  ringed
derision   Ironside
derive   reived; revied; rieved
derives   deviser; De Vries; diverse;
  revised
derma   ad rem; armed; dream
dermal   marled; medlar
dern   rend
Derna   Arden; dearn
derns   rends
derris   driers; reirds; riders; sirred
Derry   dryer; Ryder
der Tag   grated; targed
dervish   shrived
desalt   deltas; lasted; salted; slated;
  staled
descant   decants; scanted
descend   scended
descent   scented
describe   escribed
descried   deciders
description   predictions
descry   cyders
desecrate   decastere
desecrates   decasteres
desecration   considerate
desert   deters; rested
desertion   detersion
deserts   dessert; tressed
deserve   severed
desiccant   accidents
design   deigns; sdeign; signed;
  singed

designed sdeigned
designer energids; resigned
designing sdeigning
designs sdeigns
desilver delivers; silvered; slivered
desire eiders; reside
desired derides; resided
desirer Dreiser; serried
desires resides
desiring residing; ringside
desist deists; sisted
desk keds
desman amends; menads
desmans madness
Desna Andes; Danes; deans;
  sedan; snead
despair aspired; diapers; praised
despairing diaperings
despise pedesis
despiser disperse; Perseids;
  presides
despisers disperses
despites side-step
despoil diploes; dipoles; peloids;
  soliped; spoiled
despoils solipeds
despot depots; posted; stoped
dessert deserts; tressed
desserts stressed
d'Estaing sedating; steading
Desterro resorted; rostered
destiny density
desulphur sulphured
detail dilate; tailed
details dilates
detain Danite; Taiden
detainer retained
detains Danites; instead; sainted;
  stained
detent netted; tented
deter treed
deterge greeted
determines densimeter
deters desert; rested
detersion desertion
detest tested
dethrones shortened
detort rotted
detour douter; outred; red out;
  routed; toured
detours dourest; douters; outreds;
  rousted
detrain tan-ride; trade-in; trained

detrains strained; tan-rides
Detroit dottier
de trop deport; ported
deuce educe
deuced deduce; educed
deuces educes
Deurne endure; enured
doue duoc; Duse; sued; used
deva Dave; vade; Veda
devaluate evaluated
devas saved; vades; Vedas
devest vested
Devi dive; vied
deviates sedative
devil lived; vilde
devils slived
devise sieved; viséed
deviser derives; De Vries; diverse;
  revised
devisers disserve; dissever
devisor devoirs; visored; voiders
devitrify fervidity
devoid voided
devoir voider
devoirs devisor; visored; voiders
devolve evolved
devote vetoed
De Vries derives; deviser; diverse;
  revised
dew wed
Dewali wailed
dewan awned; waned
dewani wained
Dewar wader; wared
De Wet tweed
Dewey weedy
dewiness wideness
dews weds
dey dye
deys dyes; syed
Dhar hard
dhole holed
dhurrie hurried
diabetes beadiest
diadem maided
diagnose agonised; San Diego
dial Dail; dali; laid
dialect citadel; deltaic; edictal
dialects citadels
dialled dallied
dialler dallier; rallied
diallers dalliers
dials Aldis; dalis; slaid

diamante animated
diametric matricide
Diana Aidan; naiad
Diane Adeni; Andie; Denia; Edina
diaper paired; pardie; repaid
diaperings despairing
diapers aspired; despair; praised
diaries dairies
diary dairy
Dias aids; dais; Sadi; said; Sida
diastema Adamites
diaster asterid; astride; disrate;
  staired; tirades
diasters asterids; disaster; disrates
diastyle steadily
diatoms mastoid
dib bid
dibber bribed; ribbed
Diber bride; rebid
dibs bids
dice cedi; iced
diced Eddic
Dicentra crinated
dicer cider; cried; riced
dicers ciders; scried
dices cedis
diciest deistic
dickens snicked
dicker ricked
dictates acid test
didder ridded
diddle lidded
diddler riddled
didoes diodes
die ide
dieb bide
dies Ides; side
dies back backside
diesel elides; sedile; seiled
diesels idlesse
diet dite; edit; tide; tied
dieted edited
dieting editing; ignited
dietitian initiated
diets deist; dites; edits; id est; sited;
  St. Dié; stied; tides
differ riffed
dig gid
digester estridge
digesters estridges
digestions disgestion
digests disgest
digger rigged

dignity tidying
digonal loading
dika kadi
dikas kadis
diker irked
dikers risked
dikes skied
dilate detail; tailed
dilates details
dilatory adroitly; idolatry
diligence ceilinged
dilly idyll
diluent untiled
diluted luddite
dim mid
dimble limbed
dime idem
dimer mired; rimed
dimerous soredium
dimes deism
dimeter demerit; Edremit; merited
dimeters demerits
dimmer rimmed
dimness missend
dimple limped
din Ind; nid
dinar drain; Drina; Indra; nadir
dinars drains; nadirs
dindles slidden
dine Enid; nide
diner Indre
diners rinsed
dines Denis; snide
dinger dering; engird; girned;
  ringed
dingers engirds
dingle elding; engild; gilden
dingles engilds; singled
dingo doing
dingy dying
dink kind
dinks kinds
dinnle linden; linned
dinnles lindens
Dino Odin
dins sind
dint tind
dinted tinded
dinting tinding
dints tinds
diode Dodie
diodes didoes
diopter dioptre

diopters dioptres; dipteros;
  proteids; riposted
dioptre diopter
dioptres diopters; dipteros;
  proteids; riposted
dioptric tripodic
diploe dipole
diploes despoil; dipoles; peloids;
  soliped; spoiled
dipole diploe
dipoles despoil; diploes; peloids;
  soliped; spoiled
dipper ripped
Diptera pirated
dipteros diopters; dioptres;
  proteids; riposted
Dirac acrid; caird; daric
dire Reid; ride
direct credit; triced
directed credited
directing crediting
direction cretinoid
directions discretion
directives discretive
director creditor
directors creditors
directs credits
direr drier; reird; rider
direst driest; stride
dirge gride; ridge
dirges grides; grised; ridges
dirhams Midrash
dirled riddle
dirts strid
Dis Sid
disable baldies
disappear appraised
disaster asterids; diasters; disrates
disbar braids
disburse bus-rides
discern cinders; rescind
discerned rescinded
discerning rescinding
discerns rescinds
disconsolate consolidates
discount conduits
discounter introduces; reductions
discover divorces
discoverer rediscover
discoverers rediscovers
discreet discrete
discreetly discretely
discreetness discreteness

discrepant predicants
discrete discreet
discretely discreetly
discreteness discreetness
discretion directions
discretive directives
discriminator doctrinairism
disease seaside
disgest digests
disgestion digestions
disgown dowsing
dished eddish
dishes hissed
dishevel she-devil
dishevels she-devils
dishing hidings; shindig
dishonest hedonists
disinter inditers
disk kids; skid
disks skids
Disney Sidney
dispel lisped; spiled
disperse despiser; Perseids;
  presides
disperses despisers
dispone spinode
dispones spinodes
disport tripods
disprove provides
disrate asterid; astride; diaster;
  staired; tirades
disrates asterids; diasters; disaster
dissenter residents; tiredness
disserve devisers; dissever
disserves dissevers
dissever devisers; disserve
dissevers disserves
dissolute solitudes
disuse issued
dita adit
ditas adits; staid
ditcher chirted
dite diet; edit; tide; tied
dited tided
dites deist; diets; edits; id est; St.
  Dié; sited; stied; tides
dittanies daintiest
diva avid; Vida
divan Dvina; viand
divans viands
dive Devi; vied
diver drive; rived; Verdi
diverge grieved

divers   drives
diverse   derives; deviser; De Vries;
  revised
diverts   strived
dives   vised
diviner   drive-in
diviners   drive-ins
divorces   discover
Dnieper   repined
Dniester   inserted; resident;
  sintered
do   od
Döbeln   blonde; bolden
doc   cod
Doce   code; coed
docile   coiled
docker   corked; rocked
dockets   stocked
doctrinairism   discriminator
doctrine   centroid; Crediton
doctrines   centroids
dod   odd
dodger   red-dog
dodgers   gorsedd
Dodie   diode
dods   odds
doe   Deo; ode
doer   Doré; Oder; re-do; rode; roed
doers   dorse; rodes; rosed
does   dose; odes
doesn't   Donets; Ostend; stoned
dog   god
dogate   dotage; togaed
dogbane   bondage
dog-bite   bigoted
dogger   gorged
dog-leg   logged
dog-legs   slogged
dogs   gods
dog-watch   watch-dog
doh   hod
doing   dingo
doings   dosing
dolces   closed
dole   lode
dolerite   loitered
doles   Delos; lodes; soled
dolia   Idola
doline   indole; Leonid
dolines   Leonids; sondeli
dolium   Idolum
dolly   Lloyd
dolman   almond; old man

dolmans   almonds
dolmen   old men
dolt   told
Dom   mod
domain   daimon
domains   daimons; Madison
domal   modal
dome   demo; Edom; mode
domes   demos; modes
dominate   nematoid
dominates   Maidstone
domination   admonition
dominative   admonitive
dominator   admonitor
dominators   admonitors
domineers   modernise
don   nod
Donar   adorn
donate   atoned; nodate
donates   onstead
donator   odorant; tornado
done   node
done in   ondine
Donet   noted; toned
Donets   doesn't; Ostend; stoned
donga   Dagon; gonad; Gonda
dongas   gonads
Donne   end-on; on end
donor   doorn; rondo
donors   doorns; rondos
dons   nods; snod
donsie   Edison; noised; onside;
  side-on
donuts   stound
doom   mood
dooms   dsomo; moods; Sodom
Doone   Odeon
door   ordo; rood
doorbell   bordello
doorbells   bordellos
doorman   madroño
doormen   morendo
doorn   donor; rondo
doorns   donors; rondos
doors   Ordos; roods; sordo
dope   oped
doper   pedro; pored; roped
dopers   pedros; prosed
dopes   posed; spode
dopier   period
dopiest   deposit; posited; topside
doping   pongid
dor   ord; rod

Dora   Odra; road
Doras   dorsa; roads; Rodas; sorda
Doré   doer; Oder; re-do; rode; roed
doree   erode
dorees   erodes
Dorian   inroad; ordain
dormant   mordant
dormie   moider
dormies   misdoer; moiders
dorp   drop; prod
dorps   drops; prods; sprod
dors   ords; rods; sord
dorsa   Doras; roads; Rodas; sorda
dorse   doers; rodes; rosed
dorsel   drôles; solder; resold
dorsels   rodless; solders
dorser   orders
dorses   dosser; sordes
Dorset   sorted; stored; strode
Dorsten   rodents; snorted
dort   trod
dosage   dagoes; sea-dog; sea-god
dosages   sea-dogs; sea-gods
dose   does; odes
dosch   hosed; shoed
dosing   doings
doss   dsos; sods
dosser   dorses; sordes
dossil   solids
dost   dots; tods
dot   tod
dotage   dogate; togaed
dotes   tosed
doting   tin god
dots   dost; tods
dottier   Detroit
dottle   lotted
dottles   slotted
doubles   bloused
doubter   obtrude; outbred; redoubt
doubters   obtrudes; redoubts
douce   coudé
douches   choused; hocused
dour   duro; Ordu
dourer   ordure
dourest   detours; douters; outreds;
   rousted
dourness   resounds; sounders
douser   roused; soured
douter   detour; outred; red out;
   routed; toured
douters   detours; dourest; outreds;
   rousted

dover   drove; roved
dovers   droves
dovetail   violated
dowel   lowed
dowelling   well-doing
dowels   slowed; sowled
dower   rowed
dowers   dowser; drowse; worsed
dowlas   woalds
downa   adown
dowry   rowdy; wordy
dowse   sowed
dowser   dowers; drowse; worsed
dowsers   drowses
dowsing   disgown
dozen   zoned
drab   bard; brad
drabs   bards; brads
draconic   cancroid
Draconis   sardonic
draconites   redactions
drafter   redraft
drafters   redrafts
drag   darg; Gard
dragée   agreed; geared
draggle   gargled; raggled
drag-net   granted
dragon   Gondar
drags   dargs
drail   laird; Liard
drails   lairds
drain   dinar; Drina; Indra; nadir
drainage   gardenia
drainers   serranid
drains   dinars; nadirs
drake   arked; daker; raked
drakes   dakers
dramas   madras
drap   pard; prad
drape   padre; pared; raped;
   repad
draped   padder; parded; Praded
drapers   sparred
drapes   padres; parsed; rasped;
   repads; spared; spread
drapier   parried
draps   pards; prads
drat   dart; trad
drats   darts; strad
drave   raved; Revda; Varde
draw   ward
drawback   backward
drawbacks   backwards

drawer redraw; reward; warder; warred
drawers redraws; rewards; warders
draw in Darwin; inward
drawing warding
drawled dawdler; waddler
draw on onward
draws sward; wards
draws in inwards
draws on onwards
dray adry; yard
drays yards
dread adder; aredd; dared
dreads adders; sadder
dream ad rem; armed; derma
dreaming margined; mid-range; Niger Dam
dreamer rearmed
dree deer; dere; rede; reed
dreed dered
dreeing energid; reeding; reigned
drees deres; redes; reeds; Seder
dreg Derg
Dreiser desirer; serried
Dresden reddens
dresser redress
drey dyer; Ryde; yerd
dreys dyers; yerds
drib bird
driblets bristled
dribs birds
drier direr; reird; rider
driers derris; reirds; riders; sirred
dries rides; sider; sired
driest direst; stride
Drin rind
Drina dinar; drain; Indra; nadir
drive diver; rived; Verdi
drive-in diviner
drive-ins diviners
drives divers
drogue gourde; rogued; rouged
drogues gourdes; groused
droguet grouted
drôle older
drôles dorsel; resold; solder
drolling lordling
drolly lordly
dromes smored
drone ronde
droned nodder
drones rondes; snored; sorned

drongo Gordon; Grodno
droopiest depositor
drop dorp; prod
drops dorps; prods; sprod
Drosera adorers
dross sords
drove dover; roved
droves dovers
drow word
drows sword; words
drowse dowers; dowser; worsed
drowses dowsers
drub burd
drubs burds
drugged grudged
drugging grudging
drumbeat umbrated
drumble rumbled
drupe duper; Dupré; perdu; prude; pured
drupel purled
drupes dupers; perdus; prudes; pursed
druse dures
druses duress
dryer Derry; Ryder
dry ice cidery
dso sod
dsomo dooms; moods; Sodom
dsos doss; sods
dual auld; laud; udal
dub bud
dubs buds
ducal cauld; Claud
duce cued
ducker rucked
dudeen denude; Dundee
dudeens denudes
duds sudd
duel dule
duels dulse; slued
dues deus; Duse; sued; used
duetto touted
duffel duffle; luffed
duffer ruffed
duffle duffel; luffed
dugong gun dog
dugongs gun dogs
Dulcigno clouding
dule duel
dulse duels; slued
duma maud
Dumas adsum; mauds

dumpier umpired
dumple lumped; plumed
dumples slumped
Dunbar Durban
dunces secund
Dundee denude; dudeen
dune nude; unde
dunes nudes
dungaree underage; ungeared
Dunmore mourned
duo Oud; udo
duodenal unloaded
duper drupe; Dupré; perdu; prude;
  pured
dupers drupes; perdus; prudes;
  pursed
dupes pseud; spued
duple puled; upled
Dupré drupe; duper; perdu; prude;
  pured
duramen manured; maunder;
  unarmed
Durban Dunbar
dure rude; rued; urdé
dured udder
Düren runed; under; urned
Dürer ruder
dures druse
duress druses

during ungird
durmast mustard
durn rund
durns runds
duro dour; Ordu
durst turds
Duse deus; dues; sued; used
dust stud
duster rusted
dusters trussed
dusts studs
dusty study
Dvina divan; viand
dwale lawed; waled; weald
dwales swaled
dwine Edwin; widen; wined
dwined winded
dwines widens; Widnes
dwining winding
dye dey
dyed eddy
dyer drey; Ryde; yerd
dyers dreys; yerds
dyes deys; syed
dying dingy
dynamo Monday
dynamos Mondays
Dyson synod

E

ea ae
each ache
eager agree; eagre
eaglet Galtee; gelate; legate; teagle;
  telega
eaglets legates; teagles; telegas
eagre agree; eager
eagres agrees; grease
Ealing genial; linage
ean ane; Ena; nae
eanling aneling; leaning; nealing
eanlings leanings
eans sane; sean; Sena
ear are; era
eard ared; dare; dear; rade; read
earfuls refusal
earing gainer; graine; regain;
  regina
earings erasing; gainers; regains;
  searing; Seraing; seringa

earl lare; lear; râle; real
earless leasers; sealers
earliest ateliers
earls Arles; lares; laser; lears; reals;
  seral
early layer; relay
earn Arne; nare; near; Rena
earned deaner; Dearne; endear;
  neared
earner nearer
earnest eastern; nearest
earnests assenter; sarsenet
earning engrain; grannie; nearing
earnings engrains; grannies
earns nares; nears; saner; snear
earring angrier; grainer; rearing
earrings grainers
ears ares; arse; eras; rase; sear; sera
earst arets; aster; astre; rates; reast;
  resat; stare; strae; tares; tears; teras

earth Harte; hater; heart; Herat; rathe; Thera; thrae
earthborn abhorrent
earthed hearted; red-heat
earthen hearten; Teheran
earth-fed fathered
earthiness heartiness
earthing hearting; ingather
earthling haltering; lathering
earthly heartly
earthquake heartquake
earths haters; hearts; Sarthe; 'sheart
earth-shaped heart-shaped
earthy hearty
earwitness wateriness
eas sae; sea
easel lease
easels eassel; leases
easing agnise
eassel easels; leases
eassil aisles; laisse; lassie
east eats; sate; seat; seta; taes; teas
easted seated; sedate; teased
easter arêtes; eaters; reates; reseat; saeter; teaser; Teresa
Easter egg segregate
Easter eggs segregates
easterling generalist
easterlings generalists
eastern earnest; nearest
easters reseats; saeters; teasers; tessera
easting Gastein; genista; ingates; ingesta; seating; tangies; teasing; tsigane
eastings giantess
eastlin elastin; entails; salient; slàinte; staniel
eastling Galenist; genitals; stealing
eastlings Galenists
eastlins salients; staniels
Easton atones; Seaton
easy eyas; yeas
eat ate; eta; tae; tea
eater arête; reate; Taree
eaters arêtes; easter; reates; reseat; seater; teaser; Teresa
eath hate; heat; thae; Thea
eating ingate; tangie
eats east; sate; seat; seta; taes; teas
eavesdrops overpassed; passed over

ebbing Big Ben
ebon bone
Ebro Boer; bore; robe
Ebury buyer
ecarté cerate; create
Echidna chained
Echinops chopines
echoer cheero; choree; cohere; re-echo
echoers chorees; coheres
echoic choice
echt etch; tech
éclair Claire; lacier
eclat cleat; lacet
economies economise
economise economies
écritoires escritoire
ecru cure
écu cue
écus cues
Edam dame; made; mead
Eday yead
Edda dead
Eddaic caddie
Eddic diced
eddish dished
eddy dyed
Ede Dee
Eden dene; need
edentata antedate
Edenton tenoned
Edgar Gerda; grade; raged
edger greed
edges sedge
edginess seedings
Edgware ragweed; wagered
edible belied; debile
edict cited
edictal citadel; deltaic; dialect
edicts cisted
edification deification
edified deified
edifies deifies
edify deify
edifying deifying
edile elide
Edina Adeni; Andie; Denia; Diane
Edirne denier; nereid; reined
Edison donsie; noised; onside; side-on
edit diet; dite; tide; tied
edited dieted
editing dieting; ignited

edition   tenioid
editions   sedition
editor   rioted; tie-rod; triode
editors   roisted; rosited; sortied;
   steroid; storied; tie-rods; triodes
editress   resisted
edits   deist; diets; dites; id est; sited;
   St. Dié; stied; tides
Edna   Aden; Dane; dean
Edom   demo; dome; mode
Edremit   demerit; dimeter; merited
Edsel   deles; Leeds; seled
education   auctioned; cautioned
educators   Ceratodus; croustade
educe   deuce
educed   deduce; deuced
educes   deuces; seduce
eductions   seduction
eductor   courted
eductors   seductor
Edward   warded
Edwin   dwine; widen; wined
eel   lee
eelgrass   gearless; largesse
eels   else; lees; seel; sele; slee
eel-set   Steele
e'en   née
e'er   ere
eery   eyre
eft   fet
efts   fets
eftsoons   festoons
egad   aged; gade; gaed
eger   gree
egers   grees; grese; Segre; serge
egest   geste
egests   gestes
eggar   agger
eggars   aggers; sagger; seggar
eggler   legger
egglers   leggers
eggy   yegg
eglantine   inelegant
ego   geo
egocentric   geocentric
egos   goes
egress   greses
egret   greet
egrets   greets
eh   he
Eibar   Beira; Beria
eident   endite
eiders   desire; reside

eidograph   ideograph
eidographs   ideographs
eighth   height
eigne   genie
eignes   genies; seeing
eik   Ike; kie
eild   deil; idle; lied
eilding   eliding
Eire   Erie
eisel   Elsie; esile
Eisk   sike
ekes   seek; skee
e-la   ale; lea
Elam   alme; Elma; lame; leam;
   Lema; male; meal
élan   lane; lean; Lena
elance   enlace
elanced   cleaned; enlaced
elances   cleanse; enlaces; scalene
elancing   cleaning; enlacing
eland   laden; lande
elanet   lateen; La Tène
elapid   aliped; paidle; Pleiad
elapids   alipeds; lapides; paidles;
   palsied; Pleiads
Elaps   lapse; leaps; pales; peals;
   pleas; salep; sepal; spale; speal
elapse   asleep; please; sapele
elapsed   delapse; pleased
elapses   pleases
elapsing   pleasing
El Arish   hailers
elastic   astelic; Castile; laciest;
   latices
elastin   eastlin; entails; salient;
   slàinte; staniel
elate   telae
elated   delate
elater   relate; Tralee
elaterid   retailed
elaterin   entailer; treenail
elaters   Laertes; relates; stealer
elates   steale; stelae; teasel
Elath   ethal; lathe
elating   atingle; gelatin; genital
elation   toenail
Elba   Abel; able; albe; bael; bale;
   blae; Labe
elbow   below; bowel
elbow   bowel
Elbrus   rubles
Elche   leech
elchi   chiel; chile

elchis   chesil; chiels; chiles; chisel; Schlei
eld   led
eldin   lined
elding   dingle; engild; gilden
Eldred   reddle
elections   selection
electors   corselet; selector
Electra   treacle
elects   select
elegies   elegise
elegise   elegies
elegist   elegits
elegits   elegist
elfishness   fleshiness
Elgar   glare; lager; large; regal; Relga
Elgin   ingle; ligne; Nigel
Eli   lei; lie
Elian   alien; aline; anile; liane
Elias   aisle
elide   edile
elides   diesel; sedile; seiled
eliding   eilding
Eliot   toile
Elis   isle; leis; lies; seil; sile
elision   lionise
elisor   lories; oilers; oriels; Serlio
elitism   El Misti; limiest; limites
elk   lek
elks   leks; Selk
Ella   leal
Ellis   lisle
ells   sell
elm   lem
Elma   alme; Elam; iame; leam; Lema; male; meal
Elman   leman; Lemna
Elmer   merel; merle
Elmina   maline; menial
Elmira   mailer
El Misti   elitism; limiest; limites
elms   lems
elmy   Lyme; ylem
elogist   logiest
Elohist   hostile
eloins   esloin; insole; lesion; Sileno
elops   lopes; olpes; poles; slope
Elsa   ales; leas; sale; seal; slae
else   eels; lees; seel; sele; slee
Elsevier   relieves
Elsie   eisel; esile

elsin   lenis; liens; lines; nelis; Niles; silen
elsins   silens
Elstow   lowest; owlets; towels
elt   let; tel
Eltham   hamlet; Thelma
elts   lest; lets; tels
Eluard   lauder
eluded   delude
eluding   indulge
elution   outline
elvan   levan; navel; venal
Elvas   laves; salve; selva; slave; vales; valse
elver   lever; revel
elvers   levers; revels
elves   Veles
Elvis   evils; levis; lives; slive; veils
Ely   ley; lye
elytra   lyrate; realty
em   me
emanate   enemata; manatee
emanates   manatees
emanating   manganite
Emba   beam; bema
embar   amber; bream
embars   ambers; breams; Sambre
embay   beamy; maybe
emboil   bemoil; emboli; mobile
emboiled   bemoiled
emboiling   bemoiling
emboils   bemoils; mobiles
emboli   bemoil; emboil; mobile
embraced   cambered
embracing   cambering
embrues   Burmese
emend   Mende
emendation   denominate
emendator   Notre Dame
emeralds   demersal
emerged   demerge
emersed   demerse; redeems
emes   Esme; mese; seem; semé; smee
emigrants   mastering; St. Germain; streaming
emigrate   remigate
emigrated   remigated
emigrates   remigates
emigrating   remigating
emigration   remigation
émigré   regime
émigrés   regimes

Emil   lime; mile
emir   meri; mire; riem; rime
emirate   meatier
emirates   steamier
emirs   mires; miser; Reims; riems;
   rimes
emit   item; mite; time
emits   items; metis; mites; smite;
   stime; times
Emma   Mame
Emmaus   summae
emoted   demote
empanel   emplane
empanels   emplanes
empathic   emphatic
emperors   premorse
emphasis   misshape
emphatic   empathic
empire   epimer
Empire gown   empowering
empires   emprise; epimers;
   imprese; premise; spireme
emplane   empanel
emplanes   empanels
emplaster   palm trees
emplastron   Palmerston
empowering   Empire gown
emprise   empires; epimers;
   imprese; premise; spireme
emprises   impreses; premises;
   spiremes
emption   pimento
emu   meu
emus   meus; muse
en   ne
Ena   ane; ean; nae
enable   baleen
enactors   ancestor; Escatrón
enacts   ascent; secant; stance
en ami   amine; animé; Maine;
   Menai; minae
enamoured   demeanour
enarch   chenar
enarm   Marne; namer
enarmed   amender; meander;
   renamed
enarming   renaming
enarms   namers
encase   Cesena; seance; Seneca
encases   seances
encashed   enchased
encashes   enchases
encashing   enchasing

encharm   märchen
enchase   achenes
enchased   encashed
enchases   encashes
enchasing   encashing
enchoric   corniche
en clair   carline; Linacre
enclasp   spancel
enclasps   spancels
enclave   valence
enclaves   valences
enclouds   unclosed
encodes   seconde
encores   necrose
encradle   calender
encradles   calenders; esclandre
Encratism   miscreant
encrusts   curtness
encurtain   runcinate; uncertain
end   den; Ned
endarch   ranched
endart   ardent; ranted; red ant
endarting   integrand
endarts   red ants; stander
endear   deaner; Dearne; earned;
   neared
endearing   engrained; grenadine
endears   deaners
endemical   demi-lance
endews   Sweden
end-game   manèged
ending   ginned
endite   eident
enditing   indigent
endive   envied; veined
endlang   England
endodermis   modernised
end-on   Donne; on end
endorsable   banderoles; bandoleers
endow   nowed; owned; Woden
endower   re-endow
endowers   re-endows
endows   snowed
end-papers   snappered
ends   dens; send; sned
endure   Deurne; enured
endures   ensured
enduringly   underlying
end use   ensued
endwise   sinewed
enemas   enseam; seamen
enemata   emanate; manatee
enemy   Yemen

energic generic
energid reigned
energids designer; resigned
energised reseeding
energy greeny; Ygerne
enervate venerate
enervated venerated
enervates venerates
enervating venerating
enervation veneration
enerve veneer
enerves veneers
enew ween
enewed weened
enewing weening
enews sewen; weens
Enfield enfiled
enfiled Enfield
enfire ferine; Fernie; fineer; infere;
  refine
enfired refined
enfires fineers; refines
enfiring infringe; refining
enfold fondle
enfolds fondles
enforcer confrère
enforcers confrères
enforest softener
enforests softeners
enframe freeman
enframed freedman
en garde angered; derange;
  enraged; grandee; grenade
engild dingle; elding; gilden
engilds dingles singled
engird dering; dinger; girned;
  ringed
engirds dingers
England endlang
Englander Greenland
English shingle
englobed belonged
englobing belonging
englut gluten
engores Negroes
engrail aligner; learing; nargile;
  realign; reginal
engrailed Geraldine; realigned
engrailing realigning
engrailment realignment
engrailments realignments
engrails aligners; realigns;
  Salinger; sanglier; seal-ring

engrain earning; grannie; nearing
engrained endearing; grenadine
engrains earnings; grannies
engram german; manger; ragmen
engrams germans; mangers
engrave avenger
engraves avengers
Enid dine; nide
enigma gamine
enigmas gamines; seaming
enigmatist estimating
enisle ensile; nelies; senile; Silene
enisled ensiled; linseed
enisles ensiles
enisling ensiling
enlace elance
enlaced cleaned; elanced
enlaces cleanse; elances; scalene
enlacing cleaning; elancing
en l'air larine; linear; nailer
enlard aldern; darnel; lander
enlards landers; slander; snarled
enlarge general; gleaner
enlargement Greenmantle
enlarges generals; gleaners
enlight lighten
enlighted lightened
enlighting lightening
enlights lightens
enlist inlets; listen; silent; tinsel
enlisted listened
enlister Leinster; listener; re-enlist
enlisters listeners; re-enlists
enlisting listening
enlists listens; tinsels
en masse enseams
Enna Anne
Ennis nines
enodal loaned
enol leno; Leon; lone; Noel
enormous nemorous
Enos eons; noes; nose; ones; sone
enosis essoin; noesis; noises;
  ossein; sonsie
enounced denounce
enow Owen
en prise erepsin; repines
enquires squireen
enrace careen
enraces careens; caserne
enrage genera
enraged angered; derange; en
  garde; grandee; grenade

enraging angering
enrapt arpent; entrap; panter;
  parent; trepan
enrich richen
enriched richened
enriching richening
enring ginner
enrings ginners
enrol loner; Lorne; nerol
enrols loners
ens sen
ensate sateen; senate; steane
enseam enemas; seamen
enseams en masse
enshroud unhorsed
ensigns sensing
ensilage lineages
ensile enisle; nelies; senile; Silene
ensiled enisled; linseed
ensiles enisles
ensiling enisling
enslave leavens
enslaves vaneless
ensnared Andersen
ensnares nearness
ensnarl lanners
ensue Neuse
ensued end use
ensure enures
ensured endures
entailed date-line; lineated
entailer elaterin; treenail
entailers treenails
entails eastlin; elastin; salient;
  slàinte; staniel
entasis Saintes; sestina; Staines;
  tansies; tisanes
enter rente; terne; treen
entera neater; rateen
enterer re-enter; terrene
enterers re-enters; resenter;
  terrenes
enteric enticer
enters Ernest; nester; rentes;
  resent; Sterne; tenser; ternes
entia Taine; tinea
enticer enteric
entirely lientery
entires entries; Steiner; Teniers;
  trenise
entirety eternity
entitling inletting
entoiled deletion

entomic Metonic
entozoic enzootic
entrail Latiner; latrine; ratline;
  reliant; retinal; trenail
entrails Latiners; latrines; ratlines;
  trenails
entrances renascent
entrap arpent; enrapt; panter;
  parent; trepan
entraps arpents; panters; parents;
  pastern; trepans
entreat ratteen; ternate
entreats ratteens
entries entires; Steiner; Teniers;
  trenise
entropium importune
entrust nutters; test run
entrusts test runs
enumeration mountaineer
enunciated denunciate
enured Deurne; endure
enures ensure
envied endive; veined
envier Nièvre
enviers inverse; versine; Viersen
envies neives; nieves
envious niveous; veinous
enwrap pawner
enwraps pawners; spawner
enzootic entozoic
eon Neo; Noe; one
eonism Miseno; monies; Simeon;
  Simone
eons Enos; noes; nose; ones; sone
eorl lore; Orel; orle; role
eorls Leros; loser; orles; Osler;
  roles; soler; Sorel
eosin noise
Epacris Serapic
eparch preach
eparchies parcheesi
eparchy preachy
epha heap
ephod hoped
ephor hoper
epic pice
epical plaice; plicae
epics spice
epidermal impearled; impleader
epigon pigeon
epigons pigeons
epigram primage
epilate pileate

epilated   depilate; pileated
epimer   empire
epimers   empires; emprise;
   imprese; premise; spireme
Epinal   alpine; penial; pineal
Epirus   uprise
episcopal   Pepsi-Cola
epistler   peltries; reptiles
epochs   Cheops
epodes   depose; speedo
epodic   copied
epos   opes; peso; pose
épris   peris; piers; pries; prise;
   ripes; speir; spire
Epsom   mopes; poems; pomes
epulotic   poultice
equals   squeal
equators   quaestor
equip   pique
equips   piques
er   re
era   are; ear
eras   ares; arse; ears; rase; sear; sera
erased   aredes; deares; Red Sea;
   reseda; seared
erasing   earings; gainers; regains;
   searing; Seraing; seringa
Erasmus   amusers; masseur;
   mausers
Erastian   artesian; resinata
erasures   reassure
Erato   orate
erbium   imbrue
ere   e'er
erect   Crete; terce
erectable   celebrate
erection   neoteric
erections   resection; secretion
erects   certes; resect; secret
eremital   Lemaître; matériel;
   real-time
erepsin   en prise; repines
erethism   etherism
Erewhon   nowhere; whereon
erf   ref
Erfurt   returf
erg   Reg
ergo   goer; gore; ogre
ergon   Genro; goner; Negro
ergot   Roget
Erhard   harder
eric   ciré; icer; rice
Erica   ceria

erics   cries; icers; seric
Eridanus   denarius; unraised
Erie   Eire
Erin   in re; rein; Reni
eringo   ignore; Origen; region
Eris   reis; rise; sire
eristical   realistic
Erith   their
Eritrean   rain-tree; retainer
Eritreans   rain-trees; retainers;
   ternaries
Erivan   ravine; vainer; Vanier
erks   serk; sker
erne   Rene
ernes   sneer
Ernest   enters; nester; rentes;
   resent; Sterne; tenser; ternes
Ernestine   internees
Ernie   Irene
Ernst   rents; stern; terns
erode   doree
erodes   dorees
eroding   Gironde; groined; ignored;
   negroid; redoing
Eros   ores; roes; rose; sore
eroticism   isometric; meroistic
errand   darner; Renard
errands   darners; Randers
errant   ranter
erratic   Cartier; cirrate
erratum   maturer
erring   ringer
errs   serr
Erse   seer; sere
erst   rest; rets
eruct   cruet; cuter; truce
eructs   cruets; cruset; Custer; rectus;
   truces
erupted   reputed
erupting   reputing
eruptions   pertusion
erupts   purest
erven   nerve; never; Vener; Verne
eryngo   groyne
escallop   collapse
escallops   collapses
escaper   Caprese; percase
escarp   capers; Casper; crapes;
   pacers; parsec; recaps; scrape;
   spacer
escarps   parsecs; scrapes;
   spacers
Escatrón   ancestor; enactors

eschar arches; chares; chaser; raches; search
eschars chasers; crashes
escheat teaches
esclandre calenders; encradles
escolar coalers; oracles; solacer
escolars lacrosse; solacers
Escorial calories
escort corset; Cortes; coster; scoter; sector; Tresco
escorted corseted
escorting corseting
escorts corsets; costers; scoters; sectors
escribano carbonise
escribanos carbonises
escribed describe
escritoire écritoires
escroc soccer
escrow cowers
Esher herse; sheer
esile eisel; Elsie
esker reeks; skeer
eskers skeers
esloin eloins; insole; lesion; Sileno
esloins insoles; lesions; lioness
Esme emes; mese; seem; semé; smee
esne seen
Esneh sheen
esnes Essen; sense
esoteric coteries
espalier pearlies
Esperanto personate
espousal sepalous
espouser repoussé
esprit priest; Pteris; ripest; sprite; stripe; tripes
espy Spey; sype
esquire queries
esse sees
Essen esnes; sense
Essex sexes
essive sieves
essoin enosis; noesis; noises; ossein; sonsie
essoins session
estate tea-set; testae
estates tea-sets
estating tangiest
Este Sète; tees
ester reest; reset; steer; stere; teers; terse; trees

esters reests; resets; steers; steres
Esth hest; Seth; shet
Esther ethers; Hester; threes
estimating enigmatist
estocs cosset
Eston notes; onset; seton; stone; Tenos; tones
estop poets; potes; stoep; stope; topes
estops posset; stoeps; stopes
Estoril estriol; loiters; toilers
estover overset
estrade dearest; derates; reasted
estradiol idolaters
estrange grantees; greatens; reagents; segreant; sergeant
estranges greatness; sergeants
estray reasty; stayer; yarest
estrays stayers
estreat restate
estreats restates
estrepe steeper
estreped pestered
estreping perstinge; pestering; Presteign
estrich richest
estridge digester
estridges digesters
estriol Estoril; loiters; toilers
estro roset; rotes; store; tores; torse
estrous oestrus; ousters; sourest; souters; tousers; trouses; tussore
estrum muster; stumer
estrus russet; tusser
esurient retinues; reunites
eta ate; eat; tae; tea
et. al. late; leat; tael; tale; teal; tela
etalon lean-to
etalons lean-tos
etc. tec
etch echt; tech
etchers Chester; retches
eten nete; teen; tene
etens steen; teens; tense
eternal teleran
eternity entirety
eth het; the
ethal Elath; lathe
ethanol Athlone
ethe thee
Ethel Lethe
ether there; three
etherism erethism

ethers Esther; Hester; threes
ethicist itchiest; theistic
ethnical chainlet
ethnics sthenic
ethologic theologic
ethological theological
ethologist theologist
ethologists theologists
ethology theology
ethos shote; those
ethyl lythe
etna ante; Aten; neat; Tean
etnas antes; nates; Nesta; Senta;
  stane; stean; Teans
Eton note; tone
étourdi outride
étrier reiter; retire
étriers reiters; retires; retries;
  terries
Etruscan centaurs; recusant;
  untraces
Etruscans recusants
Etta tate; teat
ettles settle
etuis suite
etyma matey; meaty
eugh huge
euro roué
euros roués; rouse
Eva ave; vae
evade deave
evaded deaved
evades deaves
evading deaving
evaluated devaluate
Evan nave; Neva; vane; vena
evanishes heaviness
Evans avens; naves; Sevan; vanes
eve vee
Evelyn evenly
evenly Evelyn
evens Neves; seven
events Steven
ever veer
evert revet
everts revest; revets
eves vees
evets Steve
evict civet
evicts civets; Vectis
evidents invested
evil Levi; live; veil; vile; vlei
evilly lively; vilely

evilness vileness
evils Elvis; levis; lives; slive; veils;
  vleis
evince Venice
evites stieve
evolved devolve
Ewan anew; wane; wean
ewe wee
ewer were
ewers sewer; sweer; Weser
ewes swee; wees
ewest sweet
Ewing winge
ewk Kew
ewt tew; wet
ewts stew; tews; west; wets
exacter excreta
exalt latex
exam Xema
example exempla
except expect
excepted expected
excepting expecting
excepts expects
excides excised
excised excides
excitation intoxicate
excitor xerotic
excitors exorcist
exclaims climaxes
excreta exacter
exeem exeme
exeems exemes
exeme exeem
exemes exeems
exempla example
exerting genetrix
exertions exsertion
exerts exsert
exiles ilexes
exist exits; sixte
exists sexist
exits exist; sixte
exon oxen
exorcist excitors
exotics co-exist
expect except
expected excepted
expecting excepting
expects excepts
expires prexies
explain axle-pin
explains axle-pins

exporter re-export
exporters re-exports
exsert exerts
exsertion exertions
extend dentex
extension in extenso
extirpates sexpartite
extra taxer

extras astrex; taxers
eyas easy; yeas
eyed yede; yeed
eyelids seedily
eyra aery; Ayer; yare; year
eyras sayer; years
eyre eery
Ezra raze

F

face cafe
facer farce
facers farces
faces cafes
factional falcation
factor forçat
factories factorise
factorise factories
factors forçats
facula faucal
fad Daf
fade deaf
faeries arefies; freesia; sea-fire
Faeroes Faroese
faery arefy; Freya
fag-end fanged
faience fiancée
failed afield
fain Ifan; naif
faint Fanti
fainted defiant
fairness sanserif
fairs fiars
faithless flashiest
faker freak
fakers freaks
fakir Kafir
fakirs friska; Kafirs
fa-la alfa
falcation factional
falcon flacon
falconet conflate
falconets conflates
falcons flacons
fallout outfall
false feals; fleas; leafs
falser farles; flares; flaser
falsest fatless
Falster falters
faltered reflated
faltering reflating

falters Falster
falx flax
fameless self-same
famine infame
famines infames
fancier Francie
fancies fascine; fiancés
fanged fag-end
fangle flange
fangles flanges
fannies Fenians
Fanti faint
far fra
farce facer
farces facers
fardel Alfred; flared
fare fear; frae
fared Freda
fares farse; fears; safer
farfel raffle
farle feral; flare
farles falser; flares; flaser
farmed framed
farmer framer
farmers framers
farming framing
farmost formats
faro Afro
Faroese Faeroes
farrier Ferrari
farse fares; fears; safer
fart raft
farted dafter; rafted
farter rafter
farters rafters
farting ingraft
farts rafts
fascine fancies; fiancés
fast fats
fasten nefast; Stefan
fastener fenestra

fastens fatness
faster afters; strafe
Fastnet fattens
fat aft
fate feat
fates feast; feats; festa
fathered earth-fed
fathers shafter
fatless falsest
fatness fastens
fats fast
fatso softa
Fats Waller waterfalls
fattens Fastnet
fattrels flatters
faucal facula
faulted default
faults flatus
faunist fustian
fauns Fusan; snafu
feal flea; leaf
fealed leafed
fealing finagle; leafing
feals false; fleas; leafs
fealty featly
fear fare; frae
feared deafer
fears fares; farse; safer
feast fates; feats; festa
feasted deafest; defeats
feaster afreets; sea-fret
feasts safest
feat fate
feather terefah
featly fealty
feats fates; feast; festa
febrile Félibre
feebly bee-fly
feeder feered; reefed
feeding feigned
feel flee
feeling fine leg; fleeing
feels flees
feer fere; free; reef
feered feeder; reefed
feering feigner; freeing; reefing
feers feres; frees; reefs
feet fête
feigned feeding
feigner feering; freeing; reefing
feints finest; infest
Félibre febrile
felinity finitely

Felis files; flies; 'slife
felsite lefties
felt left
females alms-fee
feminal inflame
fen nef
fended defend
fenestra fastener
Fenians fannies
Fenris infers
fens nefs
feodal foaled; loafed
feral farle; flare
fere feer; free; reef
feres feers; frees; reefs
feria afire
ferine enfire; Fernie; fineer; infere;
  refine
ferly flyer
fermented deferment
Fermo forme; Frome
Fernie enfire; ferine; fineer; infere;
  refine
Ferrari farrier
ferrous furores
ferule refuel
ferules refuels
fervidity devitrify
festa fates; feast; feats
fester freest
festoons eftsoons
fet eft
fetal aleft
fête feet
fets efts
feuds fused
feutre refute
feutres refutes
fiancée faience
fiancés fancies; fascine
fiars fairs
fiber brief; fibre
fibers briefs; fibres
fibre brief; fiber
fibreless briefless
fibres briefs; fibers
fickled flicked
fickling flicking
fico coif; foci
Fidel field; filed
fidget gifted
fie Ife
fief fife

field Fidel; filed
fielded defiled
fielder defiler
fielders defilers
fielding defiling
field notes fieldstone
fieldstone field notes
fiend fined
fiendish finished
fierce Recife
fiery reify
fife fief
fig gif
fighter freight
fighters freights
figurate fruitage
filar flair; frail
file Leif; lief; life
filed Fidel; field
filer flier; lifer; rifle
filers fliers; lifers; rifles
files Felis; flies; 'slife
filets itself; stifle
filler refill
fillers refills
filter lifter; trifle
filters lifters; stifler; trifles
filtration flirtation
finagle fealing; leafing
finale al fine
finder friend
finders friends
fine neif; nife
fined fiend
fineer enfire; ferine; Fernie; infere; refine
fineers enfires; refines
fine leg feeling; fleeing
finer infer
fines neifs
finest feints; infest
finger fringe
fingers fringes
finished fiendish
finitely felinity
Finke knife
fino foin; info
fir Rif
fir cone conifer; inforce
fir cones conifers; forensic; forinsec; inforces
fire Frei; reif; rife
fire-back backfire

fire-backs backfires
fired fried
firelight flightier
fires fries; serif
firs fris
first frist; frits; rifts
firth frith
firths friths; shrift
fiscal califs
fisher sherif
fishers sherifs
fissure fussier
fist fits; sift
fisted sifted
fisting sifting
fists sifts
fitness infests
fits fist; sift
fitter titfer
fitters titfers
fizzing gin-fizz
flacon falcon
flacons falcons
flair filar; frail
flame fleam
flames fleams
flaneur funeral
flaneurs funerals
flange fangle
flanges fangles
flare farle; feral
flared Alfred; fardel
flares falser; farles; flaser
flaser falser; farles; flares
flashback half-backs
flashiest faithless
flashy fly ash
flatirons frost-nail
flatters fattrels
flatus faults
flax falx
flayed deafly
flea feal; leaf
fleam flame
fleams flames
fleas false; feals; leafs
flecker freckle
fleckers freckles
fled delf
flee feel
fleeing feeling; fine leg
fleer refel
fleers refels

flees   feels
Flemish   himself
flesh   shelf
flesher   herself
fleshiness   elfishness
fleshy   shelfy
flexed   deflex
flicked   fickled
flicking   fickling
flier   filer; lifer; rifle
fliers   filers; lifers; rifles
flies   Felis; files; 'slife
fling out   flouting
flirtation   filtration
flirted   trifled
flirting   trifling
flit   lift
flits   lifts
float   aloft; flota
floater   floreat; refloat
floaters   forestal; refloats
Flodden   fondled
flog   golf
flood   of old
floreat   floater; refloat
floreated   deflorate
florid   Ilford
flota   aloft; float
flounder   unfolder
flounders   unfolders
flour   fluor
flouting   fling out
flouts   Loftus
flow   fowl; wolf
flowed   fowled; wolfed
flower   fowler; reflow; wolfer
flowered   deflower; reflowed
flowering   reflowing
flowers   fowlers; reflows; wolfers
flowery   rye-wolf
flowing   fowling; wolfing
flows   fowls
flue   fuel
fluent   unfelt
flues   fuels
fluor   flour
flushing   lung-fish
fluster   fluters; restful
fluters   fluster; restful
flutinas   inflatus
fly ash   flashy
flyer   ferly
fly rail   frailly

foal   loaf; Olaf
foaled   feodal; loafed
foaling   loafing
foals   loafs; sol-fa
foci   coif; fico
fodder   forded
foetor   footer; refoot; tofore
Fogo   goof
foin   fino; info
foister   forties
Foligno   fooling; loofing
fonder   Fronde
fondle   enfold
fondled   Flodden
fondler   forlend
fondlers   forlends
fondles   enfolds
fool   loof
fooled   loofed
fooling   loofing
fools   loofs
footer   foetor; refoot; tofore
for   fro
foramen   foreman
forcat   factor
forçats   factors
forces   fresco
forded   fodder
fordo   Frodo
fore   orfe
foredo   roofed
forelies   free-soil
foreman   foramen
foremast   mort-safe
foremasts   mort-safes
fore-mean   fore-name
fore-means   fore-names; freemason
fore-name   fore-mean
fore-names   fore-means; freemason
forenight   fothering
forensic   conifers; fir cones;
    forinsec; inforces
foresight   gift horse
forest   fortes; foster
forestage   fosterage
forestal   floaters; refloats
forested   deforest; fostered
forester   fosterer
foresters   fosterers
foresting   fostering
forests   fosters
forge   gofer
forges   gofers

forinsec conifers; fir cones; forensic; inforces
forlend fondler
forlends fondlers
form from
formalin informal
formats farmost
forme Fermo, Frome
formed deform
former reform
formers reforms
Formica aciform
formulae fumarole
for sale loafers
Forst forts; frost
fortes forest; foster
forth froth
forties foister
forts Forst; frost
forward froward
forwardness frowardness
forwards frowards
foster forest; fortes
fosterage forestage
fostered deforest; forested
fosterer forester
fosterers foresters
fostering foresting
fosters forests
fothering forenight
fouled defoul
founder refound
founders refounds
foundling unfolding
fouter foutre
fouters foutres
foutre fouter
foutres fouters
fowl flow; wolf
fowled flowed; wolfed
fowler flower; reflow; wolfer
fowlers flowers; reflows; wolfers
fowling flowing; wolfing
fowls flows
fra far
fract craft
fracts crafts
frae fare; fear
frail filar; flair
frailly fly rail
fraise sea-fir
fraises sea-firs
framed farmed

framer farmer
framers farmers
framing farming
Francie fancier
frayed defray
freak faker
freaks fakers
freckle flecker
freckles fleckers
Freda fared
free feer; fere; reef
free-bench beech-fern
freebie beefier
freed defer
freedman enframed
freeing feering; feigner; reefing
freeman enframe
freemason fore-means; fore-names
freer refer
frees feers; feres; reefs
freesia arefies; faeries; sea-fire
free-soil forelies
freest fester
Frei fire; reif; rife
freight fighter
freights fighters
frenetic reinfect
fresco forces
frescoed deforces
fresher refresh
fret reft
fretful truffle
fretsaw wafters
Freya arefy; faery
fried fired
friend finder
friends finders
fries fires; serif
fringe finger
fringes fingers
fris firs
friseur frisure; surfier
friska fakirs; Kafirs
frist first; frits; rifts
frisure friseur; surfier
frith firth
friths firths; shrift
frit rift
frits first; frist; rifts
fro for
frocked defrock
Frodo fordo
from form

Frome   Fermo; forme
Fronde   fonder
froren   frorne
frorne   froren
frost   Forst; forts
frosted   defrost
frost-nail   flatirons
froth   forth
frounced   unforced
froward   forward
frowardness   forwardness
frowards   forwards
fruitage   figurate
frumenty   furmenty
fuel   flue
fuels   flues
fulmar   armful

fulmars   armfuls
fumarole   formulae
fumble   beflum
fumbles   beflums
funeral   flaneur
funerals   flaneurs
funfair   ruffian
funfairs   ruffians
furbisher   refurbish
furmenty   frumenty
furnisher   refurnish
furores   ferrous
furs   surf
Fusan   fauns; snafu
fused   feuds
fussier   fissure
fustian   faunist

G

gab   bag
gabardine   bargained
gabbler   grabble
gabblers   grabbles
gabion   bagnio
gabions   bagnios
gable   bagel; belga
gables   bagels; belgas
Gabon   obang
gabs   bags
gad   dag
gadder   graded
gade   aged; egad; gaed
gades   Degas
gadget   tagged
gadgets   stagged
gads   dags
gadso   goads
gae   age
gaed   aged; egad; gade
Gael   gale; geal; Gela
Gaels   gales; geals
gaes   ages; sage
Gail   gila; glia
gaillard   galliard
gaillards   galliards
gain   agin; Agni; Gina
gainer   earing; graine; regain;
    regina
gainers   earings; erasing; regains;
    searing; seringa
gainly   laying

gainsays   assaying
gainst   giants; sating
gair   ragi
gaiter   triage
gaiters   agister; sea-girt; stagier;
    strigae; triages
gaits   agist
gal   lag
gala   alga
Galahad   Ala Dagh
gale   Gael; geal; gela
galea   algae
Galen   angel; angle; genal; glean
galena   alnage; Angela; anlage;
    lagena
Galenic   angelic; anglice
Galenical   angelical
Galenist   eastling; genitals;
    stealing
Galenists   eastlings
gales   Gaels; geals
galilees   legalise
Galle   legal
galleon   allonge
galleons   allonges
galleries   allergies
gallery   allergy; largely; regally
galliard   gaillard
galliards   gaillards
galling   gingall
galore   gaoler
gals   lags; slag

Galtee eaglet; gelate; legate; teagle; telega
Galwegians Glaswegian
gam mag
gambler gambrel
gamblers gambrels
gambrel gambler
gambrels gamblers
game mage
game-bird Ambridge
gamed madge
gamely gleamy; mygale
gamer marge; regma
gamers marges
gamete metage
gametes Maesteg; metages
gamier imager; maigre; mirage
gamin Ngami
gamine enigma
gamines enigmas; seaming
gaming gigman
gamma magma
gammer gramme
gammers grammes
gams mags
gan nag
ganched changed
ganches changes
ganching changing
gander danger; garden; ranged
ganders dangers; gardens
gane Agen; gean; gena
ganged nagged
ganger grange; nagger
gangers granges; naggers
ganging nagging
ganister angriest; astringe; gantries; granites; inert gas; ingrates; reasting
gant gnat; tang
ganted tanged
ganting tanging
gantries angriest; astringe; ganister; granites; inert gas; ingrates; reasting
gants angst; gnats; stang; tangs
gaol goal; Olga
gaoled age-old; old age
gaoler galore
gaols goals; Lagos
gap Pag
gape page; peag
gaped paged

gaper grape; parge
gapers gasper; grapes; parges; sparge
gapes Gaspé; pages
gaping paging
gaps gasp
gar rag
garb brag; grab
garbe barge; begar; Berga
garbed badger; barged
garbes barges
garbing barging
garbler Arlberg
garbs brags; grabs
Gard darg; drag
Garda darga
garden danger; gander; ranged
Gardena Grenada
gardened deranged
gardener garnered
gardenia drainage
gardening deranging
gardens dangers; ganders
Gardner grander
gare gear; Gera; rage
garget tagger
gargle lagger; raggle
gargled draggle; raggled
gargles laggers; raggles
gargling raggling
garment margent; ragment
garments margents; ragments
garner ranger
garnered gardener
garners rangers
garnet argent
garnets Sargent; Stanger; strange
garni agrin; grain
garnish sharing
garnished degarnish
Garonne Argonne
garotter garrotte
garotters garrottes
garret garter; grater
garreted gartered; regrated; Tredegar
garrets garters; graters
garrotte garotter
garrottes garotters
gars Gras; rags
garter garret; grater
gartered garreted; regrated; Tredegar

gartering   regrating
garters   garrets; graters
garvie   Argive; rivage
garvies   Argives; rivages
Gary   gray
gas   sag
Gascon   congas
gases   sages
gash   hags; shag
gasp   gaps
Gaspé   gapes; pages
gasper   gapers; grapes; parges;
   sparge
gaspers   sparges
gas-rings   grassing
Gastein   easting; genista; ingates;
   ingesta; seating; tangies; teasing;
   tsigane
Gaston   Sontag; tangos; tongas
gat   tag
gate   geat
gates   geats; stage
gats   stag; tags
Gatun   gaunt
Gaul   gula
Gauls   gusla
Gaumont   Montagu
gaums   magus
gaunt   Gatun
gauntries   signature
gaurs   Argus; sugar
gave   Vega
gavel   Gävle
Gävle   gavel
gayer   yager
gayest   stagey
gazer   graze
gazers   grazes
geal   Gael; gale; Gela
geals   Gaels; gales
gean   Agen; gane; gena
geans   Agnes; genas; Senga
gear   gare; Gera; rage
geared   agreed; dragée
gearless   eelgrass; largesse
gears   rages; sager; sarge
geat   gate
geats   gates; stage
Geel   glee
gee-string   greetings
Geiger   Reggie
geist   geits
geits   geist

gel   leg
Gela   Gael; gale; geal
gelate   eaglet; Galtee; legate; teagle;
   telega
gelatin   atingle; elating; genital
gelatine   legatine
gelation   legation
geld   gled
gelder   ledger
gelders   ledgers; sledger
gelding   niggled
geldings   sniggled
gelds   gleds
gelid   glide
gels   legs
gem   Meg
geminates   magnesite; magnetise
gena   Agen; gane; gean
genal   angel; angle; Galen; glean
genas   Agnes; geans; Senga
genera   enrage
general   enlarge; gleaner
generalist   easterling
generalists   easterlings
generals   enlarges; gleaners
generate   green tea; renegate;
   teenager
generates   renegates; teenagers
generic   energic
genetical   clientage
genetrix   exerting
geneva   avenge
genial   Ealing; linage
genie   eigne
genies   eignes; seeing
genista   easting; Gastein; ingates;
   ingesta; seating; tangies; teasing;
   tsigane
genital   atingle; elating; gelatin
genitals   eastling; Galenist; stealing
genitival   vigilante
Genoa   agone; Onega
genre   green
genres   greens
Genro   ergon; goner; Negro
gentiles   sleeting; steeling
genuine   ingénue
geo   ego
geocentric   egocentric
Gera   gare; gear; rage
Geraint   granite; ingrate; Tangier;
   tearing
Gerald   glared

Geraldine engrailed; realigned
Gerard grader; regard
gerbe grebe
gerbes grebes
Gerda Edgar; grade; raged
gerent regent
gerents regents
Germain roaming
german engram; manger; ragmen
germane Mangere
Germanic amercing; creaming;
  Mérignac
Germans engrams; mangers
germinal maligner; malinger
germinates magnetiser
Gerona onager; orange
Gervas graves
gest gets; tegs
Gestapo postage
geste egest
gestes egests
get teg
gets gest; tegs
ghost Goths
ghoul lough
ghouls loughs; slough
giant tangi
giantess eastings
giants gainst; sating
gib big
gibbons sobbing
gibing biggin
gid dig
gif fig
gifted fidget
gift horse foresight
gigman gaming
gila Gail; glia
Gilan Laing; liang; ligan; linga
gild glid
gilded glided
gilden dingle; elding; engild
gilder girdle; glider; lidger; ridgel
gilders girdles; gliders; grisled;
  lidgers; ridgels
gilding gliding
gilt glit
Gina agin; agni; gain
gin-fizz fizzing
gingall galling
ginger nigger
gingers niggers; snigger
gingle niggle

gingles niggles; sniggle
gink king
ginks kings
ginned ending
ginnel Lingen
ginner enring
ginners enrings
gino oing; onig
gin-sling singling; slinging
gin trap parting; prating; traping
gip pig
gips pigs
girandole negroidal; reloading
girasole seraglio
gird grid
girdle gilder; glider; lidger; ridgel
girdled glidder; griddle
girdles gilders; gliders; grisled;
  lidgers; ridgels
girds grids
Giresun reusing
girkins griskin; risking
girlond lording
girn grin; ring
girned dering; dinger; engird;
  ringed
girning ringing
girns grins; rings
Giro Gori
giron groin
Gironde eroding; groined; ignored;
  negroid; redoing
girons grison; groins; rosing;
  Signor
girt grit; trig
girth grith; right
Girton roting; trigon
girts grist; grits; strig; trigs
Girvan raving
gist tigs
gite tige
gites tiges
gittern retting
gju jug
gjus jugs
glacier gracile
gladden dangled
glairin lairing; railing
glanced clanged
glancing clanging
glanders danglers
glans slang
glare Elgar; lager; large; regal; Regla

glared   Gerald
glares   lagers; regals
Glaswegian   Galwegians
glaum   algum; almug; mulga
glaums   mulgas
gleamy   gamely; mygale
glean   angel; angle; Galen; genal
gleaner   enlarge; general
gleaners   enlarges; generals
gleans   angels; angles
gled   geld
glede   gleed; ledge
gledes   gleeds; ledges; sledge
gledge   legged
gleds   gelds
glee   Geel
gleed   glede; ledge
gleeds   gledes; ledges; sledge
gleeman   mélange
glees   leges
Glenda   angled; dangle
glia   Gail; gila
glibness   blessing
glid   gild
glidder   girdled; griddle
glide   gelid
glided   gilded
glider   gilder; girdle; lidger; ridgel
gliders   gilders; girdles; grisled;
   lidgers; ridgels
gliding   gilding
glinted   tingled
glinting   tingling
glisten   singlet; tingles
glistens   singlets
glister   gristle
gilt   gilt
gloater   legator; Ortegal
gloaters   legators
gloating   goatling
globe   bogle
globes   bogles
Glos.   logs; slog
gloss   slogs
glossing   goslings
glover   grovel
glovers   grovels
glue   gule; luge
glued   luged
gluer   gruel; luger
gluers   gruels; lugers
glues   gules; luges
gluing   luging

gluten   englut
Glynis   lysing; singly
gnar   gran; rang
gnarled   dangler
gnash   hangs
gnashing   hangings
gnat   gant; tang
gnats   angst; gants; stang; tangs
gnaw   wang
gnawed   Gwenda
gnaws   swang; wangs
gneiss   singes
gnomic   coming
gnomonic   oncoming
gnostic   costing
gnu   gun
gnus   guns; snug; sung
Goa   ago
goad   dago
goads   dagos; gadso
goal   gaol; Olga
goals   gaols; Lagos
goat   Göta; toga
goatling   gloating
goats   togas
gob   bog
goblin   lobing
gobs   bogs
go by   bogy
god   dog
godets   stodge
godling   lodging
godlings   lodgings
godly   goldy
gods   dogs
godso   goods
goer   ergo; gore; ogre
goers   gores; gorse; ogres; Sergo;
   soger
goes   egos; sego
goes by   bogeys
gofer   forge
gofers   forges
goglet   toggle
goglets   toggles
goiter   goitre
goitre   goiter
Golan   along; Logan; longa
golden   longed
goldy   godly
golf   flog
gonad   Dagon; donga; Gonda
gonads   dongas

Gonda   Dagon; donga; gonad
Gondar   dragon
goner   ergon; Genro; Negro
goners   Negros
Gonvil   loving; voling
goods   godso
goof   Fogo
goop   pogo
goral   algor; argol; largo
Gordian   adoring; gradino;
   roading
Gordon   drongo; Grodno
gore   ergo; goer; ogre
gores   goers; gorse; ogres; Sergo;
   soger
gorged   dogger
Gori   Giro
goring   gringo
gorse   goers; gores; ogres; Sergo;
   soger
gorsedd   dodgers
gory   Györ; orgy
gosh   hogs; shog
goslings   glossing
got   tog
Göta   goat; toga
Goths   ghost
gourde   drogue; rogued; rouged
gourdes   drogues; groused
gouts   gusto
Goya   yoga
grab   brag; garb
grabble   gabbler
grabbles   gabblers
graben   banger
grabens   bangers
grabs   brags; garbs
graced   cadger
gracile   glacier
graddan   grandad
grade   Edgar; Gerda; raged
graded   gadder
grader   Gerard; regard
graders   regards
gradient   derating; red giant;
   treading
gradients   red giants
gradin   daring
gradine   areding; dearing; deraign;
   grained; reading
gradines   deraigns; readings
grading   niggard
gradino   adoring; Gordian; roading

graduates   date-sugar
gradus   guards
Graeme   meagre
Graham   Armagh
grail   argil; Lairg
grain   agrin; garni
graine   earing; gainer; regain;
   regina
grained   areding; dearing; deraign;
   gradine; reading
grainer   angrier; earring; rearing
grainers   earrings
grains   rasing; Sangir
grainy   raying
graith   aright
gramme   gammer
grammes   gammers
gran   gnar; rang
Granados   Sangrado
grandad   graddan
grandam   grandma
grandee   angered; derange; en
   garde; enraged; grenade
grandees   deranges; grenades
grander   Gardner
grandiose   organdies; organised
grandma   grandam
grange   ganger; nagger
granges   gangers; naggers
granite   Geraint; ingrate; Tangier;
   tearing
granites   angriest; astringe;
   ganister; gantries; inert gas;
   ingrates; reasting
grannie   earning; engrain; nearing
grannies   earnings; engrains
granted   drag-net
grantee   greaten; reagent
grantees   estrange; greatens;
   reagents; segreant; sergeant
granter   regrant
granters   regrants
grape   gaper; parge
grapes   gapers; gasper; parges;
   sparge
graphically   calligraphy
graphology   logography
Gras   gars; rags
grasp   sprag
grasped   sparged
grasper   sparger
graspers   spargers
grasping   sparging

grasps sprags
grassing gas-rings
grate great; Greta; targe; terga
grated der tag; targed
grater garret; garter
graters garrets; garters
grates Greats; stager; targes
grating targing
gratis striga
graves Gervas
gray Gary
grayling ragingly
graze gazer
grazes gazers
grease agrees; eagres
great grate; Greta; targe; terga
greaten grantee; reagent
greatens estrange; grantees;
   reagents; segreant; sergeant
greater regrate
greatness estranges; sergeants
Greats grates; stager; targes
grebe gerbe
grebes gerbes
Grecians creasing; searcing
gree eger
greed edger
green genre
Greene renege
greened reneged
greening reneging
greenish sheering
Greenland Englander
Greenmantle enlargement
greens genres
green tea generate; renegate;
   teenager
greeny energy; Ygerne
grees egers; grese; Segre; serge
greet egret
greeted deterge
greetings gee-string
greets egrets
gremlin merling; mingler
gremlins merlings; minglers
Grenaa Reagan
Grenada Gardena
grenade angered; derange; en
   garde; enraged; grandee
grenades deranges; grandees
grenadier rereading
grenadine endearing; engrained
grese egers; grees; Segre; serge

greses egress
Greta grate; great; targe; terga
grey gyre
grey-coat category
greys gyres
grid gird
griddle girdled; glidder
gride dirge; ridge
grided ridged
grides dirges; grised; ridges
griding ridging
grids girds
grieved diverge
grimaced decigram
grin girn; ring
grinder regrind
grinders regrinds
gringo goring
grinned rending
grins girns; rings
grip prig
grips prigs; sprig
gris rigs
grised dirges; grides; ridges
griskin girkins; risking
grisled gilders; girdles; gliders;
   lidgers; ridgels
grison girons; groins; rosing;
   Signor
grist girts; grits; strig; trigs
gristle glister
grit girt; trig
grith girth; right
grits girts; grist; strig; trigs
groan argon; Ongar; orang; organ
groans orangs; organs; Sargon;
   sarong
groat argot
groats argots
Grodno drongo; Gordon
groin giron
groined eroding; Gironde; ignored;
   negroid; redoing
groining ignoring
groins girons; grison; rosing;
   Signor
groma Margo
groser rogers
groove overgo
grounded underdog
groundless groundsels
groundsels groundless
grouper regroup

groupers   regroups
groupies   pirogues
grouse   orgues; rogues; rouges;
   rugose
groused   drogues; gourdes
grouted   droguet
grouty   yogurt
grovel   glover
grovels   glovers
grown   wrong
groyne   eryngo
grub   burg
grubs   burgs
grudge   rugged
grudged   drugged
grudging   drugging
gruel   gluer; luger
gruels   gluers; lugers
grunted   trudgen
grunts   strung
guards   gradus
Gueber   burgee; Guebre
Guebers   burgees; Guebres
Guebre   burgee; Gueber
Guebres   burgees; Guebers
guerdon   undergo; ungored
Guiana   iguana
guiser   regius
gula   Gaul
gulden   lunged
gule   glue; luge
gules   glues; luges
gullies   ligules
gulp   plug
gulps   plugs

guly   ugly
gum   mug
gums   mugs; smug
gun   gnu
gun dog   dugong
gun dogs   dugongs
guns   gnus; snug; sung
gunsel   lunges
gunshot   noughts; shotgun
gunshots   shotguns
gunter   gurnet; urgent
gunters   gurnets
gup   pug
gur   rug
gurgle   lugger
gurgles   luggers; slugger
gurnet   gunter; urgent
gurnets   gunters
gush   hugs
gusla   Gauls
gust   guts; tugs
Gustave   vaguest
gusted   degust
gusto   gouts
gusty   gutsy
gut   tug
guts   gust; tugs
gutsy   gusty
guy   yug
Gwenda   gnawed
Györ   gory; orgy
gyrated   tragedy
gyre   grey
gyres   greys

H

ha   ah
habitat   Tabitha
habited   Thebaid
hackles   shackle
hacks   shack
had   dah
haddocks   shaddock
Hades   heads; shade
hadji   jihad
hadjis   jihads
haeres   hearse
hafts   shaft
hags   gash; shag
hailed   halide

hailers   El Arish
hair-net   inearth
hair-nets   inearths
hairs   arish; Shari
Halden   Handel; handle
hale   heal; Leah
haled   heald
hales   halse; heals; leash; selah;
   shale; sheal
half-backs   flashback
halide   hailed
haling   Hlaing
halloo   holloa
hallows   shallow

halls shall
halma almah; hamal
halos shoal; shola; solah
Hals lash
halse hales; heals; leash; selah; shale; sheal
halsed lashed
halses hassle; lashes; shales; sheals
halsing lashing
halt iath
halted lathed
halter lather; thaler
haltered lathered
haltering earthling; lathering
halters harslet; Herstal; lathers; slather
halting Althing; lathing
halts laths; shalt; Stahl
halve Havel
hamal almah; halma
hambles shamble
Hamburg Murghab
hame ahem; Mahé
hames shame; Shema
Hamites atheism
hamlet Eltham; Thelma
hammal mahmal
hammers shammer
hams mash; sham
hamster amherst
hamsters amhersts
Handel Halden; handle
hander harden
handers hardens
handle Halden; Handel
handles handsel
handless handsels
hand-outs thousand
hands shand
handsel handles
handsels handless
handy Haydn
hangar arghan
hangings gnashing
hang-out to-hunga
hangover overhang
hangovers overhangs
hangs gnash
hank ankh; Kahn; khan
hanker harken
hankered harkened
hankering harkening

hankers harkens
hanks ankhs; khans; shank
Hans Nash; shan
hanse ashen; Shane
Hants. shan't; snath
hap pah
hapless plashes
haps hasp; pash; Shap
haram marah
hard Dhar
harden hander
hardens handers
harder Erhard
hardest dearths; hatreds; red-hats; threads; trashed
hardier harried
hards shard
hard up purdah
hardy Hydra
hare hear; Hera; rhea
hared heard
hareld harled; herald
harelds heralds
harems masher; shamer
hares hears; rheas; share; shear
haricot chariot
haricots chariots
harken hanker
harkened hankered
harkening hankering
harkens hankers
harks shark
harled hareld; herald
Harlem Mahler; Ramleh
harlot Lothar
harmed derham
harmonic choirman
harmonical monarchial
harmonicas maraschino
harms marsh
harpers sharper
harp on orphan
harps sharp
harps on orphans
harried hardier
Harris arrish; shirra; sirrah
harshest thrashes
harslet halters; Herstal; lathers; slather
hart rath; tahr; thar
Hartbees breathes
Harte earth; hater; heart; Herat; rathe; Thera; thrae

harts   raths; tahrs; thars; trash
harvest   thraves
has   ash
has-been   banshee
has-beens   banshees
hash   shah
haslet   lathes; Shelta; Thales
haslets   Hasselt, hatless
hasp   haps; pash; Shap
hasped   pashed; phased; shaped
hasping   pashing; phasing; shaping
Hasselt   haslets; hatless
hassle   halses; lashes; shales; sheals
hassled   slashed
hassles   slashes
hassling   lashings; slangish;
   slashing
hast   hats; tash
haste   ashet; hates; heats
hasted   deaths; 'sdeath; tashed
hasten   Athens; snathe; sneath;
   thanes
hastener   heartens
hastens   snathes; sneaths
hastes   ashets; tashes
hastier   sheriat
hasting   tashing
Hastings   stashing
hatches   chetahs
hate   eath; heat; thae; Thea
hated   death
hater   earth; Harte; heart; Herat;
   rathe; Thera; thrae
haters   earths; hearts; Sarthe;
   'sheart
hates   ashet; haste; heats
hating   a'thing
hatless   haslets; Hasselt
hatred   dearth; red-hat; thread
hatreds   dearths; hardest; red-hats;
   threads; trashed
hats   hast; tash
hatter   threat
hatters   rathest; shatter; threats
haunt   unhat
haunter   unearth
haunters   unearths
hauntings   unhasting
haunts   sunhat; unhats; Ushant
haut   Utah
Havel   halve
havens   Hesvan; shaven
havers   shaver

haves   shave; sheva
hawm   wham
hawms   shawm; whams
haws   shaw; wash
hawser   washer; whares
hawsers   swasher; washers
hay   yah
Haydn   handy
hayed   heady
hays   ashy; shay
hazel   Zahle
he   eh
header   adhere; hedera
headers   adheres; sheared
headings   sheading
headlamps   lampshade
heads   Hades; shade
heady   hayed
heal   hale; Leah
heald   haled
heals   hales; halse; leash; selah;
   shale; sheal
heap   epha
heaps   Pesah; phase; shape
hear   hare; Hera; rhea
heard   hared
hearer   rehear
hearers   rehears; shearer
hearings   shearing
hears   hares; rheas; share;
   shear
hearse   haeres
heart   earth; Harte; hater; Herat;
   rathe; Thera; thrae
hearted   earthed; red-heat
hearten   earthen; Teheran
heartens   hastener
heartiness   earthiness
hearting   earthing; ingather
heartly   earthly
heartquake   earthquake
hearts   earths; haters; Sarthe;
   'sheart
heart-shaped   earth-shaped
heartsome   horsemeat
hearty   earthy
heat   eath; hate; thae; Thea
heater   aether; hereat; reheat
heaters   reheats; Theresa
heaths   sheath
heats   ashet; haste; hates
heaves   sheave
heaviness   evanishes

heavy Yahve
Hebron brehon
hectare cheater; teacher
hectares cheaters; teachers
hector rochet; tocher; troche
hectored tochered
hectoring tochering
hectors rochets; tochers; torches; troches
hedera adhere; header
Hedon honed
hedonists dishonest
heeding neighed
heel hele
heeler reheel
heelers reheels
heels heles; sheel
height eighth
heinous in-house
heir hire
heirless relishes
heirs hires; shier; shire
heist shite; sithe; Thiès
heists shiest; shites; sithes; Theiss; thesis
hele heel
heles heels; sheel
helices lichees
helicon choline
Hellenic chenille
hellers sheller
hells shell
helot hotel; thole
helots hostel; hotels; tholes
helves shelve
he-man maneh
hems mesh; Shem
Henri Rhein; Rhine
hens nesh
hent then
hepar phare; raphe
hepatic aphetic
hepatical caliphate
hep-cats patches
heptads spathed
her reh; rhe
Hera hare; hear; rhea
herald hareld; harled
heralds harelds
Herat earth; Harte; hater; heart; rathe; Thera; thrae
herdic chider
herdics chiders

herds sherd; shred
hereat aether; heater; reheat
herein inhere; Rheine
Herman Arnhem
hermit mither
hermits mithers
hernial inhaler
herniated inearthed
hero hoer; Ohre; rheo
Herod horde
heroic co-heir
heroics co-heirs
heron Horne; Rhone
herons rhones; Senhor
herpes Hesper; pheers; sphere
hers rhes
herse Esher; sheer
herself flesher
herses sheers
Herstal halters; harslet; lathers; slather
Herts. Resht; tehrs
Hesper herpes; pheers; sphere
hesperid perished; shred-pie
hesperids shred-pies
Hess shes
Hessen sheens; sneesh
hest Esth; Seth; shet
Hester Esther; ethers; threes
Hesvan havens; shaven
het eth; the
hetman anthem
hetmans anthems
hewer where
hewing whinge
hewings shewing; whinges
hewn when
hews shew
hibernate inbreathe
hibernated inbreathed
hibernates inbreathes
hibernating inbreathing
hide hied
hides shied
hidings dishing; shindig
hied hide
hight thigh
hights thighs
hikers shriek; shrike
hikes sheik
hills shill
hilt lith
hilts liths

himself   Flemish
hinders   shrined
hindlegs   shingled
hing   nigh
hint   Nith; thin
hinting   in-thing
hints   thins
hip   phi
hippos   popish; shippo
hips   pish; ship
hipsters   thripses
hipt   pith
Hiram   ihram
hire   heir
hires   heirs; shier; shire
hirsel   hirsle; relish
hirsels   hirsles
hirsle   hirsel; relish
hirsles   hirsels
his   ish
hisn   shin; sinh
Hispar   parish; raphis; Shairp
hissed   dishes
hist   hits; shit; sith; this; Tshi
hists   shits
Hitler   lither
hits   hist; shit; sith; this; Tshi
hitter   tither
hitters   tithers
hivers   shiver; shrive
hives   shive
Hlaing   haling
ho   oh
hoard   Rhoda
hoarse   ashore
hoast   Athos; hosta; oaths; shoat
hoasts   hostas; shoats; Thasos
hoaxed   oxhead
hob   boh
hobo   booh
hobs   bosh
hocked   choked
hocker   choker
hockers   chokers; shocker
hocking   choking
hocks   shock
hocused   choused; douches
hocusing   chousing
hod   doh
hods   shod
hoer   hero; Ohre; rheo
hoers   horse; shoer; shore
hoes   hose; shoe

Hogmanay   mahogany
hogs   gosh; shog
hoister   shortie
hold-up   uphold
hold-ups   upholds
holed   dhole
holes   She'ol
holiday   hyaloid
holloa   halloo
Holst   holts; sloth
holster   hostler
holsters   hostlers
holt   loth
holts   Holst; sloth
homage   ohmage
homeliest   lithesome
Homer   horme
Homeric   moriche
honed   Hedon
hones   hosen; shone
honest   Sethon; Stheno
honestly   on the sly
hoo   oho
hooks   shook
hoop   pooh
hoot   Otho; toho
hooters   shooter; soother
hoots   shoot; sooth; Sotho
hop   poh
hoped   ephod
hoper   ephor
hopers   ephors; posher
Hopi   Ipoh
hoplites   isopleth
hoppers   shopper
hoppings   shopping
hops   posh; shop; soph
Horace   chorea; ochrea; orache
horde   Herod
hordes   horsed; Rhodes; shoder;
   shored
horme   Homer
hormone   moorhen
hormones   moorhens
horn   Hron
Horne   heron; Rhone
horned   dehorn
hornet   Horten; throne
hornets   shorten; thrones
horns   shorn
Hornsea   Senhora
horrent   norther
Horsa   Orsha

horse   hoers; shoer; shore
horsed   hordes; Rhodes; shoder; shored
horsemeat   heartsome
horses   shoers; shores
horsing   shoring
horst   short
horsts   shorts
Horta   Thora; Torah
Horten   hornet; throne
Hortensia   Senhorita
Horus   hours
hose   hoes; shoe
hosed   doseh; shoed
hosen   hones; shone
hoses   shoes
host   hots; shot; tosh
hosta   Athos; hoast; oaths; shoat
hostas   hoasts; shoats; Thasos
hosted   toshed
hostel   helots; hotels; tholes
hostile   Elohist
hosting   toshing
hostler   holster
hostlers   holsters
hot   tho'
hotel   helot; thole
hotels   helots; hostel; tholes
hotel suite   silhouette
hotel suites   silhouettes
hots   host; shot; tosh
hot tap   top hat
hot taps   top hats
hotter   tother
hotting   tonight
hounds   Hudson; unshod
hours   Horus
houseboat   boathouse
houseboats   boathouses
housework   workhouse
hovels   shovel
hovers   shover; shrove
hoves   shove
how   who
however   whoever
howlet   thowel
howlets   thowels

Hron   horn
hubs   bush
Hudson   hounds; unshod
huers   usher
hug   ugh
huge   eugh
Hughes   sheugh
hugs   gush
humidor   mid-hour; rhodium
humidors   mid-hours
hump   umph
humps   sumph
hums   mush
Huns   shun
hunt   Thun
hunters   shunter
huntress   shunters
hunts   shunt
hups   push
hurdle   hurled
hurled   hurdle
Hurons   onrush
hurried   dhurrie
hurries   rushier
hurst   hurts
hurt   ruth; thru; Thur
hurtful   ruthful
hurtfully   ruthfully
hurting   ungirth; unright
hurtle   Luther
hurtles   hustler; Thurles
hurtless   hustlers; ruthless
hurtlessly   ruthlessly
hurtlessness   ruthlessness
hurts   hurst
hustle   sleuth
hustler   hurtles; Thurles
hustlers   hurtless; ruthless
hustles   sleuths
hustling   sunlight
huts   shut; thus; tush
Hyads   shady
hyaloid   holiday
Hydra   hardy
hydrate   thready
hydrous   shroudy
hypnotic   pythonic

I

Iain   inia
Ian   ani

Ian Smith   isthmian
iatric   Tricia

Ibadan indaba
Iberians Siberian
Icarian Arician
icecap ipecac
iced cedi; dice
ice-hills chillies
Iceland inlaced
iceman anemic; cinema
icepack pack-ice
icepan in pace
icepans inscape; pincase
icer ciré; eric; rice
icers cries; erics; seric
ices sice
ichor choir
iciness incises
ickers scrike; sicker
Icod odic
icon coin
iconolater relocation
icons coins; scion; sonic
Ida aid; Dai
ide die
idea aide
idea'd aided
ideal ailed; Delia
idealisers serialised
idealism miladies
idealistic italicised
idealizers serialized
ideals aisled; deasil; ladies; sailed
ideas aides; aside; Sadie
ideation taenioid
idem dime
identic incited
ideograph eidograph
ideographs eidographs
ides dies; side
id est deist; diets; dites; edits; sited; St. Dié; stied; tides
idiots Idoist
idle deil; eild; lied
idler riled
idlers slider
idles deils; sidle; slide
idlesse diesels
idlest listed; silted; tildes
Idoist idiots
idol lido; Lodi; olid
Idola dolia
idolater tailored
idolaters estradiol
idolatry adroitly; dilatory

Idolum dolium
idols Isold; lidos; silo'd; sloid; soldi; solid
idyll dilly
Ifan fain; naif
Ife fie
ignaro oaring; origan
ignaros Signora; soaring
ignited dieting; editing
igniter tiering; tigrine
igniters resiting; strigine
ignorant Tir na n-Og
ignore eringo; Origen; region
ignored eroding; Gironde; groined; negroid; redoing
ignores regions; Signore
ignoring groining
iguana Guiana
ihram Hiram
Ike eik; kei
Ilagan agnail; Anglia
ileac Alice; Celia
Ilesha Sheila
ilexes exiles
Ilford florid
iliac cilia
ilk'a kail; Kali; Lika
Ilkley likely
ill Lil
Illinois illision
illision Illinois
ill-nature tellurian
ills sill
illudes ill-used; sullied
ill-used illudes; sullied
ill-uses sullies
illy lily; yill
Ilmen limen; Milne
I'm mi
imager gamier; maigre; mirage
imagers mirages
imaginer migraine
imaginers migraines
imam maim
imams maims; miasm
imarets Artemis; maestri; maister; misrate; semitar; St. Marie
imbed bedim
imbeds bedims
imbrue erbium
imbrues imburse
imburse imbrues
imitancy intimacy

immersed simmered
immersing simmering
impaled implead
impanel maniple
impanels maniples
imparl primal
impart armpit
impartial primatial
imparts armpits
impaste pastime
impastes pastimes
impearl lempira; palmier
impearled epidermal; impleader
impeding impinged
impels Milspe; simple
impetus imputes
impinged impeding
implate palmiet
implates palmiest; palmiets;
   petalism; septimal
implead impaled
impleader epidermal; impearled
impleads misplead
implored impolder
implores pelorism; sperm-oil
impolder implored
impones peonism
importers misreport
imports tropism
importune entropium
importuned minute-drop
imposer promise; semi-pro
imposers promises; semi-pros
impost impots
impots impost
imprecated mercaptide
imprecates spermaceti
impregnate permeating
impresari primaries
imprese empires; emprise;
   epimers; premise; spireme
impreses emprises; premises;
   spiremes
impress Persism; premiss; simpers
impresses premisses
impressibility permissibility
impressible permissible
impression permission
impressive permissive
impressively permissively
impressiveness permissiveness
imprest permits
imprints misprint

imps simp
impugners presuming
impugns spuming
impure umpire
imputes impetus
inaction nicotian
inane Annie
inapt paint; patin; pinta
inaptly ptyalin
inarched Red China
inarm Marin; minar
inarmed adermin; Amerind
inarms minars
inbreak Bikaner; break in
inbreaks bearskin; breaks in
inbreathe hibernate
inbreathed hibernated
inbreathes hibernates
inbreathing hibernating
inbred binder; brined; rebind
inbreed bendier
inbring brining
Inca Cain
incages ceasing
in camera American; Cinerama
Incan Cinna
in care Racine
Incas canis; Sican
incase casein
incased candies
incenses niceness
incensors corniness
incept pectin
inceptions inspection
inceptors inspector
incessant instances
incest insect; nicest; scient
inch chin
inchased cashed in
inchases Anchises
inched chined; niched
inches chines; chinse; niches
inching chining; niching
incised indices
incises iciness
incisure sciurine
incited identic
inciter citrine; crinite
inciters crinites
include nuclide
includes nuclides; unsliced
incog coign
incognita actioning

incognito cognition
incomers sermonic
incomes Comines; mesonic
inconsiderate containerised
incorporate procreation
increase resiance
increases scenarise
increate centiare; creatine; iterance
incudes incused; induces
incur runic
incused incudes; induces
incut cut in; tunic
Ind din; nid
indaba Ibadan
indeed denied
indent intend; tinned
indented intended
indenter interned
indenting intending
indents intends
India Aidin
indicate actinide
indicates actinides
indices incised
Indies inside
indigent enditing
indirectly cylindrite
indiscreet indiscrete; iridescent
indiscreetly indiscretely
indiscreetness indiscreteness
indiscrete indiscreet; iridescent
indiscretely indiscreetly
indiscreteness indiscreetness
indite tineid
inditers disinter
indole doline; Leonid
indoors Sondrio; sordino
Indore ironed
indorse rosined; sordine
Indra dinar; drain; Drina; nadir
Indre diner
induces incudes; incused
indues undies
indulge eluding
indulged deluding; ungilded
indurate daturine; ruinated;
  urinated
Indus nidus
inearth hair-net
inearthed herniated
inearths hair-nets
inelastic Catilines; sciential
inelegant eglantine

inerm miner
inert inter; nitre; Terni; trine
inert gas angriest; astringe;
  ganister; gantries; granites;
  ingrates; reasting
Ines sine
in esse Neisse; seines
in extenso extension
Inez zein
infame famine
infamed ad finem
infames famines
infarct infract
infarction infraction
infarctions infractions
infarcts infracts
infefts stiffen
infer finer
infere enfire; ferine; Fernie; fineer;
  refine
inferring infringer
infers Fenris
infest feints; finest
infests fitness
infidel infield
infield infidel
inflame feminal
inflamer rifleman
inflatus flutinas
info fino; foin
inforce conifer; fir cone
inforces conifers; fir cones;
  forensic; forinsec
informal formalin
informer reinform; reniform
informers reinforms
infract infarct
infraction infarction
infractions infarctions
infracts infarcts
infringe enfiring; refining
infringer inferring
ingate eating; tangie
ingates easting; Gastein; genista;
  ingesta; seating; tangies; teasing;
  tsigane
ingather earthing; hearting
ingénue genuine
ingénues unseeing
ingest signet; tinges
ingesta easting; Gastein; genista;
  ingates; seating; tangies; teasing;
  tsigane

ingests signets
ingle Elgin; ligne; Nigel
ingles lignes; seling; single
ingot tigon
ingots stingo; tigons; tosing
ingraft farting; rafting
ingrafts strafing
ingrain raining
ingram arming; margin
ingrate Geraint; granite; Tangier;
    tearing
ingrates angriest; astringe;
    ganister; gantries; granites; inert
    gas; reasting
ingredients tenderising
Ingres reigns; renigs; resign;
    signer; singer
ingress resigns; signers; singers
Ingrid riding
ingroup pouring; rouping
ingrowth throwing; Worthing
ingrum muring
inhaler hernial
inhere herein; Rheine
in-house heinous
inia Iain
initiated dietitian
ink kin
ink-bag baking
ink-bags basking
inkers sinker
inkle Klein; liken
inkled kilned; kindle; linked
inkles likens; silken
inkling kilning; linking
inklings sling ink; slinking
inks kins; sink; skin
Inkster stinker; tinkers
inlace ancile; Celina
inlaced Iceland
in-laws Salwin
inlayer nailery
inlets enlist; listen; silent; tinsel
inletting entitling
in love love-in
inmate tamine
inmates Samnite
inmost monist
innate tinean
inners sinner
innings inn-sign; sinning
innovate venation
inn-sign innings; sinning

inoculates inosculate
inoculations inosculation
inorb robin
inorbs robins
inosculate inoculates
inosculation inoculations
in pace icepan
inphase in shape
in re Erin; rein; Reni
inro iron; Rion
inroad Dorian; ordain
inroads ordains
inros irons; ornis; rosin
ins nis; sin
insane sienna
insatiable banalities
inscape icepans; pincase
insculp sculpin; unclips
insculps sculpins
inseam Amiens; amines; mesian
inseams samisen
insect incest; nicest; scient
insecure sinecure
insert inters; sinter; Strine; trines
inserted Dniester; resident;
    sintered
inserting sintering
inserts sinters
inset neist; set in; stein; tines
insets sets in; steins; Tessin
in shape inphase
inside Indies
insight shiting
insigne seining
insinuate annuities
insisted tidiness
insole eloins; esloin; lesion; Silone
insoles esloins; lesions; lioness
insouled delusion; unsoiled
inspect incepts; pectins
inspection inceptions
inspector inceptors
inspire pirnies; spinier
instal Latins; Stalin
instance ancients; canniest
instances incessant
instanter transient
instar santir; Sintra; strain; trains
instars santirs; strains
instate satinet
instates nastiest
instead Danites; detains; sainted;
    stained

98

instep spinet; step-in
insteps spinets; step-ins
in store orients; stonier; triones
insular urinals
insult sunlit
insulted unlisted
insulter lustrine
insure inures; rusine; ursine
insurer ruiners
insures sunrise
insurgent unresting
intaglio ligation; taglioni
intaglioed deligation
intake take-in
intakes take-ins
integer teering; treeing
integers reesting; steering; streigne
integral alerting; altering; relating; triangle
integrand endarting
integration orientating
intend indent; tinned
intended indented
intending indenting
intends indents
inter inert; nitre; Terni; trine
interests resistent; triteness
intergrade retreading
interim mintier; termini
interims minister
interlace lacertine; reclinate
interlaces centralise
interlope repletion
intern tinner
interned indenter
internees Ernestine
interns tinners
interoceptors retrospection
interosculates sansculotterie
interpage repeating
interpreter reinterpret
interpreters reinterprets
interrogatives tergiversation
inters insert; sinter; Strine; trines
in-thing hinting
intimacy imitancy
into not-I
intonated dentation
intoner ternion
intoners ternions
intones Sonnite; tension
intoxicate excitation
intra Nitra; riant; train; Trani

intradoses adroitness
in-tray Tyrian
in-trays Tyrians
intreat iterant; nattier; nitrate; tartine; tertian
intreating intrigante
intreats nitrates; straiten; tartines
intrigante intreating
introduce reduction
introduces discounter; reductions
intrude turdine; untired; untried
intruders unstirred
inundates unsainted; unstained
inure urine
inured ruined
inures insure; rusine; ursine
inuring ruining
inust suint; Tunis; units
invader ravined
invaders sandiver
Invar ravin
inveagler revealing
inveigler relieving
inverse enviers; versine; Viersen
inverses versines
invert virent
inverts striven; Ventris
invested evidents
inviter vitrine
inviters vitrines
inward Darwin; draw in
inwards draws in
ions Sion
ipecac icecap
Ipoh Hopi
Ira air; ria
irade aider; aired; redia
irades aiders; raised
Iran airn; Nair; rain; rani
irate terai
Irene Ernie
irides irised
iridescent indiscreet; indiscrete
irised irides
irked diker
irks kris; risk
iron inro; Rion
Iron Age origane
ironed Indore
ironer Renoir
ironic oniric
irons inros; ornis; rosin
Ironside derision

Irtysh shirty; thyrsi
Irun ruin
Irving riving; virgin
Irwell willer
is si
Isaacs cassia
Isar airs; Asir; rias; sair; sari
Isengrim remising
ish his
Isla ails; Lias; Lisa; sail; sial
Islam limas; mails; malis; Milas;
    salmi; Simla
isle Elis; leis; lies; seil; sile
isleman malines; menials; seminal
isles seils; siles
islet istle; steil; stile; teils; tiles
islets steils; stiles
isms miss
Isna anis; Nias; Nisa; sain; Sian
Isold idols; lidos; silo'd; sloid; soldi;
    solid
Isolde siloed; soiled
Isolt Solti; toils
isometric eroticism; meroistic
isopleth hoplites
isosceles solecises
isotherm moithers; Stroheim
Ispra pairs; Paris; Parsi
Israel sailer; serail; serial
Israelite realities

issuant sustain
issue Susie
issued disuse
issuer uresis
issues Suisse
isthmian Ian Smith
istle islet; steil; stile; teils; tiles
it ti
ita ait; tai
italicised idealistic
Italy laity
itas aits; Asti; sati; sita
itch chit
itches theics
itchiest ethicist; theistic
item emit; mite; time
items emits; metis; mites; smite;
    stime; times
iterance centiare; creatine; increate
iterant intreat; nattier; nitrate;
    tartine; tertian
iterate ariette
iterates ariettes; treaties; treatise
its sit; tis
itself filets; stifle
Ivan vain; vina
Ives vies; vise
ivresse revises
Iyar airy
iynx nixy

J

jackboot boot-jack
jackboots boot-jacks
jack-pines jack-snipe
jack-snipe jack-pines
jaded Jedda
Jaén Jane; Jean; Jena
jalouse jealous
jambul jumbal
jambuls jumbals
Jane Jaén; Jean; Jena
Jansen Nsanje
japes jaspe
jar raj
Jason Jonas
jaspe japes
jasy jays
Jat taj
jato jota
jaunt junta; Tunja

jaunts juntas
jays jasy
jealous jalouse
Jean Jaén; Jane; Jena
Jedda jaded
jeered jereed
Jena Jaén; Jane; Jean
jereed jeered
jerkin jinker
jerkins jinkers
jest jets
jetons jetson
jets jest
jetson jetons
jihad hadji
jihads hadjis
jingoist joisting
jinker jerkin
jinkers jerkins

joiner rejoin
joiners rejoins
joisting jingoist
Jonas Jason
jota jato
jotun junto
jotuns juntos
Juanita Tijuana
Judaic Judica
Judica Judaic

jug gju
jugs gjus
jumbal jambul
jumbals jambuls
junta jaunt; Tunja
juntas jaunts
junto jotun
juntos jotuns
just juts
juts just

K

kabob bobak
Kabul baulk
Kàdar Dakar
kades asked
kadi dika
kadis dikas
kae kea
kaes Aske; keas; sake
Kafir fakir
Kafirs fakirs
Kahn ankh; hank; khan
kail ilk'a; kali; laik; Lika
kails kalis; laiks; Laski; skail
kaim kami; maik
kaims kamis; maiks; smaik
Kaiser Raikes
kale lake; leak
kales lakes; leaks; slake
kali ilk'a; kail; laik; Lika
kalis kails; laiks; Laski; skail
kame make
kames makes
kami kaim; maik
kamis kaims; maiks; smaik
Kano kaon
kans sank
kant tank
kants stank; tanks
kaon Kano
karat Katar
Karen anker; naker; nerka
Karens ankers; nakers
Karl lark
Kars arks; Sark
karst karts; stark; strak
karts karst; stark; strak
kasher shaker
Kashing shaking
Kaspar parkas

Kassel slakes
kat tak
Katar karat
Kate keta; take; teak
kats skat; taks; task
Katy kyat
Kay yak
kayle leaky
kayo oaky; okay
kayoed okayed
kayoing okaying
kayos okays
kea kae
Kean Kena
Kearny yanker
keas Aske; kaes; sake
Keats skate; Skeat; stake; steak;
    takes; teaks
Kedah kheda
keds desk
keel Klee; leek
keelers sleeker
keels leeks; sleek
keen knee
keens knees; skene; Sneek
keep peek; peke
keeping peeking
keeps peeks; pekes; Speke
kegs skeg
kei eik; Ike
keir kier
keirs kiers; skier
Keltic tickle
kemi mike
ken nek
Kena Kean
Kendal ankled
kens neks
Keos okes; skeo; soke

kepi   kipe; pike
kepis   kipes; pikes; Pisek; spike
keps   skep
Kerman   Marken
kesar   asker; rakes; reaks; saker;
   skear
kesars   askers; sakers; skears
keta   Kate; take; teak
Kew   ewk
key   kye
keynotes   keystone
keys   Skye; syke; yesk
keystone   keynotes
khan   ankh; hank; Kahn
khans   ankhs; hanks; shank
kheda   Kedah
kibe   bike
kibes   bikes
kids   disk; skid
Kiel   like
kier   keir
kiers   keirs; skier
Kilbride   bird-like
kiley   kylie
kileys   kylies
kills   skill
kiln   Klin; link
kilned   inkled; kindle; linked
kilning   inkling; linking
kilns   links; slink
kin   ink
kinas   Nasik
kind   dink
kindle   inkled; kilned; linked
kinds   dinks
kine   Nike
king   gink
kingpin   pink gin; pinking
kingpins   pink gins
kings   ginks
kins   inks; sink; skin
kipe   kepi; pike
kipes   kepis; pikes; Pisek; spike
kippers   skipper
kips   skip
kirn   rink
kirns   rinks
kiss   skis
kisser   skiers
kist   kits; skit
kitchen   thicken
kitchened   thickened
kitchener   thickener

kitcheners   thickeners
kitchening   thickening
kitchens   thickens
kite   tike
kites   skite; tikes
kits   kist; skit
kitsch   thicks
Klan   lank
Klee   keel; leek
Klein   inkle; liken
Klin   kiln; link
knaps   spank
knar   kran; nark; rank
knars   krans; narks; ranks; skran;
   snark
knawel   wankle
knee   keen
knees   keens; skene; Sneek
knife   Finke
knit   tink
knits   skint; stink; tinks
knitter   trinket
knitters   trinkets
knops   knosp
knosp   knops
knots   stonk
knower   wroken
knows   snowk
knub   bunk
knubs   bunks
koa   oak; oka
koas   oaks; okas; soak
kob   bok
kobs   boks; bosk
kolo   look
kolos   looks; Sokol
Koper   poker; proke
Koran   Akron; krona
koto   toko; took
kotos   stook
kran   knar; nark; rank
krans   knars; narks; ranks; skran;
   snark
kreese   seeker
kreeses   seekers
kris   irks; risk
krona   Akron; Koran
Kroo   rook
Kroos   rooks
Krus   rusk
Kurt   Turk
kyat   Katy
kye   key

kylie kiley
kylies kileys
Kyoto Tokyo

kyte tyke
kytes skyte; tykes

L

laager alegar
laagers Alsager
lab alb
Laban Alban; banal
Labe Abel; able; albe; bael; bale;
  blae; Elba
label be-all; Bella
labiate Baalite
labiates Baalites; satiable
labile alible; Belial; Biella; liable
labis bails; basil
labrador larboard
labret albert; tabler
labrets alberts; blaster; stabler;
  tablers
labrid bridal; ribald
labrum brumal; lumbar; umbral
labs albs; slab
laburnum alburnum
lac-dye clayed
lace Alec; Clea
laced decal
lace-man Maclean; manacle
laceration creational
lacertine interlace; reclinate
laces claes; scale
lacet cleat; éclat
lacey Yecla
laches Cashel; chelas
Lachine Chilean
lacier Claire; éclair
laciest astelic; Castile; elastic;
  latices
laciness sanicles
lacing Anglic
lac insect canticles
lack calk
lacked calked
lacker calker
lackers calkers; slacker
lacking calking
lacks calks; slack
Laclos locals
laconic conical
lacrosse escolars; solacers
lacrymal clay-marl

lacrymose claymores
lacteous osculate
lactose alecost; locates; scatole;
  talcose
lacy clay
lad dal
ladder Aldred; larded; raddle
ladders raddles; saddler
laddie daidle
laddies daidles
lade dale; deal; lead; Leda
laded addle; dedal
laden eland; lande
lades dales; deals; leads; slade
ladies aisled; deasil; ideals; sailed
Ladin Linda
Ladino laid on; Olinda
ladle dalle; Della
ladles dalles
lads dals
lady yald
Laertes elaters; relates; stealer
lag gal
lagena alnage; Angela; anlage;
  galena
lager Elgar; glare; large; regal;
  Regla
lagers glares; regals
lagged daggle
lagger gargle; raggle
laggers gargles; raggles
lagniappe appealing
lagoon Loango
Lagos gaols; goals
La Grange langrage
lags gals; slag
lagunes Angelus
laid Dail; dali; dial
laid on Ladino; Olinda
laik ilk'a; kail; kali; Lika
laiks kails; kalis; Laski; skail
lain anil; nail
Laing Gilan; liang; ligan; linga
lair aril; liar; lira; rail; rial
laird drail; Liard
lairds drails

laired   derail; Lérida; railed; relaid
Lairg   argil; grail
lairing   glairin; railing
lairs   liars; liras; rails; rials
laisse   aisles; eassil; lassie
laisses   lassies
laity   Italy
lake   kale; leak
lakelets   skeletal
lakes   kales; leaks; slake
Lalin   all in
lam   mal
lama   alma
lamas   almas
lamb   balm
lambaste   blastema
lambed   ambled; balmed; bedlam;
   beldam; blamed
Lambeth   the Lamb
lambing   ambling; balming;
   blaming
lambkins   lambskin
lambs   balms
lambskin   lambkins
lame   alme; Elam; Elma; leam;
   Lema; male; meal
lamed   medal
lamely   mellay
lameness   maneless; nameless;
   salesmen
lament   mantel; mantle; mental
lamenting   alignment
laments   mantels; mantles
lamer   Ramle
lames   almes; leams; males; meals;
   Salem; samel; Selma
lamest   metals; samlet
lamina   animal; manila
laminar   railman
laminas   animals
lamination   antimonial; antinomial
laming   lingam; malign
lamp   palm
lampas   plasma
lamped   palmed
Lampeter   palm-tree
lamping   palming
lamps   palms; plasm; psalm
lampshade   headlamps
lams   alms; slam
lana   Alan; anal; nala
Lanai   liana
Lancaster   ancestral

lance   Calne; clean
lanced   candle
lancer   rancel
lancers   rancels
lances   cleans; Senlac
lancet   cantle; cental
lancets   cantles; centals
Lancs.   clans
lande   eland; laden
landed   dandle
lander   aldern; darnel; enlard
landers   enlards; slander; snarled
Landes   sendal
Landor   Arnold; lardon; Roland;
   Ronald
landrace   calendar
landraces   calendars
lane   élan; lean; Lena; neal
lanes   leans; neals; slane
Lanett   latent; latten; talent
langrage   La Grange
languid   lauding
langur   Lurgan
lank   Klan
lanker   rankle
lanners   ensnarl
Laon   loan; Nola
Laos   also; sola
Lao-tse   osteal
lap   alp; pal
Lapeer   leaper; repeal
lapel   Pella
lapides   alipeds; elapids; paidles;
   palsied; Pleiads
lapis   pails; spial
La Porte   prolate
Lapp   palp; plap
lapped   dapple; palped
lapper   rapple
lappers   rapples; slapper
lappies   applies
lapping   palping
Lapps   palps; plaps
laps   Alps; pals; salp; slap
lapse   Elaps; leaps; pales; peals;
   pleas; salep; sepal; spale; speal
lapsed   pedals; pleads
lapses   sepals; spales; speals
lapsing   palings; sapling
lapwings   spawling
larboard   labrador
larches   Charles
larded   Aldred; ladder; raddle

larding   darling
lardon   Arnold; Landor; Roland;
    Ronald
lardoon   Orlando
lardy   lyard; Rydal
lare   earl; lear; râle; real
Laredo   loader; ordeal; reload
lares   Arles; earls; laser; lears; reals;
    seral
large   Elgar; glare; lager; regal;
    Regla
largely   allergy; gallery; regally
largesse   eelgrass; gearless
largo   algor; argol; goral
lariat   Altair; atrial; latria
lariats   Al Sirat
larine   en l'air; linear; nailer
lark   Karl
larked   darkle
Larne   learn; renal
larum   mural; rumal
larums   murals; rumals
Larus   sural; Urals
larva   arval; lavra
larval   vallar
Las Bela   salable
lascar   rascal; sacral; scalar
lascars   rascals; scalars
laser   Arles; earls; lares; lears; reals;
    seral
lash   Hals
lashed   halsed
lasher   ashler
lashers   ashlers; slasher
lashes   halses; hassle; shales;
    sheals
lashing   halsing
lashings   hassling; slangish;
    slashing
Laski   kails; kalis; laiks; skail
lass   sals
lasses   salses
lassie   aisles; eassil; laisse
lassies   laisses
lasso   solas
lassoer   oarless
last   lats; salt; slat
lasted   deltas; desalt; salted; slated;
    staled
laster   alerts; alters; artels; ratels;
    salter; slater; staler; stelar; tarsel
lasters   artless; salters; slaters;
    tarsels

lasting   anglist; salting; slating;
    staling
lastly   saltly
lasts   salts; slats
Las Vegas   salvages
latches   chalets; satchel
latchet   chattel
latchets   chattels
late   et al.; leat; tael; tale; teal; tela
lated   Datel; dealt; delta
lateen   elanet; La Tène
laten   leant
La Tène   elanet; lateen
latent   Lanett; latten; talent
later   alert; alter; ratel; taler
latest   stealt
latex   exalt
lath   halt
lathe   Elath; ethal
lathed   halted
lather   halter; thaler
lathered   haltered
lathering   earthling; haltering
lathers   halters; harslet; Herstal;
    slather
lathes   haslet; Shelta; Thales
lathing   Althing; halting
laths   halts; shalt; Stahl
latices   astelic; Castile; elastic;
    laciest
Latiner   entrail; latrine; ratline;
    reliant; retinal; trenail
Latiners   entrails; latrines; ratlines;
    trenails
Latinise   alienist; litanies
Latinises   alienists
Latins   instal; Stalin
latish   tahsil
latitude   altitude
latitudes   altitudes
latitudinal   altitudinal
latitudinarian   altitudinarian
latitudinous   altitudinous
Latona   atonal
latria   Altair; atrial; lariat
latrine   entrail; Latiner; ratline;
    reliant; retinal; trenail
latrines   entrails; Latiners; ratlines;
    trenails
Latrobe   bloater
lats   last; salt; slat
latten   Lanett; latent; talent
latter   rattle; tatler

lattice tactile
Latvia avital
Latvian valiant
laud auld; dual; udal
lauder Eluard
lauding languid
lauds Aldus; udals
launce cuneal; Lucena; unlace
launces censual; unlaces; unscale
launch nuchal; unchal
launder Arundel; lurdane; rundale
launders lurdanes
Laura aural
laurel allure
laurels allures
Laurens ulnares
lava Alva; aval; Vaal
lavages salvage
lavas vasal
lave leva; vale; veal; vela
laveer leaver; reveal
laveers leavers; reveals; several
laver ravel; Reval; velar
lavers ravels; salver; serval; slaver;
  versal
laves Elvas; salve; selva; slave;
  vales; valse
lavisher shrieval
lavra arval; larva
law awl
lawed dwale; waled; weald
Lawes swale; sweal; wales; weals
lawing waling
lawk walk
lawks walks
lawned Walden
laws awls; slaw
lawyer warely
laxer relax
layer early; relay
layered delayer; relayed
layering relaying; yearling
layers relays; slayer
laying gainly
laymen meanly; namely
layover overlay
layovers overlays
lays slay
laze zeal
lazed Zelda
lea ale; e-la
leach chela
leached Chaldee; Cheadle

leaches Chelsea
lead dale; deal; lead; Leda
leaded dealed
leaden aneled; leaned; nealed
leader dealer
leaders dealers
lead-in Aldine; alined; Daniel;
  Delian; denial; nailed
leading aligned; dealing
leadings dealings
lead-ins denials; snailed
leads dales; deals; lades; slade
leadsman dalesman
leadsmen dalesmen
leady delay
leaf feal
leafed fealed
leafing fealing; finagle
leafs false; feals; fleas
Leah hale; heal
leak kale; lake
leaking linkage
leaks kales; lakes; slake
leaky kayle
leal Ella
leam alme; Elam; Elma; lame;
  Lema; male; meal
leams almes; lames; males; meals;
  Salem; samel; Selma
lean élan; lane; Lena; neal
Leander learned
leaned aneled; leaden; nealed
leaning aneling; eanling; nealing
leanings eanlings
leans lanes; neals; slane
leant laten
lean-to etalon
lean-tos etalons
leap pale; peal; pela; plea
leaped pealed
leaper Lapeer; repeal
leapers pleaser; relapse; repeals
leaping pealing
leaps Elaps; lapse; pales; peals;
  pleas; salep; sepal; spale; speal
leapt lepta; palet; pelta; petal; plate;
  pleat
lear earl; lare; râle; real
lea-rigs Algiers
learing engrail; nargile; realign;
  reginal
learn Larne; renal
learned Leander

learns ransel
learnt altern; antler; rental; ternal
lears Arles; earls; lares; laser; reals; seral
leas ales; Elsa; sale; seal; slae
lease easel
leased sealed
leaser resale; sealer; Searle
leasers earless; sealers
leases easels; eassel
leash hales; halse; heals; selah; shale; sheal
leashing shealing
leasing linages; sealing
least leats; slate; Stael; stale; steal; stela; taels; tales; teals; tesla
leat et al.; late; tael; tale; teal; tela
leather tar-heel
leathers tar-heels
leats least; slate; Stael; stale; steal; stela; taels; tales; teals; tesla
leavens enslave
leaver laveer; reveal
leavers laveers; reveals; several
leaves sleave
leavings Svengali
Leavis Aviles; valise
lebensraum mensurable
Lebu blue
lechery cheerly
led eld
Leda dale; deal; lade; lead
ledge glede; gleed
ledger gelder
ledgers gelders; sledger
ledges gledes; gleeds; sledge
lee eel
leech Elche
leeches Scheele
Leeds deles; Edsel; seled
leek keel; Klee
leeks keels; sleek
leer lere; reel
leered reeled
leeriest steelier
leering reeling
leers leres; reels
leery Leyre
lees eels; else; seel; sele; slee
leets sleet; steel; stele
left felt
lefties felsite
leg gel

legal Galle
legalise galilees
legalist stillage; tillages
legalists stillages
legate eaglet; Galtee; gelate; teagle; telega
legates eaglets; teagles; telegas
legatine gelatine
legation gelation
legator gloater; Ortegal
legators gloaters
leges glees
legged gledge
legger eggler
leggers egglers
legislator allegorist
legislators allegorists
leg-man mangel; mangle
Legnago agelong
legs gels
lei Eli; lie
Leics. ceils; ciels; Sicel; slice
Leif file; lief; life
Leinster enlister; listener; re-enlist
leir lier; lire; riel; rile
leirs liers; riels; riles; siler
leis Elis; isle; lies; seil; sile
leister sterile
leisters tireless
Leith lithe
Leitrim limiter
lek elk
leks elks; Selk
Lely yell
lem elm
Lema alme; Elam; Elma; lame; leam; male; meal
Lemaître eremital; matériel; real-time
leman Elman; Lemna
lemans Anselm; mensal
lemming Memling
Lemna Elman; leman
Lemnos lemons; melons; solemn
lemon melon
lemons Lemnos; melons; solemn
lemony myelon
lempira impearl; palmier
lems elms
Lena élan; lane; lean
lenders slender
Lenin linen
Leningrad enlarding

lenis   elsin; liens; lines; nelis; Niles;
  silen
leno   enol; Leon; lone; Noel
lenses   lessen
lenticel   lenticle
lenticels   lenticles
lenticle   lenticel
lenticles   lenticels
lentil   lintel
lentils   lintels
lentisk   tinkles
lento   olent; Olten
Leon   enol; leno; lone; Noel
Leonid   doline; indole
Leonids   dolines; sondeli
leopard   paroled
leper   repel
lepers   repels
lepid   piled; plied
lepra   paler; parle; pearl; repla
leprous   sporule
lepta   leapt; palet; pelta; petal; plate;
  pleat
lere   leer; reel
leres   leers; reels
Lérida   derail; laired; railed; relaid
Lerins   liners
Leros   eorls; loser; orles; Osler;
  roles; soler; Sorel
lesion   eloins; esloin; insole; Silone
lesions   esloins; insoles; lioness
lessen   lenses
lessened   needless
Lessing   singles
lessons   sonless
lessor   losers; solers
lest   elts; lets; tels
Lester   relets; streel
Lesvos   solves
let   elt; tel
Lethe   Ethel
let rip   triple
lets   elts; lest; tels
letters   settler; sterlet; trestle
Lettish   lithest; thistle
leva   lave; vale; veal; vela
levan   elvan; navel; venal
levanter   relevant
Levantine   Valentine
Le Vau   uveal; value
levees   sleeve
lever   elver; revel
levers   elvers; revels

Levi   evil; live; veil; vile; vlei
levin   liven
levirate   relative
levis   Elvis; evils; lives; slive; veils;
  vleis
Levoča   alcove; coeval
lewd   weld
lewder   welder
Lewes   sewel; sweel; weels; Wesel
lewis   weils; wiels; wiles
ley   Ely; lye
Leyburn   Burnley
Leyden   needly
Leyre   leery
leys   lyes; lyse; sley
liability   alibility
liable   alible; Belial; Biella; labile
Liam   lima; mail; mali
liana   Lanai
lianas   Salian; salina
liane   alien; aline; anile; Elian
lianes   aliens; alines; saline; Selina;
  silane
liang   Gilan; Laing; ligan; linga
liar   aril; lair; lira; rail; rial
Liard   drail; laird
liars   lairs; liras; rails; rials
liart   trail; trial
Lias   ails; Isla; Lisa; sail; sial
liberal   Braille
libra   brail
librae   bailer
libras   brails
librate   Alberti; triable
lice   ceil; ciel
license   selenic; silence
licensed   declines; silenced
licenser   reclines; silencer
licensers   silencers
licenses   silences
licensing   silencing
lichees   helices
licker   rickle
lickers   rickles; slicker
licks   slick
Licosa   social
lidded   diddle
lidger   gilder; girdle; glider; ridgel
lidgers   gilders; girdles; gliders;
  grisled; ridgels
lido   idol; Lodi; olid
lidos   idols; Isold; silo'd; sloid; soldi;
  solid

lids   sild; slid
lie   Eli; lei
lied   deil; eild; idle
lieder   relied
lief   file; Leif; life
liefer   relief
lien   line; Neil; Nile
liens   elsin; lenis; lines; nelis;
　　Niles; silen
lientery   entirely
lier   leir; lire; riel; rile
lierne   reline
liernes   relines
liers   leirs; riels; riles; siler
lies   Elis; isle; leis; seil; sile
Liestal   tailles; tallies
liever   relive; revile
Liévres   relives; reviles; servile
life   file; Leif; lief
lifer   filer; flier; rifle
lifers   filers; fliers; rifles
lift   flit
lifter   filter; trifle
lifters   filters; stifler; trifles
lifts   flits
ligan   Gilan; Laing; liang; linga
ligate   aiglet; taigle
ligated   taigled
ligates   aiglets; taigles
ligating   taigling
ligation   intaglio; taglioni
ligations   taglionis
liger   Rigel
lighted   delight
lighten   enlight
lightened   enlighted
lightening   enlighting
lightens   enlights
lighter   relight
lighters   relights; slighter
lightness   nightless
ligne   Elgin; ingle; Nigel
lignes   ingles; seling; single
Lignice   ceiling; cieling
lignin   lining
lignose   lingoes
ligroin   roiling
ligules   gullies
Lika   ilk'a; kail; kali; laik
like   Kiel
likely   Ilkley
liken   inkle; Klein
likens   inkles; silken

liker   Rilke
likes   Sikel
Lil   ill
lilac   Cilla
lilacs   Scilla
lilt   till
lilted   tilled
lilting   tilling
lilts   still; tills
lily   illy; yill
lima   Liam; mail; mali
limas   Islam; mails; malis; Milas;
　　salmi; Simla
limbate   timbale
limbed   dimble
lime   Emil; mile
limen   Ilmen; Milne
limens   Semlin; simnel
limes   miies; slime; smile
limestone   milestone
limiest   elitism; El Misti; limites
limited   delimit
limiter   Leitrim
limites   elitism; El Misti; limiest
limitary   military
limned   milden; Mindel
limner   merlin; Milner
limners   merlins
limp   plim
limped   dimple
limper   prelim
limpers   prelims; simpler
limpest   limpets; Mt. Siple
limpets   limpest; Mt. Siple
limps   plims
lin   nil
Linacre   carline; en clair
linage   Ealing; genial
linages   leasing; sealing
Linares   nailers
Linda   Ladin
Lindau   unlaid
linden   dinnle; linned
lindens   dinnles
line   lien; Neil; Nile
lineages   ensilage
linear   en l'air; larine; nailer
lineated   dateline; entailed
lined   eldin
linen   Lenin
liners   Lerins
lines   elsin; lenis; liens; nelis; Niles;
　　silen

line-up lupine; up-line
line-ups lupines; spinule; up-lines
linga Gilan; Laing; liang; ligan
lingam laming; malign
lingel lingle
Lingen ginnel
lingers slinger
lingle lingel
lingoes lignose
lings sling
lingual lingula
lingula lingual
lining lignin
link kiln; Klin
linkage leaking
linked inkled; kilned; kindle
linking inkling; kilning
links kilns; slink
linned dinnle; linden
lino lion; loin; noil
linos lions; loins; noils
linseed enisled; ensiled
lintel lentil
lintels lentils
lion lino; loin; noil
lionel niello; O'Neill
lionels niellos
lioness esloins; insoles; lesions
lionesses noiseless
lionise elision
lionises oiliness
lions linos; loins; noils
Lipa pail; Pali; pila
liparite reptilia
lip-read predial
lips lisp; slip
liquate tequila
lira aril; lair; liar; rail; rial
liras lairs; liars; rails; rials
lire leir; lier; riel; rile
Lisa ails; Isla; Lias; sail; sial
lisle Ellis
Lismore moilers
lisp lips; slip
lisped dispel; spiled
lisper perils; Perlis; pilers; pliers
lisping spiling
lisps slips
Lissa sails; Silas; sisal
list silt; slit
listed idlest; silted; tildes
listen enlist; inlets; silent; tinsel
listened enlisted

listener enlister; Leinster; re-enlist
listeners enlisters; re-enlists
listening enlisting
listens enlists; tinsels
lister litres; tilers
listing silting
lists silts; slits
lit til
Lita alit; Atli; tail; tali
litanies alienist; Latinise
lith hilt
lithe Leith
lither Hitler
lithesome homeliest
lithest Lettish; thistle
litho tholi
liths hilts
litotes toilets; T. S. Eliot
litre relit; tiler
litres lister; tilers
litter tilter; titler
litters slitter; stilter; testril; tilters;
    titlers
littoral tortilla
littorals tortillas
live evil; Levi; veil; vile; vlei
lived devil; vilde
lively evilly; vilely
liven levin
livens Sliven; snivel
liver livre; rivel
livered deliver; relived; reviled
livers livres; rivels; silver; sliver
livery verily
lives Elvis; evils; levis; slive; veils;
    vleis
livre liver; rivel
livres livers; rivels; silver; sliver
Lleyn Nelly
Lloyd dolly
load alod; odal
loader Laredo; ordeal; reload
loaders ordeals; reloads; sea-lord
loading digonal
loads alods; odals
loaf foal; Olaf
loafed feodal; foaled
loafers for sale
loafing foaling
loafs foals; sol-fa
loamier Morelia
loams salmo
loan Laon; Nola

loaned enodal
loaner Lorena; reloan
loaners orleans; reloans; Salerno
Loango lagoon
loans salon; sloan; solan; Solna
loath lotah
loather rat-hole
loathers rat-holes
loathly tally-ho
lobate oblate
lobated bloated
lobation oblation
lobbied bilobed
lobbies bilboes
lobe bole; Loeb
lobes boles
lobi boil
lobing goblin
lobose sobole
lobs Bols; slob
lobster bolster; bolters
lobsters bolsters
lobules soluble
lobus bolus
locals Laclos
Locarno coronal
locate Alecto
located cold tea
locates alecost; lactose; scatole; talcose
location colation
loci Clio; coil
Locke cloke
locked cloked
locking cloking
loco cool
locoed cooled
locoing cooling
locos cools
Locrian clarino; clarion
Locrians clarinos; clarions
locus clous
locust clouts
lode dole
lodes Delos; doles; soled
lodge ogled
lodging godling
lodgings godlings
Lodi idol; lido; olid
Loeb bole; lobe
loess loses; sloes; soles
loftier trefoil
Loftus flouts

Logan along; Golan; longa; NALGO
loge ogle
loges ogles; segol
logged dog-leg
loggers slogger
logiest elogist
logography graphology
logs Glos.; slog
loin lino; lion; noil
loins linos; lions; noils
Loire oiler; oriel
Loiret loiter; toiler
Lois oils; silo; soil; soli
loiter Loiret; toiler
loitered dolerite
loiters Estoril; estriol; toilers
Lomé mole
loment melton; molten
lone enol; leno; Leon; Noel
loner enrol; Lorne; nerol
loners enrols
longa along; Golan; Logan; NALGO
longed golden
longships sploshing
Looe oleo
loof fool
loofed fooled
loofing Foligno; fooling
loofs fools
looing olingo
look kolo
looked out outlooked
looking out outlooking
lookout outlook
lookouts looks out; outlooks
looks kolos; Sokol
looks out lookouts; outlooks
loom mool
looms mools; sloom
looniest oilstone
loons snool; Solon
loop polo; pool
looped poodle; pooled
loopers spooler
looping pooling
loops pools; sloop; spool
loos Oslo; solo
loose oleos; soole
loosed oodles; sooled
looses sooles
loosing olingos; sooling

loot tool
looted Toledo; tooled
looter Loreto; rootle; tooler
looters rootles; toolers
looting tooling
loots lotos; stool; tools
lope olpe; Opel; pole
loped poled
lopes elops; olpes; poles; slope
loping poling
lopper propel
loppers propels
lops slop
loran Arlon; Lorna
Lorca carol; claro; coral
lorcha choral
lorchas scholar
lording girlond
lordling drolling
lordly drolly
lore eorl; Orel; orle; role
Lorena loaner; reloan
Loreto looter; rootle; tooler
Loretta retotal
lorica caroli
loricates sectorial
lories elisor; oilers; oriels; Serlio
loris roils
L'Orme morel
Lorna Arlon; loran
Lorne enrol; loner; nerol
lose Ösel; sloe; sole
loser eorls; Leros; orles; Osler;
  roles; soler; Sorel
losers lessor; solers
loses loess; sloes; soles
losing soling
loss sols
lost lots; slot; St. Lô
lot Olt
lota alto; tola
lotah loath
lote tole
lotes toles
loth holt
Lothar harlot
Loti toil
lotos loots; stool; tools
lots lost; slot; St. Lô
lotted dottle
Lottie toilet
lotus louts; Soult
loud ludo

louden nodule; Oundle
loudens nodules
louder loured
loudest tousled
lough ghoul
loughs ghouls; slough
lounder roundel; roundle
lounders roundels; roundles
loured louder
louse ousel; Seoul
loused souled
louses ousels; soleus
lousy Louys
lout tolu; Toul
louts lotus; Soult
louver louvre; velour
louvers louvres; velours
louvre louver; velour
louvres louvers; velours
Louys lousy
love vole
loved voled
love-in in love
lovely volley
lovers solver
loves slove; solve; voles
loving Gonvil; voling
low owl
lowbred Bowdler
lowed dowel
lower owler; rowel
lowers owlers; rowels; slower
lowery owlery
lowest Elstow; owlets; towels
lows owls; slow; sowl
loyal alloy
lubber burble; rubble
lubbers burbles; slubber
Lubeck buckle
lucarne nuclear; unclear
Lucas cauls
luce clue
Lucena cuneal; launce; unlace
luces clues; cluse
Lucian Alcuin; Lucina; uncial
Lucina Alcuin; Lucian; uncial
lucre cruel; ulcer
luddite diluted
ludo loud
luffed duffel; duffle
luge glue; gule
luged glued
luger gluer; gruel

lugers gluers; gruels
luges glues; gules
lugger gurgle
luggers gurgles; slugger
luging gluing
lugs slug
lumbar brumal; labrum; umbral
lumber rumble
lumbers Burslem; rumbles; slumber
lumen Melun
lump plum
lumped dumple; plumed
lumpen plenum
lumper replum; rumple
lumpers rumples
lumping pluming
lumps plums; slump
lumpy plumy
lums slum
Luna ulan; ulna
lunar ulnar; urnal
lunarist Luristan
lunatics sultanic
lunettes unsettle
lunged gulden
lunges gunsel
lung-fish flushing
lungs slung
luniest utensil
lupine line-up; up-line
lupines line-ups; spinule; up-lines
lurch churl
lurdane Arundel; launder; rundale
lurdanes launders
lure rule
lured ruled
lures rules
Lurgan langur
luring ruling

Luristan lunarist
lush shul; Suhl
lust slut
luster lustre; luters; result; rustle; sutler; ulster
lusters lustres; results; rustles; sutlers; ulsters
lusting singult
lustre luster; luters; result; rustle; sutler; ulster
lustred rustled; strudel
lustres lusters; results; rustles; sutlers; ulsters
lustrine insulter
lustring rustling
lusts sluts
lute tule
iuters luster; lustre; result; rustle; sutler; ulster
lutes tules
Luther hurtle
Lutonian Ultonian
Lutonians Ultonians
lyard lardy; Rydal
Lydia daily
lye Ely; ley
lyes leys; lyse; sley
Lyme elmy; ylem
Lyon only
Lyra aryl; ryal
lyrate elytra; realty
lyre rely
lyres slyer
lyric Cyril
Lys sly
lyse leys; lyes; sley
lyses sleys; Yssel
lysing Glynis; singly
lysol Solly
lythe ethyl

M

ma am
ma'am mama
Ma'an Mana
Maasin animas; manias; Manisa; Samian
Mab bam
Mabel amble; blame; Melba
mac cam
macaronic carcinoma

mace acme; came
macer Ceram; crame; cream; Crema; Merca
macerated camerated; demarcate
maceration cameration
macers crames; creams; scream
maces acmes
mach cham
machairs archaism; charisma

Machen   Manche
macks   smack
macle   camel
Maclean   lace-man; manacle
macled   calmed
macles   camels; mascle; mescal
macs   cams
mad   dam
madden   damned; demand
maddened   demanded
maddening   demanding
maddens   demands
made   dame; Edam; mead
Maderno   roadmen
madge   gamed
Madison   daimons; domains
madness   desmans
madras   dramas
madrasahs   madrassah
madrassah   madrasahs
madroña   mandora
madroñas   mandoras
madroño   doorman
mads   dams
maenad   anadem
maenads   anadems
Maesteg   gametes; metages
maestri   Artemis; imarets; maister;
   misrate; semitar; St. Marie
maestro   amorets
mag   gam
mage   game
magenta   magnate
Magians   siamang
Maginot   moating
magister   migrates; sterigma
magma   gamma
magnate   magenta
magnesite   geminates; magnetise
magnetise   geminates; magnesite
magnetiser   germinates
magneto   megaton; montage
magnetos   megatons;
   montages
mags   gams
magus   gaums
Mahé   ahem; hame
Mahler   Harlem; Ramleh
mahmal   hammal
mahogany   Hogmanay
mahsir   marish
maid   amid
maided   diadem

maiden   daimen; Damien; demain;
   median; Medina
maidens   demains; medians;
   sideman
maids   Midas
Maidstone   dominates
maigre   gamier; imager; mirage
Maigret   migrate; ragtime
maik   kaim; kami
maiks   kaims; kamis; smaik
mail   Liam; lima; mali
mailed   medial
mailer   Elmira
mailers   realism
mails   Islam; limas; Milas; salmi;
   Simla
maim   imam
maims   imams; miasm
main   Amin; mina
Maine   amine; animé; en ami;
   Menai; minae
mainor   Marino; Marion; Mirano
mains   Manis; minas
mainyard   dairyman
maire   Marie; ramie; rimae
maires   armies
Mais   aims; Amis; Siam; sima
maister   Artemis; imarets; maestri;
   misrate; semitar; St. Marie
maisters   asterism; misrates;
   semitars
Makarios   romaikas
make   kame
makes   kames
mal   lam
malar   alarm; ramal
malate   tamale
malates   tamales
Malay   Yamal
male   alme; Elam; Elma; lame; leam;
   Lema; meal
maleic   malice
males   almes; lames; leams; meals;
   Salem; samel; Selma
mali   Liam; lima; mali
malic   claim
malice   maleic
malign   laming; lingam
maligner   germinal; malinger
maligners   malingers
maline   Elmina; menial
malines   isleman; menials; seminal
malinger   germinal; maligner

malingers maligners
malis Islam; limas; Milas; salmi; Simla
malison Osmanli; Soliman
malisons Osmanlis
malls small
Malone melano
Malta tamal
malts smalt
maltster martlets
mama ma'am
Mame Emma
man mna; nam
Mana Ma'an
manacle lace-man; Maclean
manage agname
managed agnamed
managers Semarang
manages agnames; Mesagna
manatee emanate; enemata
manatees emanates
Manche Machen
mandatory damnatory
mandora madroña
mandoras madroñas
mane amen; mean; Mena; name
maned amend; Medan; menad; named
manège menage
manèged end-game
manèges menages
maneh he-man
maneless lameness; nameless; salesman
manes amens; manse; means; Mensa; names; samen
Manet meant
manganite emanating
mange Megan
mangel leg-man; mangle
mangels mangles
manger engram; german; ragmen
Mangere germane
mangers engrams; germans
mangle leg-man; mangel
mangles mangels
mango among
mania amian; amnia; anima
maniac caiman
maniacs caimans
manias animas; Maasin; Manisa; Samian
Manichees mechanise

manila animal; lamina
manioc camion
maniple impanel
maniples impanels
Manis mains; minas
Manisa animas; Maasin; manias; Samian
manlier marline; mineral; railmen
manliest ailments; aliments; salt-mine
manna Annam
mannered Menander
manor Morna; Norma; Ramon; Roman
manors ramson; ransom; Romans
manred red-man; remand
manreds remands
Mansart artsman; mantras
manse amens; manes; means; Mensa; names; samen
manses messan
mansion onanism
mantas Tasman
mantel lament; mantle; mental
mantels laments; mantles
mantes aments; stamen
manticore cremation
mantis matins
mantissa Satanism
mantle lament; mantel; mental
mantles laments; mantels
mantras artsman; Mansart
manual alumna
manure murena
manured duramen; maunder; unarmed
manures surname
many myna
Maoist Taoism
Maori Mario; Moira; moria
map amp; pam
maple ample; pelma
maples sample
mapper pamper
mappers pampers
maps amps; pams; samp; spam
mar arm; ram
mara Aram; Rama
maracas marasca; mascara
marah haram
Maranta amarant
Maras Samar
marasca maracas; mascara

maraschino harmonicas
Marat Tamar
marble ambler; blamer; ramble
marbled rambled
marbler rambler
marblers ramblers
marbles amblers; blamers; rambles
marbling rambling
marc cram
marcel calmer; Carmel
march charm
marched charmed
märchen encharm
marcher charmer
marchers charmers
marches mesarch
marchese cashmere
marching charming
marchioness monarchises
Marconi Minorca; Romanic
Marcos caroms
mare ream
mares maser; reams; smear
margarines misarrange
Margate regmata
marge gamer; regma
margent garment; ragment
margents garments, ragments
marges gamers
margin arming; ingram
marginal alarming
marginally alarmingly
margined dreaming; mid-range;
  Niger Dam
Margo groma
Mari amir; Mira; rami; rima
Marian airman; marina
Marianne Armenian
Marie ramie; rimae
Marin inarm; minar
marina airman; Marian
marine airmen; Marnie; remain
mariner rein-arm
mariners rein-arms
marines remains; seminar; sirname
Marinist martinis
Marino mainor; Marion; Mirano
Mario Maori; Moira; moria
Marion mainor; Marino; Mirano
marish mahsir
Marist Ramist
Marists Ramists; tsarism
marital martial

Marken Kerman
marker remark
markers remarks
marled dermal; medlar
marline manlier; mineral; railmen
marlines minerals
Marlon normal
Marne enarm; namer
Marnie airmen; marine; remain
Maronites matronise
maroon Monaro
Maros moras; roams
Marple ampler; palmer
Marples palmers; sampler
Marree reamer
married admirer
marries simarre
mars arms; rams
marsh harms
Marston matrons; transom
mart tram
martel armlet
martels armlets
martens artsmen; sarment;
  smarten
martensite terminates
Martha Matrah
martial marital
martian tamarin
martians tamarins
martin Antrim
martinets stream-tin
martinis Marinist
martlets maltster
Martos Mostar; stroam; stroma
marts smart; trams
Mary army; Myra
mascara maracas; marasca
mascle camels; macles; mescal
mascon socman
mascot comsat
mascots comsats
masculine calumnies
maser mares; reams; smear
masers Ramses; smears
Maseru amuser; mauser
mash hams; sham
mashed shamed
masher harems; shamer
mashers shamers; smasher
mashes shames
mashies Messiah
mashing shaming

mason   moans; monas; Osman
masons   Namsos; Samson
massa   amass; Assam
massé   mesas; seams
Massenet   tameness
masseter   sea-terms; steamers
masseur   amusers; Erasmus;
mausers
Massine   Messina
mast   mats; tams
master   armets; maters; stream;
tamers
mastered   streamed
mastering   emigrants; St. Germain;
streaming
masterless   streamless
masters   streams
master-work   work-master
mastery   streamy
masticot   stomatic
mastics   miscast
mastoid   diatoms
masty   mayst
mat   tam
mate   meat; Meta; tame; team; Tema
mated   tamed
mateless   meatless; tameless
mater   armet; tamer; trema
matériel   eremital; Lemaître;
real-time
maters   armets; master; stream;
tamers
mates   meats; Mesta; steam; tames;
teams
matey   etyma; meaty
matin   tamin
matinees   seminate
mating   taming
matins   mantis
Matisse   asteism; samites; tamises
Matrah   Martha
matrices   ceramist
matricide   diametric
matronise   Maronites
matrons   Marston; transom
matross   stroams
mats   mast; tams
matters   smatter
mattress   smartest; smatters
maturation   natatorium
maturer   erratum
matures   strumae
maud   duma

mauds   adsum; Dumas
maugre   murage
maul   alum; Mula
maund   Munda; undam
maunder   duramen; manured;
unarmed
maundered   undreamed
maundering   undreaming
maunders   surnamed
maunds   Mundas; undams
mauser   amuser; Maseru
mausers   amusers; Erasmus;
masseur
mawr   warm
mawrs   swarm; warms
maws   swam
may   Amy; Mya; yam
maybe   beamy; embay
Mayen   meany; yamen
mayest   steamy
mayo   Amoy
mayor   moray
mayors   morays
mays   yams
mayst   masty
mazy   azym
M'Bao   ambo; boma; Moab
me   em
meads   dame; Edam; made
meads   dames
meagre   Graeme
meal   alme; Elam; Elma; lame; leam;
Lema; male
mealiness   messaline
meals   almes; lames; leams; males;
Saiem; samel; Selma
mean   amen; mane; Mena; name
meander   amender; enarmed;
renamed
meanders   amenders
meaner   rename
meaning   amening
meanly   laymen; namely
means   amens; manes; manse;
Mensa; names; samen
meant   ament; Manet
meany   Mayen; yamen
measly   samely
measures   reassume
meat   mate; Meta; tame; team; Tema
Meath   Thame
meatier   emirate
meatiness   amnesties; seminates

meatless   mateless; tameless
meats   mates; Mesta; steam; tames; teams
meaty   etyma; matey
mebos   besom
mechanics   mischance
mechanise   Manichees
medal   lamed
medals   damsel
Medan   amend; maned; menad; named
meddle   melded
Mede   deem; deme; meed
Medea   adeem
Medes   deems; demes; meeds
media   aimed; amide
medial   mailed
medials   misdeal; mislead
median   daimen; Damien; demain; maiden; Medina
medians   demains; maidens; sideman
medical   claimed; decimal; declaim
medically   decimally
medicals   decimals; declaims
medicaster   miscreated
medicate   decimate
medicated   decimated
medicates   decimates
medicating   decimating
medication   decimation
medicinal   adminicle
Medina   daimen; Damien; demain; maiden; median
Medise   demise
Medised   demised; misdeed
Medises   demises
Medising   demising
medlar   dermal; marled
Medusa   amused
meed   deem; deme; Mede
meeds   deems; demes; Medes
meer   mere
meercat   ceramet; cremate
meercats   ceramets; cremates
meers   meres; Merse
meet   mete; teem; Teme
meeting   teeming
meets   metes; teems; Temes; temse
Meg   gem
Megan   mange
megasse   message
megaton   magneto; montage

megatons   magnetos; montages
Megiddo   demigod
Meilhac   Michael
mein   mine
meins   mines
Meissen   misseen; nemesis; siemens
mélange   gleeman
melano   Malone
Melba   amble; blame; Mabel
melded   meddle
melding   mingled
mêlées   Semele
melic   clime
Melissa   aimless; mesails; samiels; seismal
mellay   lamely
mells   smell
melodies   melodise
melodise   melodies
meloid   moiled
melon   lemon
melons   Lemnos; lemons; solemn
Melos   moles
melters   smelter
melton   loment; molten
melts   smelt
Melun   lumen
Memling   lemming
memo   mome
memories   memorise
memorise   memories
memos   momes; Somme
Mena   amen; mane; mean; name
menad   amend; maned; Medan; named
Menado   daemon; moaned; Modane; Modena; nomade
menads   amends; desman
ménage   manège
ménages   manèges
Menai   amine; animé; en ami; Maine; minae
Menander   mannered
men-at-arms   armaments
Mende   emend
mender   red-men
menes   mense; mesne; semen
menial   Elmina; maline
menials   isleman; malines; seminal
meno   nome; omen
Menorca   Cameron; Cremona; romance

Mensa amens; manes; manse; means; names; samen
mensal Anselm; lemans
mense menes; mesne; semen
mensurable lebensraum
mensural numerals
mental lament; mantel; mantle
montally tallymon
mentioners minestrone
mentor Merton; montre
mentors monster; montres; Ore Mtns.
Merano moaner; monera
Merca Ceram; crame; cream; Crema; macer
mercaptide imprecated
Mercator cremator
merceries mercerise
mercerise merceries
Mercia Crimea
Mercian carmine; Crimean
merciful crimeful
merciless crimeless
mere meer
merel Elmer; merle
merels merles
meres meers; Merse
merest Mestre; meters; metres; Termes
meri emir; mire; riem; rime
Mérida admire
Mérignac amercing; creaming; Germanic
meril miler
Merill miller
merils milers; smiler
merinos mersion
merism mimers; simmer
meristem mimester; mismetre
merit mitre; remit; timer
merited demerit; dimeter; Edremit
merits mister; mitres; remits; smiter; timers
merle Elmer; merel
merles merels
merlin limner; Milner
merling gremlin; mingler
merlings gremlins; minglers
merlins limners
meroistic eroticism; isometric
Merops mopers; proems
merriest rimester; triremes
Merse meers; meres

Mersea ameers; seamer
Mersin miners
mersion merinos
mersions minoress
Merton mentor; montre
Meru mure
mesa same; seam
Mesagna agnames; manages
mesail mesial; Salemi; samiel; Sliema
mesails aimless; Melissa; samiels; seismal
mesaraic Americas
mesarch marches
mesas massé; seams
mescal camels; macles; mascle
mese emes; Esme; seem; semé; smee
mesh hems; Shem
mesial mesail; Salemi; samiel; Sliema
mesian Amiens; amines; inseam
mesne menes; mense; semen
mesocarp compares; compears
meson nomes; omens
mesonic Comines; incomes
mesotron Montrose
message megasse
messaline mealiness
messan manses
Messiah mashies
messier remises
Messina Massine
mess-tin missent
Mesta mates; meats; steam; tames; teams
mesto motes; smote; tomes
Mestre merest; meters; metres; Termes
Meta mate; meat; tame; team
metage gamete
metages gametes; Maesteg
metals lamest; samlet
metamer ammeter
metamers ammeters
mete meet; teem; Teme
meteor remote
meter metre
metering regiment
meters merest; Mestre; metres; Termes
metes meets; teems; Temes; temse
metis emits; items; mites; smite; stime; times

Metol motel
metonic entomic
metre meter
metres merest; Mestre; meters;
  Termes
metrician criminate
metricians criminates
metrics cretism
metronome monometer;
  monotreme
metronomes monometers;
  monotremes
Metsu mutes
meu emu
meus emus; muse
mew Wem
mews smew
mho ohm
mhos ohms
Mhow whom
mi I'm
Mia aim
miasm imams; maims
mica amic
micate acmite
Michael Meilhac
miche Chiem; chime
miched chimed
miches chimes
miching chiming
microclimates commercialist
mid dim
Midas maids
midden minded
mid-hour humidor; rhodium
mid-hours humidors
mid-range dreaming; margined;
  Niger Dam
Midrash dirhams
mid-sea amides
mid-term trimmed
mien mine
Mieres misère; remise
migraine imaginer
migraines imaginers
migrants smarting
migrate Maigret; ragtime
migrates magister; sterigma
mihrab Brahmi
mike Kemi
miladies idealism
Milas Islam; limas; malis; salmi;
  Simla

milden limned; Mindel
mildness mindless
mile Emil; lime
miler meril
milers merils; smiler
miles limes; slime; smile
Milesian alienism
milestone limestone
military limitary
milks sklim
miller Merill
millets mistell
millstone stone-mill
Milne Ilmen; limen
Milner limner; merlin
Milo moil
Milos moils
milreis slimier
Milspe impels; simple
mimers merism; simmer
mimester meristem; mismetre
mimesters mismetres
Min nim
mina Amin; main
minae amine; animé; en ami;
  Maine; Menai
minar inarm; Marin
minaret raiment
minars inarms
minas mains; Manis
minded midden
Mindel limned; milden
minder remind
minders reminds
mindless mildness
mine mien
mined denim
miner inerm
mineral manlier; marline; railmen
minerals marlines
miners Mersin
Minerva vermian
mines Nimes
minestrone mentioners
mingled melding
mingler gremlin; merling
minglers gremlins; merlings
minister interims
minks Minsk
Minnesota nominates
Minorca Marconi; Romanic
minoress mersions
Minos Simon

Minot Timon
Minsk minks
minster minters
minsters trimness
mintage teaming; tegmina
mintages steaming
minters minster
mintier interim; termini
minuend unmined
minuet minute; mutine
minuets minutes; mistune;
  mutinès
minute minuet; mutine
minute-drop importuned
minutely untimely
minutes minuets; mistune;
  mutines
minxes mixens
mir rim
Mira amir; Mari; rami; rima
Mirabel balmier; mirable; remblai
mirable balmier; Mirabel; remblai
miracle Almeric; Carmiel; claimer;
  reclaim
miracles claimers; reclaims
mirage gamier; imager; maigre
mirages imagers
Mirano mainor; Marino; Marion
mire emir; meri; riem; rime
mired dimer; rimed
mires emirs; miser; Reims; riems;
  rimes
mirier rimier
miriest mistier; rimiest
miring riming
Miro Riom
mirs rims; smir
miry rimy; Ymir
misarrange margarines
misaunter ruminates
miscast mastics
mischance mechanics
miscreant Encratism
miscreated medicaster
miscredit misdirect
miscredited misdirected
miscrediting misdirecting
miscredits misdirects
misdeal medials; mislead
misdealing misleading
misdeals misleads
misdeed demised; Medised
misdirect miscredit

misdirected miscredited
misdirecting miscrediting
misdirects miscredits
misdo odism
misdoer dormies; moiders
mise Seim; semi
misease Siamese
Miseno eonism; monies; Simeon;
  Simone
miser emirs; mires; Reims; riems;
  rimes
misère Mieres; remise
misers remiss
mises seism; semis
misfield misfiled
misfiled misfield
mishap pashim
mislead medials; misdeal
misleader misleared
misleading misdealing
misleads misdeals
misleared misleader
misled slimed; smiled
mismate tammies
mismetre meristem; mimester
mismetres mimesters
misplead impleads
misprint imprints
misprise pismires
misrate Artemis; imarets; maestri;
  maister; semitar; St. Marie
misrates asterism; maisters;
  semitars
misread admires
misreads sidearms
misreport importers
miss isms
missa amiss
missal salmis
misseen Meissen; nemesis;
  siemens
missel slimes; smiles
missend dimness
missent mess-tin
misses seisms
misset smites; stimes; tmesis
misshape emphasis
missile similes
missioner remission
mist smit
misteach tachisme
misted demits; stimed
mistell millets

mister merits; mitres; remits; smiter; timers
mistery smytrie
mistier miriest; rimiest
misting smiting; stiming; timings
mistrained administer
mistune minuets; minutes; mutines
misuser mussier; surmise
misusers surmises
mite emit; item; time
mites emits; items; metis; smite; stime; times
mither hermit
mithers hermits
mitre merit; remit; timer
mitres merits; mister; remits; smiter; timers
mittens smitten
mixens minxes
mna man; nam
Moab ambo; boma; M'Bao
moan Amon; mona; Oman
moaned daemon; Menado; Modane; Modena; nomade
moaner Merano; monera
moaners Romanes; San Remo
moans mason; monas; Osman
moas Amos; soma
moat atom
moating Maginot
moats atoms; stoma
mobbed bombed
mobbing bombing
mobile bemoil; emboil; emboli
mobiles bemoils; emboils
Mocha Mohác
mocks smock
mod Dom
modal domal
Modane daemon; Menado; moaned; Modena; nomade
Modder Modred
mode demo; dome; Edom
models seldom
Modena daemon; Menado; moaned; Modane; nomade
modern rodmen
modernise domineers
modernised endodermis
moderns rodsmen
modes demos; domes
Modred Modder

Moers mores; morse; omers; smore
Mohác Mocha
moider dormie
moiders dormies; misdoer
moidore moodier
moil Milo
moiled meloid
moilers Lismore
moils Milos
Moira Maori; Mario; moria
Moissac mosaics
moist omits
moister mortise
moithers isotherm; Stroheim
mokes smoke
molal molla
molar moral
molars morals; morsal
molders smolder
mole Lomé
moles Melos
molest motels; St. Elmo
Molina monial; oil-man
moline oil-men
molla molal
molten loment; melton
mome memo
moment montem
momes memos; Somme
mona Amon; moan; Oman
monacid monadic; nomadic
monad Damon; nomad
monades daemons; nomades
monadic monacid; nomadic
monads damson; nomads
monals salmon
monandry Normandy
monarch nomarch
monarchial harmonical
monarchies monarchise; nomarchies
monarchise monarchies; nomarchies
monarchises marchioness
monarchs nomarchs
monarchy nomarchy
Monaro maroon
monas mason; moans; Osman
Monastir Romanist
Monday dynamo
Mondays dynamos
moner morne
monera Merano; moaner

Monet monte
monger morgen
mongers morgens
monial Molina; oil-man
monies eonism; Miseno; Simeon;
  Simone
monism nomism
monist inmost
monistic nomistic
monists Stimson
mono moon
monodactylous condylomatous
monogram nomogram
monograms nomograms
monograph phonogram
monographs phonograms
monometer metronome;
  monotreme
monometers metronomes;
  monotremes
monopolies monopolise
monopolise monopolies
monosis simoons
monotones moonstone
monotreme metronome;
  monometer
monotremes metronomes;
  monometers
Monroe mooner
monster mentors; montres; Ore
  Mtns.
montage magneto; megaton
montages magnetos; megatons
Montagu Gaumont
Montargis sigmatron; stroaming
monte Monet
montem moment
montre mentor; Merton
montres mentors; monster; Ore
  Mtns.
Montrose mesotron
monture mounter; remount
montures mounters; remounts
moo oom
mood doom
moodier moidore
moods dooms; dsomo; Sodom
mool loom
mools looms; sloom
moon mono
mooner Monroe
moons nomos
moonstone monotones

moor Moro; room
Moore Romeo
moored roomed
moorhen hormone
moorhens hormones
mooring rooming
moorings smooring
moors Moros; Ormos; rooms;
  smoor
moos soom
moot toom
mooted toomed
mooting tooming
moots smoot; tooms
mop pom
mope poem; pome
moper proem; Prome
mopers Merops; proems
mopes Epsom; poems; pomes
mopish Ophism
mops poms
mora Omar; roam; Roma
moraines Romanies; Romanise
moral molar
morals molars; morsal
moras Maros; roams
moray mayor
morays mayors
mordant dormant
more omer; Rome
morel L'Orme
Morelia loamier
morels morsel
morendo doormen
mores Moers; morse; omers; smore
morgen monger
morgens mongers
moria Maori; Mario; Moira
moriche Homeric
Moringa roaming
morn norm
Morna manor; Norma; Ramon;
  Roman
mornay romany
morne moner
mornes sermon
morns norms
Moro moor; room
moronic omicron
Moros moors; Ormos; rooms;
  smoor
morose Romeos
morsal molars; morals

morse   Moers; mores; omers; smore
morsel   morels
morses   smores
mortise   moister
morts   storm; Troms
mort-safe   foremast
mort-safes   foremasts
mosaics   Moissac
most   mots; toms
Mostar   Martos; stroam; stroma
mot   tom
mote   tome
motel   Metol
motels   molest; St. Elmo
motes   mesto; smote; tomes
motet   motte; totem
motets   mottes; totems
mothers   smother; thermos
motmot   tomtom
motmots   tomtoms
motors   Tromsö
mots   most; toms
motte   motet; totem
mottes   motets; totems
moues   mouse
moulder   remould
mouldered   remoulded
mouldering   remoulding
moulders   remoulds; smoulder
mount   muton; notum
mountaineer   enumeration
mounted   demount
mounter   monture; remount
mounters   montures; remounts
mounts   mutons
Moura   amour
mourn   Munro; Muron
mourned   Dunmore
mouse   moues
moused   soumed; Usedom
mousers   smouser
mousing   souming
mousse   smouse
mousses   smouses
moutan   amount
moutans   amounts
mover   vomer
movers   vomers
mows   sowm
Mt. Siple   limpest; limpets
much   chum
Mucor   mucro

mucro   Mucor
mud-cones   consumed
muddies   dedimus
mudstone   demounts
mug   gum
muggers   smugger
mugs   gums; smug
Mula   alum; maul
mulga   algum; almug; glaum
mulgas   glaums
mumble   bummle
mumbled   bummled
mumbles   bummles
mumbling   bummling
Munda   maund; undam
mundane   unnamed
Mundas   maunds; undams
Munro   mourn; Muron
Munster   sternum
Mur   rum
murage   maugre
mural   larum; rumal
murals   larums; rumals
murder   Red Rum
murdered   demurred
murderer   demurrer
murderers   demurrers
murdering   demurring
murders   smurred
mure   Meru
mured   demur
murena   manure
mures   muser; Remus; serum; Sumer
Murex   Rumex
Murghab   Hamburg
muring   ingrum
Muron   mourn; Munro
Mus   sum
Musca   Camus; caums; sumac
muscadin   scandium
muscatel   calumets
Musci   music
muscone   consume
muse   emus; meus
mused   sedum
muser   mures; Remus; serum; Sumer
muses   musse
mush   hums
music   Musci
muss   sums
musse   muses

nussels sumless
nussier misuser; surmise
nust smut; stum; tums
mustard durmast
muster estrum; stumer
musters stumers
muteness tenesmus
mutes Metsu
mutilate ultimate
mutilates stimulate
mutilators stimulator
mutine minuet; minute

mutines minuets; minutes;
  mistune
muton mount; notum
mutons mounts
mutual umlaut
Mya Amy; may; yam
myelon lemony
mygale gamely; gleamy
myna many
myotic comity
Myra army; Mary
myrtle termly

N

na an
nab ban
Nabeul nebula; unable
nabk bank
nabks banks
nabs bans; snab
nache caneh
naches canehs
nacre crane; crena; rance
nacreous carneous
nacrite Catrine; ceratin; certain;
  crinate
nadir dinar; drain; Drina; Indra
nadirs dinars; drains
nae ane; ean; Ena
nag gan
nagged ganged
nagger ganger; grange
naggers gangers; granges
nagging ganging
Nagina angina
nags sang; snag
naiad Aidan; Diana
naïf fain; Ifan
nail anil; lain
nailed Aldine; alined; Daniel;
  Delian; denial; lead-in
nailer en l'air; larine; linear
nailers Linares
nailery inlayer
nailing alining
nails salin; snail
Nair airn; Iran; rain; rani
Nairn Narni
naker anker; Karen; nerka
nakers ankers; Karens
nala Alan; anal; lana

nalas nasal
nalla Allan
nam man; mna
name amen; mane; mean; Mena
nameable amenable
named amend; maned; Medan;
  menad
nameless lameness; maneless;
  salesmen
namely laymen; meanly
namer enarm; Marne
namers enarms
names amens; manes; manse;
  means; Mensa; samen
Namsos masons; Samson
Namur unarm
Nan Ann
nana anan; anna
nanas annas
Nancy canny
nap pan
nape neap; pane
napes aspen; neaps; panes; peans;
  sneap; spane; spean
Napier rapine
Naples panels; planes
napped append
napper parpen
nappers parpens; parsnep;
  snapper
naps pans; snap; span
Nara Aran; rana
narcotism romantics
nard darn; rand
narded dander; darned
narding darning
Nardo radon

nards darns; rands
nare Arne; earn; near; Rena
nares earns; nears; saner; snare
Narew awner
narghile nargileh
nargile aligner; engrail; learing;
  realign; reginal
nargileh narghile
nark knar; kran; rank
narked danker; darken; ranked
narking ranking
narks knars; krans; ranks; skran;
  snark
Narni Nairn
nary Ryan; yarn
nasal nalas
Nash Hans; shan
Nasik kinas
Nasser sarsen; snares
nastier ratines; resiant; retains;
  retinas; retsina; stainer; starnie;
  stearin
nastiest instates
nastily saintly
nasty tansy
nasute unseat
nasutes unseats
Nat ant; tan
natatorium maturation
natch chant
natches chasten
nates antes; etnas; Nesta; Senta;
  stane; stean; Teans
nation anoint
nations anoints; onanist
natively venality
nativist visitant
nativists visitants
natter ratten
nattered rattened
nattering rattening
natters rattens
nattier intreat; iterant; nitrate;
  tartine; tertian
nature aunter; Neutra; tea-urn
natures aunters; saunter; tea-urns
nautch chaunt
nave Evan; Neva; vane; vena
navel elvan; levan; venal
naves avens; Evans; Sevan; vanes
navigate vaginate
nawab bwana
nawabs bwanas

Naxos axons; Saxon
nay any
nazes senza
Nazi azin
Ndola nodal; Öland
ne en
neal élan; lane; lean; Lena
nealed aneled; leaden; leaned
nealing aneling; eanling; leaning
neals lanes; leans; slane
neap nape; pane
neaped peaned
neaping peaning
neaps aspen; napes; panes; peans;
  sneap; spane; spean
near Arne; earn; nare; Rena
neared deaner; Dearne; earned;
  endear
nearer earner
nearest earnest; eastern
nearing earning; engrain; grannie
nearly anerly
nearness ensnares
nears earns; nares; saner; snare
nearside arsenide
neat ante; Aten; etna; Tean
neater entera; rateen
neath thane
neatherd adherent
neatherds adherents
neb ben
Nebit-Dag debating
nebris brines
nebs bens; sneb
nebula Nabeul; unable
nebulose bluenose
Neckar canker
necks sneck
necrose encores
necrotic concerti
nectar canter; carnet; creant;
  Cretan; recant; tanrec; trance
nectared cantered; crenated;
  decanter; recanted
nectarines transience
nectarous courtesan; outrances
Ned den; end
née e'en
need dene; Eden
needers sneered
needless lessened
needly Leyden
needs denes; dense

126

nef fen
nefast fasten; Stefan
nefs fens
negation Antigone
negativism time-saving
Negev venge
Negro ergon; Genro; goner
Negroes engores
negroid eroding; Gironde; groined;
     ignored; redoing
negroidal girandole; reloading
Negros goners
neif fine; nife
neifs fines
neighed heeding
Neil lien; line; Nile
Neisse in esse; seines
neist inset; set in; stein; tines
neither therein
Neiva avine
neive nieve
neives envies; nieves
nek ken
neks kens
nelies enisle; ensile; senile; Silene
nelis elsin; lenis; liens; lines; Niles;
     silen
Nelly Lleyn
nematoid dominate
nemesis Meissen; misseen;
     siemens
nemoral almoner
nemorous enormous
Neo eon; Noe; one
neon none
neoteric erection
neotropical percolation
nep pen
Nepal panel; penal; plane; plena
neper preen
nepers preens
nephological phenological
nephologist phenologist
nephologists phenologists
nephology phenology
nephric phrenic; pincher
nephrite trephine
nephritis phrenitis
nepotism pimentos
nereid denier; Edirne; reined
nereids deniers
Nerita ratine; retain; retina; Tiranë
nerka anker; Karen; naker

Nero Nore; oner; Orne; Reno; rone
nerol enrol; loner; Lorne
nerval vernal
nervation vernation
nerve erven; never; Vener; Verne
nerved Denver; vender; Verden
nerves Nevers; Severn
nerviest reinvest; servient; sirvente
nesh hens
ness Sens
nest nets; sent; sten; tens
Nesta antes; etnas; nates; Senta;
     stane; stean; Teans
nested sedent; tensed
nester enters; Ernest; rentes;
     resent; Sterne; tenser; ternes
nesters resents
nesting tensing
Neston nonets; sonnet; stonen;
     tenons; tenson; tonnes
Nestos onsets; setons; sets on;
     stones
nests stens
net ten
nete eten; teen; tene
nether threne
nets nest; sent; sten; tens
nett tent
netted detent; tented
netting tenting
netty tenty
Neuquen unqueen
neural ulnare; unreal
neurosis resinous
Neuse ensue
Neustadt unstated; untasted
Neustria urinates
neuter retune; tenure; tureen
neuters retunes; tenures; tureens
Neutra aunter; nature; tea-urn
neutral Renault
Neva Evan; nave; vane; vena
never erven; nerve; Vener; Verne
Nevers nerves; Severn
Neves evens; seven
Nevis veins; vines; visne
new wen
Newark wanker
newish whines
new rich wincher
New Ross worsens
news sewn; wens
newt went

Ney yen
Ngami gamin
Nias anis; Isna; Nisa; sain; Sian
Niassa Asians
nib bin
nibs bins; snib
Nicastro cast-iron
niceness incenses
nicer crine
nicest incest; insect; scient
niche chine
niched chined; inched
niches chines; chinse; inches
niching chining; inching
nickels slicken
nickers snicker
nicks snick
Nicol Colin
Nicole cineol
nicotian inaction
nictate tetanic
nid din; Ind
nide dine; Enid
nidget tinged
nidor Rodin
nidus Indus
niello lionel; O'Neill
niellos lionels
nieve neive
nieves envies; neives
Nièvre envier
nife fine; neif
niffs sniff
Nigde deign
Nigel Elgin; ingle; ligne
Niger reign; renig
Niger Dam dreaming; margined;
  mid-range
niggard grading
nigger ginger
niggers gingers; snigger
niggle gingle
niggled gelding
niggles gingles; sniggle
nigh hing
night thing
nightcap patching
nightless lightness
night-robe bothering
nights things
nigrescent centerings; centreings
Nike kine
nil lin

Nile lien; line; Neil
Niles elsin; lenis; liens; lines; nelis;
  silen
nilgai ailing
nilgais sailing
nim Min
Nimes mines
nines Ennis
ninety-seven seventy-nine
ninety-six sixty-nine
Ningbo boning
niobic bionic
nip pin
Nipa pain; piña
Nipigon opining
nippers snipper
nips pins; snip; spin
nipter Pinter; pterin
nis ins; sin
Nisa anis; Isna; Nias; sain; Sian
nisse sines
nit tin
Nith hint; thin
Nitra intra; riant; train; Trani
nitrate intreat; iterant; nattier;
  tartine; tertian
nitrates intreats; straiten; tartines
nitre inert; inter; Terni; trine
nitric citrin
nits tins
nival Alvin; anvil; Vilna
niveous envious; veinous
nixy iynx
no on
nob bon
Nobel noble
noble Nobel
noblesse boneless
nobs bos'n; snob
nock conk
nocked conked
nocking conking
nocks conks
nod don
nodal Ndola; Öland
nodate atoned; donate
nodder droned
node done
nodes nosed; sonde
no dice codein; coined
nodose noosed
nods dons; snod
nodule louden; Oundle

nodules loudens
nodus sound
Noe eon; Neo; one
Noel enol; leno; Leon; lone
noes Enos; eons; nose; ones; sone
noesis enosis; essoin; noises; ossein; sonsie
noetic notice
nogs snog; song
noil lino; lion; loin
noils linos; lions; loins
noise eosin
noised donsie; Edison; onside; side-on
noiseless lionesses
noises enosis; essoin; noesis; ossein; sonsie
Nola Laon; loan
nomad Damon; monad
nomade daemon; Menado; moaned; Modane; Modena
nomades daemons; monades
nomadic monacid; monadic
nomads damson; monads
nomarch monarch
nomarchies monarchies; monarchise
nomarchs monarchs
nomarchy monarchy
nome meno; omen
nomes meson; omens
nominates Minnesota
nomism monism
nomistic monistic
nomogram monogram
nomograms monograms
nomos moons
none neon
nonesuch unchosen
nonet tenon; tonne
nonets Neston; sonnet; stonen; tenons; tenson; tonnes
non-glare Algernon
Nono noon
non-U noun
nooks snook
noon Nono
noosed nodose
nope open; peon; pone
nor Ron
Nora Arno; Oran; roan; Rona
Norah Rhona

Nore Nero; oner; Orne; Reno; rone
norm morn
Norma manor; Morna; Ramon; Roman
normal Marlon
Normandy monandry
norms morns
Norse noser; oners; rones; Ronse; Señor; seron; snore
north thorn
northed thorned; throned
norther horrent
northing thorning; throning
norths thorns
North Sea Sheraton
nos. son
nose Enos; eons; noes; ones; sone
nosed nodes; sonde
noseless soleness
noser Norse; oners; rones; Ronse; Señor; seron; snore
nosers Señors; sensor; serons; snores
noses sones; sonse
nosier senior; soneri
nostalgia analogist
not ton
notal talon; tolan; tonal
notarial rational
notarially rationally
notaries Señorita
notary aroynt
note Eton; tone
Notec cento; conte
noted Donet; toned
noteless toneless
noter tenor; trone
noters Reston; stoner; tenors; tensor; Terson; trones
notes Eston; onset; seton; stone; Tenos; tones
not-I into
notice noetic
noticer Citroen
notices section
noting toning
Noto onto; oont; toon
Notre Dame emendator
notum mount; muton
noughts gunshot; shotgun
noun non-U
noup Puno; upon
nous onus

nova Avon
Nova Scotia avocations
novel Venlo; Vlonë
novels sloven
now own; won
nowed endow; owned; Woden
nowhere Erewhon; whereon
Nowra rowan
nowt town; wont
noy yon
Nsanje Jansen
nub bun
nubs buns; snub
nuchal launch; unchal
nuclear lucarne; unclear
nuclide include

nuclides includes; unsliced
nude dune; unde
nudes dunes
nudges snudge
nudity untidy
numerals mensural
nuns sunn
nur run; urn
nurled rundle
nurs runs; urns
nurse runes
nursed sunder
nut tun
nuts stun; tuns; Unst
nutters entrust; test run
nuzzles snuzzle

O

oafs sofa
oak koa; oka
oaks koas; okas; soak
oaky kayo; okay
oar ora
oared adore; oread
oaring ignaro; origan
oarless lassoer
oars Oras; osar; Rosa; soar; sora
oast oats; Sato; stoa; Taos
oasts assot; stoas; Tasso
oat Tao
oaten Aneto; atone; Onate
oaths Athos; hoast; hosta; shoat
oats oast; Sato; stoa; Taos
ob bo
obang Gabon
obdurate taboured
Obed bode
obelus blouse; boules
Oberland banderol
Oberon Borneo
obeying biogeny
obeys syboe
obit bito
oblast bloats
oblate lobate
oblation lobation
obligant bloating; bog-Latin
oboes boose
Obok boko; book
observe obverse; verbose
obsess bosses

obsigns bossing
obtainer baritone
obtainers baritones
obtains bastion
obtested besotted
obtesting besotting
obtrude doubter; outbred; redoubt
obtrudes doubters; redoubts
obturate tabouret
obturates tabourets
obverse observe; verbose
ocarina Aaronic
ocean canoe
oceanic cocaine
oceans canoes
ocellated decollate
ocelli collie
ocelots coolest
ochery ochrey
ochre chore
ochrea chorea; Horace; orache
ochres chores; cosher
ochrey ochery
ocrea Corea
Octan acton; canto; cotan
octane at once
octanes costean
Octans actons; cantos
octave avocet
octaves avocets
octillion cotillion
octillions cotillions
octuple couplet

octuples couplets
od do
odal alod; load
odaliques odalisque
odalisque odaliques
odals alods; loads
odd dod
Odda dado
odder roded
odds dods
ode Deo; doe
Odeon Doone
Oder doer; Doré; re-do; rode; roed
odes does; dose
odic Icod
Odin Dino
odism misdo
odorant donator; tornado
Odra Dora; road
odyle yodel; yodle
o'er ore; roe
oestrus estrous; ousters; sourest;
  souters; tousers; trouses; tussore
offset set-off
offsets set-offs
ogle loge
ogled loged
ogles loges; segol
ogre ergo; goer; gore
ogres goers; gores; gorse; Sergo;
  soger
ogress sogers
oh ho
ohm mho
ohmage homage
ohms mhos
oho hoo
Ohre hero; hoer; rheo
oiler Loire; oriel
oilers elisor; lories; oriels; Serlio
oiliness lionises
oil-lamp oil-palm; palm-oil
oil-lamps oil-palms
oilman Molina; monial
oilmen moline
oil-palm oil-lamp; palm-oil
oil-palms oil-lamps
oil-press spoilers
oils Lois; silo; soil; soli
oilstone looniest
oka koa; oak
okas koas; oaks; soak
okay kayo; oaky

okayed kayoed
okaying kayoing
okays kayos
okes Keos; skeo; soke
Olaf foal; loaf
Öland Ndola; nodal
Olav oval; vola
old age age old; gaoled
older drôle
old man almond; dolman
old men dolmen
Olean alone
oleander reloaned
olent lento; Olten
oleo Looe
oleos loose; soole
Olga gaol; goal
olid idol; lido; Lodi
Olinda Ladino; laid on
olingo looing
olingos loosing; sooling
Oliva viola
olivaceous violaceous
olive voile
olives solive
olivet violet
olivets violets
Olivier rilievo
olpe lope; Opel; pole
olpes elops; lopes; poles; slope
Olt lot
Olten lento; olent
Oman Amon; moan; mona
Omar mora; roam; Roma
ombre brome
ombú umbo
ombús umbos
omen meno; nome
omens meson; nomes
omer more; Rome
omers Moers; mores; morse; smore
omicron moronic
omits moist
omneity omniety
omniety omneity
on no
onager Gerona; orange
onagers oranges
onanism mansion
onanist anoints; nations
Onate Aneto; atone; oaten
once cone
oncer Creon; crone

oncers censor; crones
oncoming gnomonic
ondine done in
ondines Denison
one eon; Neo; Noe
Onega agone; Genoa
O'Neill lionel; niello
on-end Donne; end-on
oner Nero; Nore; Orne; Reno; rone
oners Norse; noser; rones; Ronse;
  Señor; seron; snore
ones Enos; eons; noes; nose; sone
Ongar argon; groan; orang; organ
oniric ironic
only Lyon
onrush Hurons
onset Eston; notes; seton; stone;
  Tenos; tones
onsets Nestos; setons; sets on;
  stones
onside donsie; Edison; noised;
  side-on
onst snot; tons
onstead donates
on tap panto
Ontario oration
on the sly honestly
onto Noto; oont; toon
onus nous
onward draw on
onwards draws on
oodles loosed; sooled
oom moo
oons soon
oont Noto; onto; toon
op Po
opal Pola
opals Palos
op art porta; Prato
ope Poe
oped dope
Opel lope; olpe; pole
open nope; peon; pone
opened depone
opener perone; reopen; repone
openers perones; reopens; repones
opens peons; pones; Posen; snoep
operand padrone; pandore
operands padrones; pandores; San
  Pedro; Sarpedon
operant Paterno; pronate; protean
operants Paterson; pronates
operas Pesaro

operates protease
operating orange-tip
operator poor-rate
operators poor-rates
operettas poetaster
opes epos; peso; pose
Ophism mopish
opining Nipigon
Opole Poole
opposer propose
opposers proposes
oppressor proposers
oppugn pop-gun
oppugns pop-guns
ops pos; sop
opt pot; top
optant Patton
opted depot; poted; toped
optic picot; topic
optical Capitol; coal-pit; pit-coal;
  topical
optically topically
optics picots; topics
opting poting; toping
option potion
options potions
optology topology
opts post; pots; spot; stop; tops
Opuntia Utopian
opus soup
opuscle close-up; couples; upclose
ora oar
orach roach
orache chorea; Horace; ochrea
oraches roaches
orachs Cahors
oracle Carole; coaler
oracles coalers; escolar; solacer
orals soral
Oran Arno; Nora; roan; Rona
orang argon; groan; Ongar; organ
orange Gerona; onager
oranges onagers
orange-tip operating
orangs groans; organs; Sargon;
  sarong
orant toran; trona
Oras oars; osar; Rosa; soar; sora
orate Erato
orating tragion
oration Ontario
oratress assertor; roasters
orb bor; rob

orbed   bored; robed
orbing   boring; robing
orbited   debitor
orbits   bistro
orbs   robs; sorb
orc   cor; roc
Orca   arco; Cora; Roca
orcein   coiner; orcine
orchestra   cart-horse
orchestras   cart-horses
orchis   choirs
orcine   coiner; orcein
orcs   cors; rocs
Orcus   scour
ord   dor; rod
ordain   Dorian; inroad
ordainer   reordain
ordainers   reordains
ordains   inroads
ordeal   Laredo; loader; reload
ordeals   loaders; reloads; sea-lord
orderer   reorder
orderers   reorders
orderless   solderers
orders   dorser
ordinals   Rosalind
ordinate   deration; rationed;
  Rodentia
ordo   door; rood
Ordos   doors; roods; sordo
ords   dors; rods; sord
Ordu   dour; duro
ordure   dourer
ore   o'er; roe
oread   adore; oared
oreads   adores; soared
Oregon   orgone
Orel   eorl; lore; orle; role
Ore Mtns.   mentors; monster;
  montres
ores   Eros; roes; rose; sore
Orestes   osseter
Öresund   resound; sounder;
  undoers
orfe   fore
organ   argon; groan; Ongar; orang
organdies   grandiose; organised
organise   origanes
organised   grandiose; organdies
organist   roasting
organs   groans; orangs; Sargon;
  sarong
orgeat   Tagore

orgone   Oregon
orgue   rogue; rouge
orgues   grouse; rogues; rouges;
  rugose
orgy   gory; Györ
oriel   Loire; oiler
oriels   elisor; lories; oilers; Serlio
oriental   relation
Orientals   Orleanist; relations
orientating   integration
orients   in store; stonier; triones
origan   ignaro; oaring
origane   Iron Age
origanes   organise
Origen   eringo; ignore; region
Orkneys   Yonkers
Orlando   lardoon
orle   eorl; lore; Orel; role
Orleanist   Orientals; relations
orleans   loaners; reloans; Salerno
orles   eorls; Leros; loser; Osler;
  roles; soler; Sorel
Ormos   moors; Moros; rooms;
  smoor
ornate   atoner
Orne   Nero; Nore; oner; Reno; rone
ornis   inros; irons; rosin
orphan   harp on
orphans   harps on
Orpheus   shore up
orpine   Pinero; rope in
orpines   ropes in
orpins   prison
orra   roar
Orrell   roller
orsellic   colliers
Orsha   Horsa
ort   rot; tor
Orta   rota; taro; Tora
Ortegal   gloater; legator
Orton   Troon
orts   rots; sort; tors
os   so
osar   oars; Oras; Rosa; soar; sora
Osbert   sorbet; strobe
Oscars   across
oscillation   colonialist
oscillations   colonialists
oscine   conies; cosine
Oscines   cession; cosines
osculate   lacteous
Ösel   lose; sloe; sole
osier   Rosie; Siero

Osler eorls; Leros; loser; orles; roles; soler; Sorel
Oslo loos; solo
Osman mason; moans; monas
Osmanli malison; Soliman
Osmanlis malisons
osmiate atomies; atomise
osmiates atomises
ossein enosis; essoin; noesis; noises; sonsie
osseter Orestes
osteal Lao-tse
Ostend doesn't; Donets; stoned
ostent Totnes
ostents stetson; St. Neots
ostler sterol
ostlers sterols
ostracon cartoons; corantos
ostrich chorist
other throe
others Rothes; throes; tosher
otherwise white rose
Otho hoot; toho
Otsu oust; outs
ottar tarot
otters Troste
Otto toot
ouch chou
ouches chouse
Oud duo; udo
ought tough
ounce Cuneo
Oundle louden; nodule
ours sour
ousel louse; Seoul
ousels louses; soleus
oust Otsu; outs
ousted toused
ouster outers; routes; souter; touser; trouse
ousters estrous; oestrus; sourest; souters; tousers; trouses; tussore
ousting outings; tousing
outbreak break out
outbreaking breaking out
outbreaks breaks out
outbred doubter; obtrude; redoubt
outbroke broke out
outcast cast out
outcasts casts out
outcome come out
outcomes comes out
outcried cried out

outcries citreous; cries out
outcry cry out
outcrying congruity; crying out
outdare read-out
outdares read-outs
outer outré; route; Touré
outers ouster; routes; souter; touser; trouse
outfall fallout
outings ousting; tousing
outline elution
outlook lookout
outlooked looked out
outlooking looking out
outlooks lookouts; looks out
outrances courtesan; nectarous
outré outer; route; Touré
outred detour; douter; red out; routed; toured
outreds detours; dourest; douters; rousted
outride étourdi
outrides outsider
outs Otsu; oust
outsell sell-out
outsells sell-outs
outside tedious
outsider outrides
outspring posturing; sprouting
outstep toupets
outswear outwears
outwears outswear
outwith without
outwork work-out
oval Olav; vola
ovals salvo
ovates avoset
ovenbird bind over
ovenbirds binds over
over rove
overacts overcast
overbusy overbuys
overbuys overbusy
overcast overacts
overdoes overdose
overdose overdoes
overgo groove
overhang hangover
overhangs hangovers
overland rondavel
overlay layover
overlays layovers
overlie relievo

overpass Passover
overpassed eavesdrops; passed over
overpost overtops
overrated overtrade
overs roves; Serov; servo; verso
overset estover
overspin provines
overt trove; voter
overtops overpost
overtower overwrote
overtrade overrated
overture trouvère
overtures trouvères
overturn turnover
overturns turnovers
overwrote overtower
Ovid void
owe woe
Owen enow
ower owre; wore
owers serow; sower; swore; worse
owes woes

owl low
owler lower; rowel
owlers lowers; rowels; slower
owlery lowery
owlet towel
owlets Elstow; lowest; towels
owls lows; slow; sowl
own now; won
owned endow; nowed; Woden
owner rowen
owners rowens; worsen
owns snow; sown
owre ower; wore
oxen exon
oxers Sorex
oxhead hoaxed
oyer yore
oyez Yezo
oyster rosety; storey; Troyes; tyroes; Yes Tor
oysters storeys
Oz zo

P

pacable capable
pace cape
paced caped
pacer caper; crape; recap
pacers capers; Casper; crapes; escarp; parsec; recaps; scrape; spacer
paces capes; Caspe; scape; space
pacing caping
packer repack
packers repacks
pack-ice icepack
paction caption; Pontiac
pactioned captioned
pactioning captioning
pactions captions
pad dap
padang pad-nag
padangs pad-nags
padder draped; parded; Praded
pad-nag padang
pad-nags padangs
padre drape; pared; raped; repad
padres drapes; parsed; rasped; repads; spared; spread
padrone operand; pandore

padrones operands; pandores; San Pedro; Sarpedon
pads daps
Pag gap
pagan panga
pagans pangas
page gape; peag
paged gaped
pages gapes; Gaspé
paging gaping
pah hap
Pai pia
paidle aliped; elapid; Pleiad
paidles alipeds; elapids; lapides; palsied; Pleiads
paik pika
paiks pikas
pail Lipa; Pali; pila
paillasse palliasse
paillasses palliasses
pails lapis; spial
pain Nipa; piña
painless spaniels
pains piñas; Spain; spina
paint inapt; patin; pinta
painted patined

painter Patenir; pertain; pine-tar; repaint
painters pantries; Parentis; pertains; pinaster; repaints
paintress pinasters
paints patins; pintas; ptisan
paired diaper; pardie; repaid
pairs Ispra; Paris; Parsi
pais Apis; Pias; Pisa
pal alp; lap
pale leap; peal; pela; plea
paled pedal; plead
paler lepra; parle; pearl; repla
pales Elaps; lapse; leaps; peals; pleas; salep; sepal; spale; speal
palest palets; pastel; petals; plates; pleats; septal; staple
Palestine penalties
palet leapt; lepta; pelta; petal; plate; pleat
palets palest; pastel; petals; plates; pleats; septal; staple
palette peltate
Pali Lipa; pail; pila
palings lapsing; sapling
palliasse paillasse
palliasses paillasses
palls spall
palm lamp
palmary palmyra
palmated date-palm
palmed lamped
palmer ampler; Marple
palmers Marples; sampler
Palmerston emplastron
palmette template
palmettes templates
palmier impearl; lempira
palmiest implates; palmiets; petalism; septimal
palmiet implate
palmiets implates; palmiest; petalism; septimal
palming lamping
palmists psalmist
palm-oil oil-lamp; oil-palm
palms lamps; plasm; psalm
palm-tree Lampeter
palm-trees emplaster
palmy amply
palmyra palmary
Palos opals
palp Lapp; plap

palped dapple; lapped
palping lapping
palps Lapps; plaps
palpus slap-up
pals Alps; laps; salp; slap
palsied alipeds; elapids; lapides; paidles; Pleiads
palsy plays; splay
palsying splaying
palter plater
palterers plasterer
palters per-salt; plaster; platers; psalter; Spartel; stapler
paltry partly
paly play
pam amp; map
pamper mapper
pampers mappers
pams amps; maps; samp; spam
pan nap
pance pecan
pances pecans
pander repand
pandoors spadroon
pandore operand; padrone
pandores operands; padrones; San Pedro; Sarpedon
pandy Pydna
pane nape; neap; pean
panel Nepal; penal; plane; plena
panels Naples; planes
panes aspen; napes; neaps; peans; sneap; spane; spean
panga pagan
pangas pagans
pangs spang
panicle capelin; pelican
panicles capelins; pelicans
panics panisc
panisc panics
pans naps; snap; span
panted pedant; pentad
panter arpent; enrapt; entrap; parent; trepan
panters arpents; entraps; parents; pastern; trepans
panther Penarth
panties patines; sapient; spinate
pantiles plainest
pantine pinnate
pantler planter; replant
pantlers planters; replants
panto on tap

pantries painters; Parentis; pertains; pinaster; repaints
papal appal
papers sapper
papery prepay
par Arp; rap
parables sparable
parades aspread
paradise Sparidae
parasite aspirate; septaria
parasites aspirates; satrapies
parcel carpel; placer
parcels carpels; clasper; placers; scalper
parcheesi eparchies
parchesi seraphic
pard drap; prad
parded draped; padder; Praded
pardie diaper; paired; repaid
pards draps; prads
pare pear; Pera; rape; reap
pared drape; padre; raped; repad
parent arpent; enrapt; entrap; panter; trepan
parental paternal; prenatal
Parentis painters; pantries; pertains; pinaster; repaints
parents arpents; entraps; panters; pastern; trepans
parers parser; rasper; sparer
pares asper; parse; pears; prase; presa; rapes; reaps; spaer; spare; spear
paresis aspires; praises; Serapis
parge gaper; grape
parges gapers; gasper; grapes; sparge
paries aspire; Persia; praise
paring raping
parings parsing; rasping; sparing
Paris Ispra; pairs; Parsi
parish Hispar; raphis; Shairp
parkas Kaspar
parks spark
parle lepra; paler; pearl; repla
parled pedlar
parles pearls
parley pearly; player; replay
parleyed replayed
parleying replaying
parleys parsley; players; replays; sparely
Parmesan spearman

parodic picador
parol polar
paroled leopard
paroles reposal
Paros proas; psora; sapor; sopra
parpen napper
parpens nappers; parsnep; snapper
parried drapier
parries praiser; rapiers; raspier; repairs
parrot raptor
parroted predator; prorated; tear-drop
parroting prorating
parrots raptors
parse asper; pares; pears; prase; presa; rapes; reaps; spaer; spare; spear
parsec capers; Casper; crapes; escarp; pacers; recaps; scrape; spacer
parsecs escarps; scrapes; spacers
parsed drapes; padres; rasped; repads; spared; spread
Parsees asperse
parser parers; rasper; sparer
parsers raspers; sparers; sparser
parses aspers; passer; repass; spaers; spares; sparse; spears
Parsi Ispra; pairs; Paris
parsing parings; rasping; sparing
parsley parleys; players; replays; sparely
parsnep nappers; parpens; snapper
parsneps snappers
parson aprons; Prosna
part prat; rapt; trap
parted depart; petard; prated; traped
parter prater
parters praters
parti atrip; tapir
partial patrial
partialism patrialism
parties piastre; pirates; praties; traipse
parting gin trap; prating; traping
partisan aspirant
partisans aspirants
partite tear-pit
partitioned trepidation

partlet platter; prattle
partlets platters; prattles; splatter;
  sprattle
partly paltry
parts prats; spart; sprat; strap;
  traps
party praty
parure uprear
parures uprears
parvis Privas
pas asp; sap; spa
Pasch chaps
pash haps; hasp; Shap
pashed hasped; phased; shaped
pashes phases; shapes
pashim mishap
pashing hasping; phasing; shaping
Pashto pathos; potash
paspy sappy
pass asps; saps; spas
passé apses; spaes
passed sepads; spades
passed over eavesdrops;
  overpassed
passer aspers; parses; repass;
  spaers; spares; sparse; spears
Passeres asperses; repasses
passive pavises
passman sampans
Passover overpass
past pats; spat; stap; taps
paste pates; septa; spate; speat;
  tapes
pasted adepts
pastel palest; palets; petals; plates;
  pleats; septal; staple
pastels staples
paster paters; Praest; prates; repast;
  tapers; trapes
pastern arpents; entraps; panters;
  parents; trepans
pasters repasts
pastes spates; speats; stapes
Pasteur pasture
pastime impaste
pastimes impastes
pastor asport; portas; sap-rot
pastors asports
pastries piastres; raspiest; Tarsipes;
  traipses
pasts spats; staps
pasture Pasteur
pasty patsy; pyats

pat apt; tap
Patarine Tarpeian
patcher chapter
patchers chapters
patches hep-cats
patchier chapiter; phreatic
patching nightcap
pate peat; tape
pated adept; taped
paten tapen
Patenir painter; pertain; pine-tar;
  repaint
patent patten
patented pattened
patents pattens
pater apert; peart; Petra; prate;
  taper; trape
paternal parental; prenatal
Paterno operant; pronate; protean
paternoster penetrators
paters paster; Praest; prates; repast;
  tapers; trapes
Paterson operants; pronates
pates paste; septa; spate; speat;
  tapes
path Ptah
pathos Pashto; potash
patin inapt; paint; pinta
patined painted
patines panties; sapient; spinate
patins paints; pintas; ptisan
patly aptly
patness aptness
Patras satrap; Sparta
patrial partial
patrialism partialism
patrol portal
patrols portals
patron tarpon
patroness transpose
pats past; spat; stap; taps
patsy pasty; pyats
patten patent
pattened patented
pattens patents
patterns transept
patters spatter; tapster
Patti Pitta
pattles peltast
Patton optant
Paul Pula
paves Vespa
pavid vapid

pavise spavie
pavises passive
paw wap
pawls spawl
pawner enwrap
pawners enwraps; spawner
pawns spawn
paws spaw; swap; waps; wasp
pay pya; yap
payer apery; Peary; repay
payers repays; speary
pays spay; yaps
pea ape
peach chape; cheap
peachers preaches; sea-perch
peag gape; page
peaks spake; speak
peal leap; pale; pela; plea
pealed leaped
pealing leaping
peals Elaps; lapse; leaps; pales;
  pleas; salep; sepal; spale; speal
pean nape; neap; pane
peaned neaped
peaning neaping
peans aspen; napes; neaps; panes;
  sneap; spane; spean
pear pare; Pera; rape; reap
pearl lepra; paler; parle; repla
pearled pleader
pearlers relapser
pearlies espalier
pearlin plainer; praline
pearls parles
pearly parley; player; replay
pears asper; pares; parse; prase;
  presa; rapes; reaps; spaer; spare;
  spear
peart apert; pater; Petra; prate;
  taper; trape
pear-tree repartee; repeater
pear-trees repeaters
Peary apery; payer; repay
peas apes; apse; spae
peasant anapest
peasants anapests
peat pate; tape
pecan pance
pecans pances
peches cheeps; speech
Pechora poacher
pecks speck
Pecos copes; copse; scope

pecs spec
pectin incept
pectins incepts; inspect
peculates speculate
peculation unpoetical
peculations speculation
peculators speculator
pedal paled; plead
pedals lapsed; pleads
pedant panted; pentad
pedantries pedestrian
pedants pentads
pederast predates; trapesed
pedesis despise
pedestrian pedantries
pedicel pedicle
pedicels pedicles
pedicle pedicel
pedicles pedicels
pedlar parled
pedro doper; pored; roped
pedros dopers; prosed
peds sped
peed deep
peek keep; peke
peeking keeping
peeks keeps; pekes; Speke
peel Pele
peelers sleeper; speeler
peelings sleeping; speeling
peels sleep; speel
peened deepen
peer pree
peered deeper; De Pere
peering preeing
peerless sleepers; speelers
peers perse; prees; prese; speer;
  spree
pees seep
peke keep; peek
pekes keeps; peeks; Speke
Pekin Penki
pela leap; pale; peal; plea
Pelagians Pelasgian
Pelasgian Pelagians
Pele peel
pelican capelin; panicle
pelicans capelins; panicles
Pella lapel
pells spell
pelma ample; maple
pelmet temple
pelmets stempel; stemple; temples

peloids despoil; diploes; dipoles; soliped; spoiled
Pelops peplos
pelorism implores; sperm-oil
pelta leapt; lepta; palet; petal; plate; pleat
peltast pattles
peltate palette
pelter petrel
pelters petrels; spelter
peltries epistler; reptiles
peltry pertly
pelts slept; spelt
pen nep
penal Nepal; panel; plane; plena
penalties Palestine
Penarth panther
penates pesante
pencils splenic
pended depend
pends spend
pendular uplander
penetrant repentant
penetrators paternoster
penial alpine; Epinal; pineal
penis pines; snipe; spine
Penistone stone-pine
Penki Pekin
pensil Pilsen; spinel; spline
pensils spinels; splines
pentad panted; pedant
pentads pedants
peon nope; open; pone
peonism impones
peons opens; pones; Posen; snoep
peopling popeling
pepla appel; apple
peplos Pelops
peplus supple
pepo pope
pepos popes
Pepsi-Cola episcopal
per rep
Pera pare; pear; rape; reap
percale replace
percase Caprese; escaper
percept precept
perceptive preceptive
percepts precepts
percolation neotropical
percuss spruces
percussion supersonic

perdu drupe; duper; Dupré; prude; pured
perdues perused
perdus drupes; dupers; prudes; pursed
perfect prefect
perfects prefects
perform preform
performed preformed
performing preforming
performs preforms
peri pier; ripe
pericopes periscope
peril piler; plier
perils lisper; Perlis; pilers; pliers
Perim prime
period dopier
peripatetic precipitate
periplus supplier
perique re-equip; repique
peris épris; piers; pries; prise; ripes; speir; spire
periscope pericopes
perish reship; seriph
perished hesperid; shred-pie
peristome temporise
peristomes temporises
Perlis lisper; perils; pilers; pliers
perlite reptile
permeating impregnate
permissibility impressibility
permissible impressible
permission impression
permissive impressive
permissively impressively
permissiveness impressiveness
permits imprest
permitter pretermit
permitters pretermits
perms sperm
Pernod ponder
Peron prone
perone opener; reopen; repone
perones openers; reopens; repones
per pro proper
perries reprise; respire
perry pryer; ryper
per-salt palters; plaster; platers; psalter; Spartel; stapler
per-salts plasters; psalters; staplers
perse peers; prees; prese; speer; spree
Perseid predies; preside; speired

Perseids despiser; disperse; presides
Perseus peruses
Persia aspire; paries; praise
Persic cripes; precis; prices; spicer
persico copiers
Persism impress; premiss; simpers
persist priests; sprites; stirpes; stripes
persistent prettiness
persisting springiest
person prones
personate Esperanto
perstringe estreping; pestering; Presteign
pertain painter; Patenir; pine-tar; repaint
pertains painters; pantries; Parentis; pinaster; repaints
pertinacity antipyretic
pertly peltry
pertness presents; serpents
pertuse reputes
pertusion eruptions
Peru puer; pure
perusal serpula
peruse purées; rupees
perused perdues
perusers pressure
peruses Perseus
pervade deprave
pervaded depraved
pervades depraves
pervading depraving
perverse preserve
pervert Prévert
pervious previous; viperous
Pesah heaps; phase; shape
pesante penates
Pesaro operas
peso epos; opes; pose
pesos poses; posse; speos
pest pets; sept; step
pester peters; preset
pestered estreped
pestering estreping; perstinge; Presteign
pesters presets
pests septs; steps
Pétain pineta
petal leapt; lepta; palet; pelta; plate; pleat
petaline tapeline

petalism implates; palmiest; palmiets; septimal
petals palest; palets; pastel; plates; pleats; septal; staple
petard depart; parted; prated; traped
petards departs
peter petre
peters pester; preset
petitioner repetition
Petra apert; pater; peart; prate; taper; trape
petre peter
petrel pelter
petrels pelters; spelter
petri piert; tripe
petrochemical cephalometric
petrography typographer
petrosal prolates
petrous posture; pouters; Proteus; septuor; spouter; troupes
pets pest; sept; step
pews spew
phaetons Stanhope; Stephano
phanerogam anemograph
phare hepar; raphe
phares phrase; raphes; seraph; shaper; Sherpa; sphaer
Pharisees apheresis
phase heaps; Pesah; shape
phased hasped; pashed; shaped
phases pashes; shapes
phasing hasping; pashing; shaping
phasmid dampish
pheers herpes; Hesper; sphere
phenological nephological
phenologist nephologist
phenologists nephologists
phenology nephology
pheon phone
pheons phones
phese sheep
phi hip
philter philtre
philters philtres
philtre philter
philtres philters
phoca poach
pholades asphodel
phonautographs anthropophagus
phone pheon
phones pheons
phonetics Ctesiphon

phonic chopin
phonics chopins
phonogram monograph
phonograms monographs
phrase phares; raphes; seraph; shaper; Sherpa; sphaer
phrased sharped
phraser harpers; sharper
phrasers sharpers
phrases seraphs; shapers; Sherpas; sphaers
phrasing sharping
phreatic chapiter; patchier
phrenic nephric; pincher
phrenitis nephritis
physic scyphi
pia Pai
Pias Apis; pais; Pisa
piastre parties; pirates; praties; traipse
piastres pastries; raspiest; Tarsipes; traipses
picador parodic
picadors sporadic
picas aspic; Capis; spica
pice epic
picker ripeck
pickers ripecks
pickets skeptic
pickler prickle
picklers prickles
picks spick
picot optic; topic
picoté poetic
picots optics; topics
picrates crispate; practise
Picton Pontic
picture cuprite
piecer pierce; recipe
piecers pierces; precise; recipes
pieces specie
piece-work workpiece
piend pined
piends sniped; spined
pier peri; ripe
pierce piecer; recipe
pierces piecers; precise; recipes
piers épris; peris; pries; prise; ripes; speir; spire
piert petri; tripe
pies pisé; sipe
piets piste; spite; stipe
pig gip

pigeon epigon
pigeons epigons
pigs gips
pigskin spiking
pigsny spying
pika paik
pikas paiks
pike kepi; kipe
pikelets spikelet
pikes kepis; kipes; Pisek; spike
pila Lipa; pail; Pali
Pilar April; prial
pilaster plaister; plaiters
pilastered plaistered
pilasters plaisters
Pilate aplite
pileate epilate
pileated depilate; epilated
piled lepid; plied
piler peril; plier
pilers lisper; perils; Perlis; pliers
piles plies; slipe; spiel; spile
pillagers aspergill
pillages spillage
pills spill
pilots pistol; postil; spoilt
Pilsen pensil; spinel; spline
pilules pullies
piment pitmen
pimento emption
pimentos nepotism
pin nip
piña Nipa; pain
piñas pains; Spain; spina
pinaster painters; pantries; Parentis; pertains; repaints
pinasters paintress
pincase icepans; inscape
pincer prince
pincers Crespin; princes
pincher nephric; phrenic
pinchers pinscher
pinches sphenic
pineal alpine; Epinal; penial
pined piend
Pinero orpine; rope in
pines penis; snipe; spine
pineta Pétain
pine-tar painter; Patenir; pertain; repaint
pingers springe
pingle pin-leg
pingles pin-legs; spignel

pink gin   kingpin; pinking
pink gins   kingpins
pinking   kingpin; pink gin
pinks   Pinsk; spink
pin-leg   pingle
pin-legs   pingles; spignel
pinnate   pantine
pinners   spinner
pins   nips; snip; spin
Pinsk   pinks; spink
pinscher   pinchers
pinta   inapt; paint; patin
pintails   alpinist
pintas   paints; patins; ptisan
Pinter   nipter; pterin
pintles   plenist
pinto   piton; point; Ponti; potin
pintos   piston; pitons; points
piny   pyin
piolets   pistole; Ploesti
pipers   sipper
pique   equip
piques   equips
Piraeus   spuriae; upraise
Piran   Pirna
pirate   pratie; pteria
pirated   diptera
pirates   parties; piastre; praties;
    traipse
piratically   capillarity
Pirna   Piran
pirnies   inspire; spinier
pirogue   groupie
pirogues   groupies
Pisa   Apis; pais; Pias
piscator   apricots
pisces   spices
pisé   pies; sipe
Pisek   kepis; kipes; pikes; spike
pish   hips; ship
pismires   misprise
piss   sips
pisses   sepsis; speiss
piste   piets; spite; stipe
pistes   spites; stipes
pistol   pilots; postil; spoilt
pistole   piolets; Ploesti
pistols   postils
piston   pintos; pitons; points
pit   tip
pitchers   spitcher
pit-coal   Capitol; coal-pit; optical;
    topical

pith   hipt
pitmen   piment
piton   pinto; point; Ponti; potin
pitons   pintos; piston; points
pits   spit; tips
pit-saw   sawpit
pit-saws   sawpits
Pitta   Patti
pitters   spitter; tipster
placatory   play-actor
place   caple
placer   carpel; parcel
placers   carpels; clasper; parcels;
    scalper
places   caples
plaice   epical; plicae
plainer   pearlin; praline
plainest   pantiles
plains   spinal
plaint   pliant
plaister   pilaster; plaiters
plaistered   pilastered
plaisters   pilasters
plaiters   pilaster; plaister
plaits   spital
plane   Nepal; panel; penal; plena
planes   Naples; panels
planet   platen
planets   platens
planta   platan
planter   pantler; replant
planters   pantlers; replants
plap   Lapp; palp
plaps   Lapps; palps
plashes   hapless
plasm   lamps; palms; psalm
plasma   lampas
plasms   psalms
plaster   palters; per-salt; platers;
    psalter; Spartel; stapler
plasterer   palterers
plasters   per-salts; psalters; staplers
plastery   psaltery
platan   planta
platanes   pleasant
platans   saltpan
plate   leapt; lepta; palet; pelta; petal;
    pleat
platen   planet
platens   planets
plater   palter
platers   palters; per-salt; plaster;
    psalter; Spartel; stapler

plates palest; palets; pastel; petals; pleats; septal; staple
platinous pulsation
plats spalt; splat
platter partlet; prattle
platters partlets; prattles; splatter; sprattle
play paly
play-actor placatory
player parley; pearly; replay
players parleys; parsley; replays; sparely
plays palsy; splay
plea leap; pale; peal; pela
pleach chapel
plead paled; pedal
pleader pearled
pleaders relapsed
pleads lapsed; pedals
pleas Elaps; lapse; leaps; pales; peals; salep; sepal; spale; speal
pleasant platanes
please asleep; elapse; sapele
pleased delapse; elapsed
pleaser leapers; relapse; repeals
pleasers relapses
pleases elapses
pleasing elapsing
pleat leapt; lepta; palet; pelta; petal; plate
pleats palest; palets; pastel; petals; plates; septal; staple
Pleiad aliped; elapid; paidle
Pleiads alipeds; elapids; lapides; paidles; palsied
plena Nepal; panel; penal; plane
plenist pintles
plenum lumpen
pliant plaint
plicae epical; plaice
plied lepid; piled
plier peril; piler
pliers lisper; perils; Perlis; pilers
plies piles; slipe; spiel; spile
plim limp
plims limps
plissé slipes; spiels; spiles
Ploesti piolets; pistole
plot polt
Plotinus unspoilt
plots polts; Stolp
ploys slopy; Pylos
plug gulp

plug-in puling
plugs gulps
plum lump
plumed dumple; lumped
pluming lumping
plums lumps; slump
plumy lumpy
pluteus pustule
Po op
poach phoca
poacher Pechora
poachy pochay
pochay poachy
pocks Spock
poco coop
podex poxed
Poe ope
poem mope; pome
poems Epsom; mopes; pomes
poesy sepoy
poet pote; tope
poetaster operettas
poetic picoté
poets estop; potes; stoep; stope; topes
pogo goop
poh hop
point pinto; piton; Ponti; potin
pointe pontie
pointel pontile; top-line
pointer protein; pterion; tropine
pointers proteins
points pintos; piston; pitons
poises posies
poisons poisson
poisson poisons
pokal polka
pokals polkas
poker Koper; proke
pokers prokes
pokes spoke
Pola opal
polar parol
pole lope; olpe; Opel
poled loped
polemic compile
polemics compiles; complies
poler prole
polers proles; splore
poles elops; lopes; olpes; slope
poling loping
polka pokal
polkas pokals

polo   loop; pool
polt   plot
polts   plots; Stolp
polyps   sloppy
polyester   proselyte
polyesters   proselytes
polythene   telephony
pom   mop
pome   mope; poem
pomes   Epsom; mopes; poems
poms   mops
ponder   Pernod
ponders   respond
pone   nope; open; peon
pones   opens; peons; Posen; snoep
pongid   doping
Ponti   pinto; piton; point; potin
Pontiac   caption; paction
Pontic   Picton
pontie   pointe
pontile   pointel; top-line
pontoons   spontoon
poodle   looped; pooled
poodles   spooled
poofs   spoof
pooh   hoop
pool   loop; polo
Poole   Opole
pooled   looped; poodle
pooling   looping
pools   loops; sloop; spool
poor   proo; roop
poorest   Pooters
poor-rate   operator   -
poor-rates   operators
poort   Porto; troop
poorts   troops
Pooters   poorest
pope   pepo
popeling   peopling
poperin   propine
poperins   propines
popery   pyrope
popes   pepos
pop-gun   oppugn
pop-guns   oppugns
popish   hippos; shippo
popsy   soppy
porches   Porsche
pore   rope
pored   doper; pedro; roped
porer   prore; roper
porers   prores; proser; ropers

pores   poser; prose; ropes; Soper;
   spore
porgies   serpigo
poring   roping
Porsche   porches
porta   op art; Prato
portal   patrol
portals   patrols
portas   asport; pastor; sap-rot
Porte   repot; toper; trope
ported   deport; de trop
portend   protend
portends   protends
porter   pretor; report
porterage   reportage
porters   pretors; reports; sporter
portions   positron
Porto   poort; troop
portrayed   predatory
portress   sporters
ports   sport; strop
Portslade   Adlestrop
pos   ops; sop
pose   epos; opes; peso
posed   dopes; spode
Posen   opens; peons; pones; snoep
poser   pores; prose; ropes; Soper;
   spore
posers   proses; spores
poses   pesos; posse; speos
posh   hops; shop; soph
posher   ephors; hopers
posies   poises
posit   topis
posited   deposit; dopiest; topside
positional   spoliation
positron   portions
poss   sops
posse   pesos; poses; speos
posset   estops; stoeps; stopes
post   opts; pots; spot; stop; tops
postage   Gestapo
postboy   pot-boys
posted   depots; despot; stoped
poster   presto; repost; repots;
   topers; tropes
postern   Preston
posters   reposts
postil   pilots; pistol; spoilt
postils   pistols
posting   stoping
postings   signpost; stopings
postman   tampons

posts spots; stops
posture petrous; pouters; Proteus; septuor; spouter; troupes
postured proudest; sprouted
postures spouters
posturing outspring; sprouting
pot opt; top
potamic Tampico
potash Pashto; pathos
pot-boys postboy
pote poet; tope
poted depot; opted; toped
potes estop; poets; stoep; stope; topes
pother thorpe
pothers strophe; thorpes
potin pinto; piton; point; Ponti
poting opting; toping
potion option
potions options
potman tampon
pots opts; post; spot; stop; tops
pottered repotted
pottering pottinger; repotting
potters protest; spotter
potties tiptoes
pottiness stone-pits
pottinger pottering; repotting
pottingers protesting
potty typto
poules souple
poultice epulotic
pounce uncope
pounced uncoped
pounces uncopes
pouncing uncoping
pour roup
poured rouped
pouring ingroup; rouping
pours roups
pouter troupe
pouters petrous; posture; Proteus; septuor; spouter; troupes
pouts spout; stoup
pow wop
pows sowp; swop; wops
poxed podex
practise crispate; picrates
practised crispated
prad drap; pard
Praded draped; padder; parded
prads draps; pards

Praest paster; paters; prates; repast; tapers; trapes
praetors Raptores
praise aspire; paries; Persia
praised aspired; despair; diapers
praiser parries; rapiers; raspier; repairs
praises aspires; paresis; Serapis
praising aspiring
praline pearlin; plainer
pram ramp
prams ramps
prangs sprang
prase asper; pares; parse; pears; presa; rapes; reaps; spaer; spare; spear
prat part; rapt; trap
prate apert; pater; peart; Petra; taper; trape
prated depart; parted; petard; traped
prater parter
praters parters
prates paster; paters; Praest; repast; tapers; trapes
pratie pirate; pteria
praties parties; piastre; pirates; traipse
prating gin trap; parting; traping
Prato op art; porta
prats parts; spart; sprat; strap; traps
prattle partlet; platter
prattles partlets; platters; splatter; sprattle
praty party
prayers respray; sprayer
prays raspy; spray
preach eparch
preaches peachers; sea-perch
preachy eparchy
precast carpets; spectra
precept percept
preceptive perceptive
precepts percepts
precipitate peripatetic
precis cripes; Persic; prices; spicer
precise piecers; pierces; recipes
precursor procurers
predate red tape; tapered
predates pederast; trapesed
predator parroted; prorated; tear-drop
predators tear-drops

predatory portrayed
predial lip-read
predicants discrepant
predictions description
predictiveness vice-presidents
predicts scripted
predies Perseid; preside; speired
pree peer
preeing peering
preen neper
preens nepers
prees peers; perse; prese; speer;
  spree
prefect perfect
prefects perfects
preform perform
preformed performed
preforming performing
preforms performs
prelim limper
prelims limpers; simpler
preludes repulsed
prelusive pulverise; repulsive
premiers simperer
premise empires; emprise;
  epimers; imprese; spireme
premised demireps; simpered
premises emprises; impreses;
  spiremes
premising simpering
premiss impress; Persism; simpers
premisses impresses
premorse emperors
prenatal parental; paternal
prentices prescient; reinspect
prep repp
prepare repaper
prepares repapers
prepay papery
Prerov prover
presa asper; pares; parse; pears;
  prase; rapes; reaps; spaer; spare;
  spear
presage asperge
presaged asperged
presager asperger
presagers aspergers
presages asperges
presaging asperging
prescient prentices; reinspect
prese peers; perse; prees; speer;
  spree
present repents; serpent

presented serpented
presenter repenters; represent
presenters represents
presenting serpenting
presentive vespertine
presents pertness; serpents
preserve perverse
preses speers; sperse; sprees
preset pester; peters
presets pesters
preside Perseid; predies; speired
presides despiser; disperse;
  Perseids
pressed depress; spersed
presser repress
pressing spersing; springes
pression ropiness
pressure perusers
Prestea repeats
Presteign estreping; perstinge;
  pestering
presto poster; repost; repots;
  topers; tropes
Preston postern
presume supreme
presuming impugners
pretense terpenes
preterist preterits
preterit prettier
preterits preterist
pretermit permitter
pretermits permitters
pretor porter; report
Pretoria priorate
pretors porters; reports; sporter
prettier preterit
prettiness persistent
Prévert pervert
previous pervious; viperous
prewar warper
prexies expires
prexy Pyrex
prey pyre; rype
preys pyres; Ypres
prial April; Pilar
prials spiral
Priam prima
prices cripes; Persic; precis; spicer
prickle pickler
prickles picklers
pride pried; redip; riped
prides prised; redips; risped;
  spider; spired

pried   pride; redip; riped
prier   riper
pries   épris; peris; piers; prise; ripes;
   speir; spire
priest   esprit; ripest; Pteris; sprite;
   stripe; tripes
priestly   spritely
priests   persist; sprites; stirpes;
   stripes
prig   grip
prigs   grips; sprig
prima   Priam
primage   epigram
primal   imparl
primaries   impresari
primatial   impartial
prime   Perim
primes   simper
primrose   promiser
primroses   promisers
prims   prism
primus   purism
prince   pincer
princes   Crespin; pincers
printer   reprint
printers   reprints
printless   splinters
prints   sprint
priorate   Pretoria
Pripet   tipper
prise   épris; peris; piers; pries; ripes;
   speir; spire
prised   prides; redips; rispled;
   spider; spired
prises   speirs; spires
prising   risping; spiring
prism   prims
prison   orpins
Privas   parvis
proas   Paros; psora; sapor; sopra
probationer   reprobation
probe   rebop
probed   bedrop
procedure   reproduce
procedures   reproduces
process   corpses
procreant   copartner
procreation   incorporate
procure   crouper
procured   producer
procurers   precursor
procures   croupers
prod   dorp; drop

prods   dorps; drops; sprod
produce   crouped
producer   procured
proem   moper; Prome
proems   Merops; mopers
proke   Koper; poker
prokes   pokers
prolate   La Porte
prolates   petrosal
prole   poler
proles   polers; splore
prom   romp
Prome   moper; proem
promise   imposer; semi-pro
promiser   primrose
promisers   primroses
promises   imposers; semi-pros
proms   romps
pronate   operant; Paterno; protean
pronates   operants; Paterson
prone   Peron
prones   person
pronto   proton
proo   poor; roop
propel   lopper
propels   loppers
proper   per pro
propine   poperin
propines   poperins
propose   opposer
proposers   oppressor
proposes   opposers
prorated   parroted; predator;
   tear-drop
prorating   parroting
prore   porer; roper
prores   porers; proser; ropers
prose   pores; poser; ropes; Soper;
   spore
prosed   dopers; pedros
proselyte   polyester
proselytes   polyesters
proser   porers; prores; ropers
proses   posers; spores
prosit   tripos
Prosna   aprons; parson
protean   operant; Paterno; pronate
proteas   seaport
protease   operates
proteids   diopters; dioptres;
   dipteros; riposted
protein   pointer; pterion; tropine
proteins   pointers

protend   portend
protends   portends
protest   potters; spotter
protesting   pottingers
protests   spotters
Proteus   petrous; posture; pouters;
　septuor; spouter; troupes
prothesis   sophister; store-ship
protist   tropist
protists   tropists
proton   pronto
proud   pudor
proudest   postured
Proust   sprout; stroup; stupor
prover   Prerov
provides   disprove
provines   overspin
proxies   Siporex
prude   drupe; duper; Dupré; perdu;
　pured
prudent   uptrend
prudes   drupes; dupers; perdus;
　pursed
pruners   spurner
prussic   Scirpus
pryer   perry; ryper
psalm   lamps; palms; plasm
psalmist   palmists
psalms   plasms
psalter   palters; per-salt; plaster;
　platers; Spartel; stapler
psalters   per-salts; plasters; staplers
psaltery   plastery
psaltress   strapless
pseud   dupes; spued
psi   sip
psittacine   antiseptic
psoas   apsos; soaps
psora   Paros; proas; sapor; sopra
Ptah   path
ptarmic   crampit
ptarmics   crampits
pteria   pirate; pratie
pterin   nipter; Pinter
pterion   pointer; protein; tropine
Pteris   esprit; priest; ripest; sprite;
　stripe; tripes
pteryla   apertly
ptisan   paints; patins; pintas
ptomain   tampion
ptyalin   inaptly
publisher   republish
pudent   punted

pudic   cupid
pudicity   cupidity
pudor   proud
puds   spud
puer   Peru; pure
puers   pures; purse; sprue; super
pug   gup
puisne   supine
Pula   Paul
puled   duple; upled
pules   pulse; spule
puling   plug-in
pullies   pilules
pulper   purple; repulp
pulpers   purples; repulps
pulsation   platinous
pulse   pules; spule
pulverise   prelusive; repulsive
puncher   unperch
punier   purine; unripe
puniest   punties
punish   unship
punks   spunk
punnet   unpent
punnets   unspent
Puno   noup; upon
puns   spun
punster   punters
punted   pudent
punters   punster
punties   puniest
puntos   unstop
pupils   slip up
purdah   hard up
pure   Peru; puer
pured   drupe; duper; Dupré; perdu;
　prude
purée   rupee
purées   peruse; rupees
purely   Purley
pures   puers; purse; sprue; super
purest   erupts
purine   punier; unripe
purism   primus
purist   spruit; stir up; uprist
purists   spruits; stirs up
puritan   uptrain
puritans   Rasputin; uptrains
purled   drupel
Purley   purely
purple   pulper; repulp
purples   pulpers; repulps
purposes   supposer

purs spur
purse puers; pures; sprue; super
pursed drupes; dupers; perdus;
  prudes
purses sprues; supers
purslane supernal
pursued usurped
pursuer usurper
pursuers usurpers
pursuing usurping
pursy Pyrus; syrup
pus sup; ups
push hups
Pushtu shut up
puss sups
pustule pluteus
put tup

puts tups
putters sputter
putti titup
pya pay; yap
pyats pasty; patsy
Pydna pandy
Pye yep
pyin piny
Pylos ploys; slopy
pyre prey; rype
pyres preys; Ypres
Pyrex prexy
pyrogenic recopying
pyrope popery
Pyrus pursy; syrup
pythonic hypnotic

Q

quads squad
quaestor equators
quails squail
quakes squeak
quantise antiques
quartets squatter
quartile requital
quartiles requitals
queries esquire
querist requits
quester request
questers requests
questor quoters; roquets; torques
quickest quickset

quickset quickest
quids squid
quiet quite
quieter requite
quills squill
quinate antique
quince cinque
quires Quseir; risqué; squire
quite quiet
quits squit
quoter roquet; torque
quoters questor; roquets; torques
Quseir quires; risqué; squire

R

Ra ar
Raab Arab; arba
Rab bar; bra
rabbet barbet
rabbets barbets; stabber
rabble barbel
rabbled dabbler
rabbles barbels; slabber
rabi Bari
rabic baric; Carib
rabid Baird; braid
rabies braise; Serbia

Rabot abort; boart; tabor
race acer; acre; care
raced acred; arced; cadre; cared;
  cedar
raceme amerce
racemed amerced; creamed
racemes amerces
racer crare
racers crares
races acers; acres; cares; carse;
  scare; scrae; sérac
rach arch; char

rache   Caher; chare; reach
raches   arches; chares; chaser;
  eschar; search
rachis   chairs; Charis
racial   Alaric
racialist   satirical
Racine   in care
racing   arcing; caring
racists   sacrist
rack   cark
racked   arcked; carked; dacker
racket   tacker
rackets   stacker; tackers
racking   arcking; carking
racks   carks
racoon   corona
racoons   coronas
racy   Cary
raddle   Aldred; ladder; larded
raddles   ladders; saddler
rade   ared; dare; dear; eard; read
radian   Adrian; Andria
radians   Sindara
radiate   tiaraed
radicel   decrial; radicle
radicels   radicles
radices   sidecar
radicle   decrial; radicel
radicles   radicels
radicule   auricled
radio   aroid
radios   aroids
radius   Darius
radome   roamed
radon   Nardo
Raf   far; fra
raffia   affair
raffle   farfel
raft   fart
rafted   dafter; farted
rafter   farter
rafters   farters
rafting   farting
rafts   farts
rag   gar
raga   agar; Agra
ragas   Sagar
rage   gare; gear; Gera
raged   Edgar; Gerda; grade
rager   regar
rages   gears; sager; sarge
ragged   dagger
raggle   gargle; lagger

raggled   draggle; gargled
raggles   gargles; laggers
raggling   gargling
ragi   gair
ragingly   grayling
ragmen   engram; german; manger
ragment   garment; margent
ragments   garments; margents
rags   gars; Gras
rag-tag   tagrag
ragtime   Maigret; migrate
ragweed   Edgware; wagered
raid   arid; dari
raider   arride
raiders   arrides
raids   Sidra
raik   raki
raiked   daiker
Raikes   Kaiser
rail   aril; lair; liar; lira; rial
railed   derail; laired; Lérida; relaid
railer   rerail
railers   rerails
railing   glairin; lairing
railman   laminar
railmen   manlier; marline; mineral
rails   lairs; liars; liras; rials
raiment   minaret
rain   airn; Iran; Nair; rani
rained   Dairen; Darien; randie
raininess   sirenians
raining   ingrain
rains   ranis
rain-tree   Eritrean; retainer
rain-trees   Eritreans; retainers;
  ternaries
raise   aesir; Aries; arise; Riesa; serai;
  Seria
raised   aiders; irades
raiser   airers; Sérrai; sierra
raisers   sierras
raises   arises; serais
raising   arising
rait   airt
raited   airted; tirade
raits   airts; astir; sitar; Sitra; stair;
  stria; tarsi; Trias
raj   jar
raja   ajar
rake   reak
raked   arked; daker; drake
rakes   asker; kesar; reaks; saker;
  skear

151

raki raik
raking arking
rakish shikar
râle earl; lare; lear; real
rallied dallier; dialler
ram arm; mar
Rama Aram; mara
ramal alarm; malar
ramble ambler; blamer; marble
rambled marbled
rambler marbler
ramblers marblers
rambling marbling
Rameses seamers
rami amir; Mari; Mira; rima
ramie maire; Marie; rimae
ramis simar
Ramist Marist
Ramists Marists; tsarism
Ramle lamer
Ramleh Harlem; Mahler
Ramon manor; Morna; Norma;
  Roman
ramp pram
ramped damper
ramps prams
rams arms; mars
Ramses masers; smears
ramson manors; ransom; Romans
ramsons ransoms
ramus arums; rusma; Sarum
rana Aran; Nara
rance crane; crena; nacre
ranced cedarn; craned; dancer
rancel lancer
rancels lancers
rances casern; cranes
ranched endarch
ranches chenars
rancho anchor; archon; Charon
ranchos anchors; archons
rancing craning
rand darn; nard
Randers darners; errands
randie Dairen; Darien; rained
random rodman
rands darns; nards
rang gnar; gran
range anger; Regan; renga
ranged danger; gander; garden
ranger garner
rangers garners
ranges angers; Sanger; serang

ranginess angriness
rangy angry
rani airn; Iran; Nair; rain
ranis rains
rank knar; kran; nark
ranked danker; darken; narked
ranking narking
rankle lanker
ranks knars; krans; narks; skran;
  snark
ransel learns
ransom manors; ramson; Romans
ransoms ramsons
rant tarn
ranted ardent; endart; red ant
ranter errant
rants starn; tarns
rap Arp; par
rape pare; pear; Pera; reap
raped drape; padre; pared; repad
rapes asper; pares; parse; pears;
  prase; presa; reaps; spaer; spare;
  spear
raphe hepar; phare
raphes phares; phrase; seraph;
  shaper; Sherpa; sphaer
raphis Hispar; parish; Shairp
rapids spraid
rapier repair
rapiers parries; praiser; raspier;
  repairs
rapine Napier
raping paring
rapist tapirs
rapparee reappear
rapparees reappears
rapped dapper
rappel lapper
rappels lappers; slapper
raps rasp; spar
rapt part; prat; trap
raptor parrot
Raptores praetors
raptors parrots
rare rear
rarebit arbiter
rarebits arbiters
ras sar
rascal lascar; sacral; scalar
rascals lascars; scalars
rase Ares; arse; ears; eras; sear; sera
rased dares; dears; reads
rases arses; rasse; sears

rasher sharer
rashers sharers
rashes shares; shears
rasing grains; Sangir
rasp raps; spar
rasped drapes; padres; parsed; repads; spared; spread
rasper parers; parser; sparer
raspers parsers; sparers; sparser
raspier parries; praiser; rapiers; repairs
raspiest pastries; piastres; Tarsipes; traipses
rasping parings; parsing; sparing
raspingly sparingly
rasps spars
Rasputin puritans; uptrains
raspy prays; spray
rasse arses; rases; sears
raster arrest; arrêts; raters; Sartre; starer; terras
rasters arrests; starers
Rastus Straus; sutras; Tarsus
rat art; tar
rata tara
ratable Alberta
ratal altar; talar
ratan antra
ratas tasar
ratbite battier; biretta
ratbites birettas
ratch chart
ratchet chatter
ratchets chatters
rate aret; tare; tear
rated adret; dater; tared; trade; tread
rateen entera; neater
ratel alert; alter; artel; later; taler
ratels alerts; alters; artels; laster; salter; slater; staler; stelar; tarsel
rater arrêt; terra
raters arrest; arrêts; raster; Sartre; starer; terras
rates arets; aster; astre; earst; reast; resat; stare; strae; tares; tears; teras
rath hart; tahr; thar
rathe earth; Harte; hater; heart; Herat; Thera; thrae
rathest hatters; shatter; threats
rat-hole loather
rat-holes loathers
raths harts; tahrs; thars; trash

ratine Nerita; retain; retina; Tiranë
ratines nastier; resiant; retains; retinas; retsina; stainer; starnie; stearin
rating taring
ratings staring
ratio ariot
ration aroint
rational notarial
rationale alienator
rationalise realisation
rationally notarially
rationed deration; ordinate; Rodentia
rations aroints
ratios Artois
ratite attire; Tiaret
ratlin trinal
ratline entrail; Latiner; latrine; reliant; retinal; trenail
ratlines entrails; Latiners; latrines; trenails
ratlings starling
rats arts; star; tars; tsar
ratsbane ant-bears
rattan Tantra; tartan
rattans Tantras; tartans
ratted tarted; tetrad
ratteen entreat; ternate
ratteens entreats
ratten natter
rattened nattered
rattening nattering
rattens natters
ratters restart; starter
rattle latter; tatler
rattlers startler
rattles slatter; starlet; startle; tatlers; Telstar
rattlings startling
ratton rottan
rattons rottans
ratty tarty
raun Arun
rave Arve; aver; vare; Vera
raved drave; Revda; Varde
ravel laver; Reval; velar
ravels lavers; salver; serval; slaver; versal
raves avers; saver; vares
Ravi riva; vair
ravin Invar
ravine Erivan; vainer; Vanier

ravined invader
ravines Servian
raving Girvan
raw war
rawing waring
rawn warn
rawness answers
rawns warns
ray ary; Ayr
rayed deary; deray; ready; yeard
raying grainy
rayless slayers
rays Syra
raze Ezra
razed zerda
re er
reabsorb absorber
reabsorbs absorbers
reach Caher; chare; rache
reached Ardèche
reachers research; searcher
react caret; carte; cater; crate; recta; trace
reacted catered; cedrate; created
reacting argentic; catering; citrange; creating
reaction creation
reactions creations
reactive creative
reactively creatively
reactivity creativity
reactor acroter; creator
reactors acroters; creators
reacts carets; cartes; caster; caters; crates; Cresta; recast; traces
read ared; dare; dear; eard; rade
readdress addresser
Reade arede; deare; eared
reader dearer; reared; reread
readers redsear; rereads
readies dearies
readiest steadier
reading areding; dearing; deraign; gradine; grained
readings deraigns; gradines
readjust adjuster
readjusts adjusters
read-out outdare
read-outs outdares
reads dares; dears; rased
ready deary; deray; rayed; yeard
readying deraying; yearding
reaffirm affirmer

reaffirms affirmers
Reagan Grenaa
reagent grantee; greaten
reagents estrange; grantees; greatens; segreant; sergeant
reak rake
reaks asker; kesar; rakes; saker; skear
real earl; lare; lear; râle
realign aligner; engrail; learing; nargile; reginal
realigned engrailed; Geraldine
realigning engrailing
realignment engrailment
realignments engrailments
realigns aligners; engrails; Salinger; sanglier; seal-ring
realisation rationalise
realised sidereal
realism mailers
realist Alister; retails; saltier; saltire; slatier
realistic eristical
realists saltiers; saltires; slaister
realities Israelite
reals Arles; earls; lares; laser; lears; seral
re-alter relater
re-alters relaters
real-time eremital; Lemaître; matériel
realtor relator
realtors relators
realty elytra; lyrate
ream mare
reamed remade
reamer Marree
reaming Germain
reams mares; maser; smear
reap pare; pear; Pera; rape
reappear rapparee
reappears rapparees
reaps asper; pares; parse; pears; prase; presa; rapes; spaer; spare; spear
rear rare
reared dearer; reader; reread
rearing angrier; earring; grainer
rearmed dreamer
rearrest arrester
rearrests arresters
rears Sarre; serra
reascend ascender

reascends   ascenders
reascent   sarcenet
reason   Señora
reasons   Señoras
reassert   asserter; serrates
reasserts   asserters
reassume   measures
reassure   orassuree
reast   arets; aster; astre; earst; rates;
    resat; stare; strae; tares; tears; teras
reasted   dearest; derates; estrade
reasting   angriest; astringe;
    ganister; gantries; granites; inert
    gas; ingrates
reasts   assert; asters; astres; stares;
    Stresa
reasty   estray; stayer; yarest
reate   arête; eater; Taree
reates   arêtes; easter; eaters; reseat;
    saeter; teaser; Teresa
reaves   averse; Varese
reaving   vinegar
reback   backer
rebacks   backers
rebate   beater; berate
rebated   berated; betread; debater
rebates   beaters; berates
rebating   berating
rebid   bride; Diber
rebids   brides
rebind   binder; brined; inbred
rebinds   binders
rebit   biter; Tiber; tribe
rebloom   bloomer
reblooms   bloomers
reboil   boiler
reboils   boilers
rebop   probe
rebound   bounder; unrobed
rebounds   bounders; suborned
rebroadcast   broadcaster
rebroadcasts   broadcasters
rebuff   buffer
rebuffed   buffered
rebuffing   buffering
rebuffs   buffers
rebuild   builder
rebuilds   builders
rebus   burse; suber
rebut   brute; tuber
rebuts   brutes; buster; tubers
rebuttal   burletta
rebutted   buttered

rebutting   buttering
recall   caller; cellar
recalled   cellared
recalling   cellaring
recalls   callers; cellars; scleral
recant   canter; carnet; creant;
    Cretan; nectar; tanrec; trance
recanted   cantered; crenated;
    decanter; nectared
recanter   recreant
recanters   recreants
recanting   cantering
recants   canters; carnets; Cretans;
    tanrecs; trances
recap   caper; crape; pacer
recaps   capers; Casper; crapes;
    escarp; pacers; parsec; scrape;
    spacer
recast   carets; cartes; caster; caters;
    crates; Cresta; reacts; traces
recasting   citranges
recasts   actress; casters; Castres
recede   decree
receded   decreed
recedes   decrees; seceder
received   deceiver
recent   center; centre; tenrec
recentness   sentencers
recepts   respect; sceptre; spectre
recessed   seceders
Rechab   Béchar; breach
Recife   fierce
recipe   piecer; pierce
recipes   piecers; pierces; precise
recital   article
recitals   articles; sterical
recite   cerite; tierce
recites   tierces
recked   decker
reckon   conker
reckons   conkers
reclaim   Almeric; claimer; miracle
reclaimed   declaimer
reclaims   claimers; miracles
reclinate   interlace; lacertine
reclines   licenser; silencer
recloses   coreless; sclerose
recluses   cureless
reclusion   Cornelius
recognise   congeries
recomfort   comforter
recomforts   comforters
recondition   conditioner

reconditions conditioners
reconvert converter
reconverts converters
reconvey conveyer
reconveys conveyers
recopying pyrogenic
recount cornute; counter; trounce
recounted countered
recounting countering
recounts construe; cornutes;
  counters; trounces
recoup couper; croupe; cuerpo
recoups coupers; croupes
recourse resource
recreant recanter
recreants recanters
recross crosser
recruits crustier
recta caret; carte; cater; crate; react;
  trace
rectal cartel; claret; tarcel
recti trice
rectifiable certifiable
rectification certification
rectified certified
rectifier certifier
rectifiers certifiers
rectifies certifies
rectify certify
rectifying certifying
rectitude certitude
rectus cruets; cruset; Custer; eructs;
  truces
recur curer
recures rescuer; securer
recurs curers; curser
recusant centaurs; Etruscan;
  untraces
recusants Etruscans
recuse Cereus; ceruse; Creuse;
  rescue; secure
recused reduces; rescued; secured;
  seducer
recuses rescues; secures
recusing rescuing; securing
redact carted; crated; Dectra; traced
redactions draconites
redans sander; snared
red ant ardent; endart; ranted
red ants endarts; stander
Red Bay brayed
red-book brooked
redbreast bestarred

rebud budder
redbuds budders
redcap carped; craped
redcaps scarped; scraped
Redcar carder
red cent centred; credent
Red China inarched
redcoat cordate
reddens Dresden
reddle Eldred
red-dog dodger
reddy ydred
rede deer; dere; dree; reed
redeems demerse; emersed
redeliver deliverer
redelivers deliverers
redes deres; drees; reeds; Seder
red giant derating; gradient;
  treading
red giants gradients
red-hat dearth; hatred; thread
red-hats dearths; hardest; hatreds;
  threads; trashed
redhead adhered
red-heat earthed; hearted
red-hot dehort
redia aider; aired; irade
redip pride; pried; riped
redips prides; prised; risped;
  spider; spired
rediscover discoverer
rediscovers discoverers
red-man manred; remand
red-men mender
redness senders
Red Nile relined
re-do doer; Doré; Oder; rode; roed
redoubt doubter; obtrude; outbred
redoubts doubters; obtrudes
redound rounded; underdo
redounding underdoing
red out detour; douter; outred;
  routed; toured
redraft drafter
redrafts drafters
redraw drawer; reward; warder;
  warred
redraws drawers; rewards;
  warders
redress dresser
Red Rum murder
Red Sea aredes; deares; erased;
  reseda; seared

156

redsear   readers; rereads
red tape   predate; tapered
reduces   recused; rescued; secured;
  seducer
reduction   introduce
reductions   discounter; introduces
redwing   wringed
reech   cheer
re-echo   cheero; choree; cohere;
  echoer
reechy   cheery
reed   deer; dere; dree; rede
reedily   yielder
reeding   dreeing; energid: reigned
re-edit   retied
re-editing   reignited
re-edits   reisted; re-sited
reeds   deres; drees; redes; Seder
reedstop   reposted
reef   feer; fere; free
reefed   feeder; feered
reefing   feering; feigner; freeing
reefs   feers; feres; frees
reeks   esker; skeer
reel   leer; lere
reeled   leered
reeling   leering
reels   leers; leres
re-endow   endower
re-endows   endowers
re-enlist   enlister; Leinster;
  listener
re-enlists   enlisters; listeners
re-enter   enterer; terrene
re-enters   enterers; resenter;
  terrenes
re-equip   perique; repique
re-equips   repiques
reest   ester; reset; retes; steer; stere;
  teers; terse; trees
reested   steered
reesting   integers; steering; streigne
reests   esters; resets; steers; steres
reeved   veered
reeves   severe
reeving   veering
re-export   exporter
re-exports   exporters
ref   erf
refel   fleer
refels   fleers
refer   freer
refill   filler

refills   fillers
refine   enfire; ferine; Fernie; fineer;
  infere
refined   enfired
refines   enfires; fineers
refining   enfiring; infringe
refits   sifter; strife
reflated   faltered
reflating   faltering
refloat   floater; floreat
refloats   floaters; forestal
reflow   flower; fowler; wolfer
reflowed   deflower; flowered
reflowing   flowering
reflows   flowers; fowlers; wolfers
refoot   foetor; footer; tofore
reform   former
reformed   deformer
reforms   formers
refound   founder
refounds   founders
refresh   fresher
reft   fret
refuel   ferule
refuels   ferules
refunded   underfed
refurbish   furbisher
refurnish   furnisher
refusal   earfuls
refute   feutre
refutes   feutres
Reg   erg
regain   earing; gainer; graine;
  regina
regains   earings; erasing; gainers;
  searing; Seraing; seringa
regal   Elgar; glare; lager; large;
  Regla
regalia   Algeria
regalian   Algerian
regally   allergy; gallery; largely
regals   glares; lagers
Regan   anger; range; renga
regar   rager
regard   Gerard; grader
regards   graders
regelate   relegate
regelated   relegated
regelates   relegates
regelating   relegating
regelation   relegation
regent   gerent
regents   gerents

Reggie Geiger
regime émigré
regiment metering
regimes émigrés
regina earing; gainer; graine;
  regain
reginal aligner; engrail; learing;
  nargile; realign
region eringo; ignore; Origen
regions ignores; Signore
regius guiser
Regla Elgar; glare; lager; large;
  regal
regma gamer; marge
regmata Margate
regnal angler
regrant granter
regrants granters; stranger
regrate greater
regrated gartered; garreted;
  Tredegar
regrating gartering
regrind grinder
regrinds grinders
regroup grouper
regroups groupers
reh her
rehear hearer
reheard adherer
rehears hearers; shearer
reheat aether; heater; hereat
reheats heaters; Theresa
reheel heeler
reheels heelers
rehoused rose-hued
Reid dire; ride
reif fire; Frei; rife
reify fiery
reign Niger; renig
reigned dreeing; energid; reeding
reignited re-editing
reigns Ingres; renigs; resign;
  signer; singer
Reims emirs: mires; miser; riems;
  rimes
rein Erin; in re; Reni
rein-arm mariner
rein-arms mariners
reined denier; Edirne; nereid
reinfect frenetic
reinforce confrérie
reinforces confréries
reinform informer; reniform

reinforms informers
reins resin; rinse; risen; serin; siren
reinsert reinters; rentiers; terrines
reinspect prentices; prescient
reinsured surreined
reinter rentier; terrine
reinterpret interpreter
reinterprets interpreters
reinters reinsert; rentiers; terrines
reinvest nerviest; servient; sirvente
reird direr; drier; rider
reirds derris; driers; riders; sirred
reis Eris; rise; sire
reist resit; rites; Siret; tiers; tires;
  tries
reisted re-edits; re-sited
reists resist; resits; sister
reiter étrier; retire
reiters étriers; retires; retries;
  terries
reive revie; rieve
reived derive; revied; rieved
reiver riever
reivers rievers
reives revies; revise; rieves
reiving rieving
rejoin joiner
rejoins joiners
relaid derail; laired; Lérida; railed
relapse leapers; pleaser; repeals
relapsed pleaders
relapser pearlers
relapses pleasers
relate elater; Tralee
related alerted; altered; treadle
relater re-alter
relaters re-alters
relates elaters; Laertes; stealer
relating alerting; altering; integral;
  triangle
relation oriental
relations Orientals; Orleanist
relative levirate
relatives versatile
relator realtor
relators realtors
relax laxer
relay early; layer
relayed delayer; layered
relaying layering; yearling
relays layers; slayer
releasing Algerines
relegate regelate

relegated regelated
relegates regelates
relegating regelating
relegation regelation
relets Lester; streel
relevant levanter
reliably Bareilly
reliance cinereal
reliant entrail; Latiner; latrine;
    ratline; retinal; trenail
relic Creil
relics slicer
relict Tricel
relied lieder
relief liefer
relies resile
relieves Elsevier
relieving inveigler
relievo overlie
relight lighter
relights lighters; slighter
reline lierne
relined Red Nile
relines liernes
relish hirsel; hirsle
relishes heirless
relit litre; tiler
relive liever; revile
relived deliver; livered; reviled
relives Liévres; reviles; servile
reliving reviling
reload Laredo; loader; ordeal
reloading girandole; negroidal
reloads loaders; ordeals; sea-lord
reloan loaner; Lorena
reloaned oleander
relocation iconolater
reluct culter; cutler
relucts cluster; culters; cutlers;
    custrel
rely lyre
remade reamed
remain airmen; marine; Marnie
remains marines; seminar; sirname
remand manred; red-man
remanded demander
remands manreds
remark marker
remarks markers
remblai balmier; Mirabel; mirable
remigate emigrate
remigated emigrated
remigates emigrates

remigating emigrating
remigation emigration
remind minder
reminds minders
remise Mieres; misère
remises messier
remising Isengrim
remiss misers
remission missioner
remit merit; mitre; timer
remits merits; mister; mitres;
    smiter; timers
remitter trimeter
remitters trimester; trimeters
remodel Delorme
remora roamer
remoras roamers
remote meteor
remould moulder
remoulded mouldered
remoulding mouldering
remoulds moulders; smoulder
remount monture; mounter
remounts montures; mounters
Remus mures; muser; serum;
    Sumer
Rena Arne; earn; nare;
    near
renal Larne; learn
rename meaner
renamed amender; enarmed;
    meander
renaming enarming
Renard darner; errand
renascent entrances
Renault neutral
renay yearn
renayed deanery; yearned
renaying yearning
renays senary; yearns
rend dern
rending grinned
rends derns
Rene erne
renegate generate; green tea;
    teenager
renegates generates; teenagers
renege Greene
reneged greened
reneging greening
renga anger; range; Regan
Reni Erin; in re; rein
reniform informer; reinform

renig Niger; reign
renigs Ingres; reigns; resign; signer; singer
rennet tenner
rennets tenners
Reno Nero; Nore; oner; Orne; rone
Renoir ironer
rent tern
rental altern; antler; learnt; ternal
rentals antlers; saltern; sternal
rente enter; terne; treen
rented tender; terned
rentes enters; Ernest; nester; resent; Sterne; tenser; ternes
rentier reinter; terrine
rentiers reinsert; reinters; terrines
renting ringent; terning
rents Ernst; stern; terns
renvois version
reopen opener; perone; repone
reopens openers; perones; repones
reordain ordainer
reordains ordainers
reorder orderer
reorders orderers
rep per
repack packer
repacks packers
repad drape; padre; pared; raped
repads drapes; padres; parsed; rasped; spared; spread
repaid diaper; paired; pardie
repaint painter; Patenir; pertain; pine-tar
repaints painters; pantries; Parentis; pertains; pinaster
repair rapier
repairs parries; praiser; rapiers; raspier
repand pander
repaper prepare
repapers prepares
repartee pear-tree; repeater
repass aspers; parses; passer; spaers; spares; sparse; spears
repassed aspersed
repasses asperses; Passeres
repassing aspersing
repast paster; paters; Praest; prates; tapers; trapes
repasts pasters
repasture apertures

repay apery; payer; Peary
repays payers; speary
repeal Lapeer; leaper
repeals leapers; pleaser; relapse
repeater pear-tree; repartee
repeaters pear-trees
repeating interpage
repeats Prestea
repel leper
repels lepers
repentant penetrant
repenters presenter; represent
repents present; serpent
repetition petitioner
repined Dnieper
repines en prise; erepsin
repique perique; re-equip
repiques re-equips
repla lepra; paler; parle; pearl
replace percale
replant pantler; planter
replants pantlers; planters
replay parley; pearly; player
replayed parleyed
replaying parleying
replays parleys; parsley; players; sparely
repletion interlope
replica caliper
replicas calipers; spiracle
replies spieler
replum lumper; rumple
repone opener; perone; reopen
repones openers; perones; reopens
report porter; pretor
reportage porterage
reports porters; pretors; sporter
reposal paroles
reposing spongier
reposit riposte
reposits ripostes
repost poster; presto; repots; topers; tropes
reposted reedstop
reposts posters
repot Porte; toper; trope
repots poster; presto; repost; topers; tropes
repotted pottered
repotting pottering; pottinger
repoussé espouser
repp prep
represent presenter; repenters

represents presenters
repress presser
reprint printer
reprints printers; sprinter
reprise perries; respire
reprised respired
reprises respires
reprising respiring; springier
reprobation probationer
reproduce procedure
reproduces procedures
reptile perlite
reptiles epistler; peltries
Reptilia liparite
republish publisher
repulp pulper; purple
repulps pulpers; purples
repulsed preludes
repulsive prelusive; pulverise
reputed erupted
reputes pertuse
reputing erupting
request quester
requests questers
requital quartile
requitals quartiles
requite quieter
requits querist
rerail railer
rerails railers
re-rate tearer
re-rates serrate; tearers
reread dearer; reader; reared
rereading grenadier
rereads readers; redsear
resale leaser; sealer; Searle
resat arets; aster; astre; earst; rates; reast; stare; strae; tares; tears; teras
rescale cereals
rescaled declares
rescind cinders; discern
rescinded discerned
rescinding discerning
rescinds discerns
rescuable securable
rescue Cereus; ceruse; Creuse; recuse; secure
rescued recused; reduces; secured; seducer
rescuer recures; securer
rescuers securers
rescues recuses; secures
rescuing recusing; securing

research reachers; searcher
reseat arêtes; easter; eaters; reates; saeter; teaser; Teresa
reseating stingaree
reseats easters; saeters; teasers; tessera
resect certes; erects; secret
resected secreted
resecting secreting
resection erections; secretion
resections secretions
resects cresset; secrets
reseda aredes; deares; erased; Red Sea; seared
reseeding energised
resell seller
resells sellers
resent enters; Ernest; nester; rentes; Sterne; tenser; ternes
resenter enterers; re-enters; terrenes
resents nesters
reserve reveres; reverse
reserved reversed
reserves reverses
reserving reversing
reset ester; reest; retes; steer; stere; teers; terse; trees
resets esters; reests; steers; steres
reshape sphaere
reshapes sphaeres
reship perish; seriph
reships seriphs
Resht Herts.; tehrs
resiance increase
resiant nastier; ratines; retains; retinas; retsina; stainer; starnie; stearin
reside desire; eiders
resided derides; desired
resident Dniester; inserted; sintered
residents dissenter; tiredness
resides desires
residing desiring; ringside
resign Ingres; reigns; renigs; signer; singer
resigned designer; energids
resigns ingress; signers; singers
resile relies
resiling Riesling
resin reins; rinse; risen; serin; siren
Resina arisen; arsine
resinata artesian; Erastian

resinous neurosis
resins rinses; serins; sirens
resist reists; resits; sister
resistant straitens
resisted editress
resistent interests; triteness
resistor roisters; sorriest
resists sisters
resit reist; rites; Siret; tiers; tires; tries
re-site reties
re-sited re-edits; reisted
re-siting igniters; strigine
resits reists; resist; sister
resold dorsel; drôles; solder
resort roster; sorter; storer
resorted Desterro; restored; rostered
resorter restorer; retrorse
resorting restoring; rostering
resorts rosters; sorters; storers
resound Öresund; sounder; undoers
resounds dourness; sounders
resource recourse
respect recepts; sceptre; spectre
respects sceptres; spectres
respell speller
respells spellers
respire perries; reprise
respired reprised
respires reprises
respiring reprising; springier
respond ponders
respray prayers; sprayer
resprays sprayers
rest erst; rets
restart ratters; starter
restarts starters
restate estreat
restates estreats
rest-day strayed
rested desert; deters
restful fluster; fluters
restiff stiffer
resting stinger
restive veriest
restless tressels
restocking stockinger
Reston noters; stoner; tenors; tensor; Terson; trones
restored Desterro; resorted; rostered

restorer resorter; retrorse
restoring resorting; rostering
restrain strainer; terrains; trainers; transire
restrains strainers; transires
restrict critters; stricter
rests tress
resty Steyr; treys; tyres
restyle tersely
result luster; lustre; luters; rustle; sutler; ulster
resulted ulstered
results lusters; lustres; rustles; sutlers; ulsters
retail retial
retailed elaterid
retails Alister; realist; saltier; saltire; slatier
retain Nerita; ratine; retina; Tiranë
retained detainer
retainer Eritrean; rain-tree
retainers Eritreans; rain-trees; ternaries
retains nastier; ratines; resiant; retinas; retsina; stainer; starnie; stearin
retakes sakeret
retard darter; dartre; tarred; trader
retards darters; starred; traders
retches Chester; etchers
rete teer; tree
retell teller
retells tellers
retes ester; reest; reset; steer; stere; teers; terse; trees
rethink thinker
rethinks thinkers
retial retail
retied re-edit
reties re-site
retina Nerita; ratine; retain; Tiranë
retinae Aintree; trainee
retinal entrail; Latiner; latrine; ratline; reliant; trenail
retinas nastier; resiant; ratines; retains; retsina; stainer; starnie; stearin
retinue reunite; uterine
retinues esurient; reunites
retiral retrial; trailer
retire étrier; reiter
retired retried

retires étriers; reiters; retries; terries
retort rotter; torret
retorts rotters; torrets
retotal Loretta
retouch toucher
retour router; tourer
retours routers; tourers; trouser
retrace caterer; terrace
retraced terraced
retraces caterers; terraces
retracing terracing
retread treader
retreading intergrade
retreads serrated; treaders
retreat treater
retreats treaters
retrench trencher
retrial retiral; trailer
retrials trailers
retried retired
retries étriers; reiters; retires; terries
retrieves River Tees
retrorse resorter; restorer
retrospection interoceptors
retry terry; tryer
rets erst; rest
retsina nastier; resiant; ratines; retains; retinas; stainer; starnie; stearin
retting gittern
retund turned
retune neuter; tenure; tureen
retunes neuters; tenures; tureens
returf Erfurt
return turner
returns turners
reunite retinue; uterine
reunites esurient; retinues
Reus rues; ruse; sure; ures; user
reusing Giresun
Reuss ruses; users
reutter utterer
reutters utterers
Reval laver; ravel; velar
revamp vamper
revamps vampers
Revda drave; raved; Varde
reveal laveer; leaver
revealing inveagler
reveals laveers; leavers; several
revel elver; lever

revels elvers; levers
reveres reserve; reverse
revers server; verser
reversal slaverer
reversals slaverers
reverse reserve; reveres
reversed reserved
reverses reserves
reversi reviser
reversing reserving
revest everts; revets
revet evert
revets everts; revest
revie reive; rieve
revied derive; reived; rieved
revies reives; revise; rieves
review viewer
reviews viewers
revile liever; relive
reviled deliver; livered; relived
reviles Liévres; relives; servile
reviling reliving
revise reives; revies; rieves
revised derives; deviser; De Vries; diverse
reviser reversi
revises ivresse
revolute true-love
Rewa ware; wear
reward drawer; redraw; warder; warred
rewards drawers; redraws; warders
Rewari warier
rewind winder
rewinds winders
rewords sworder
rework worker
reworks workers
rewound wounder
rhaetic rich tea
rhe her; reh
rhea hare; hear; Hera
rheas hares; hears; share; shear
Rhein Henri; rhine
Rheine herein; inhere
rheo hero; hoer; Ohre
rhes hers
rheous rushes; ushers
rhine Henri; Rhein
rhines shiner; shrine
Rhoda hoard

Rhodes hordes; horsed; shoder; shored
rhodium humidor; mid-hour
Rhona Norah
rhone heron; Horne
rhones herons; Senhor
Rhus rush
rhyton thorny
ria air; Ira
rial aril; lair; liar; lira; rail
rials lairs; liars; liras; rails
Rialto tailor
riant intra; Nitra; train; Trani
rias airs; Asir; Isar; sair; sari
ribald bridal; labrid
ribbed bribed; dibber
ribbing bribing
Ribe bier; Brie
Ribera Barrie
Ribes biers; birse
ribless birsles
rice ciré; eric; icer
riced cider; cried; dicer
richen enrich
richened enriched
richening enriching
richer chirre
richest estrich
rich tea rhaetic
ricked dicker
rickets Sickert; sticker; tickers
rickle licker
rickles lickers; slicker
ridable bedrail
riddance cider-and
ridded didder
ridden rinded
riddle dirled
riddled diddler
riddles slidder
ride dire; Reid
rident tinder; trined
rider direr; drier; reird
ridered Deirdre; derider
riders derris; driers; reirds; sirred
rides dries; sider; sired
ridge dirge; gride
ridged grided
ridgel gilder; girdle; glider; lidger
ridgels gilders; girdles; gliders; grisled; lidgers
ridges dirges; grides; grised
ridging griding

riding Ingrid
riel leir; lier; lire; rile
riels leirs; liers; riles; siler
riem emir; meri; mire; rime
riems emirs; mires; miser; Reims; rimes
Riesa aesir; Aries; arise; raise; serai; Seria
Riesling resiling
Riet rite; tier; tire
rieve reive; revie
rieved derive; reived; revied
riever reiver
rievers reivers
rieves reives; revies; revise
rieving reiving
Rif fir
rife fire; Frei; reif
riffed differ
rifle filer; flier; lifer
rifleman inflamer
rifles filers; fliers; lifers
rift frit
rifts first; frist; frits
Rigel liger
rigged digger
right girth; grith
rigs gris
rile leir; lier; lire; riel
riled idler
riles leirs; liers; riels; siler
rilievo Olivier
Rilke liker
rillet tiller
rillets stiller; tillers; trellis
rim mir
rima amir; Mari; Mira; rami
rimae maire; Marie; ramie
rime emir; meri; mire; riem
rimed dimer; mired
rimes emirs; mires; miser; Reims; riems
rimester merriest; triremes
rimier mirier
rimiest miriest; mistier
riming miring
rimless smilers
rimmed dimmer
rims mirs; smir
rimy miry; Ymir
rind Drin
rinded ridden
ring girn; grin

ringed dering; dinger; engird; girned
ringent renting; terning
ringer erring
ringing girning
ringless slingers
ringlet tingler; tringle
ringlets sterling; tinglers; tringles
ring out routing; touring
rings girns; grins
ringside desiring; residing
ringtail trailing
rink kirn
rinks kirns
rinse reins; resin; risen; serin; siren
rinsed diners
rinses resins; serins; sirens
Riom Miro
Rion inro; iron
riot tiro; tori; trio
rioted editor; tie-rod; triode
rioters roister
riots roist; rosit; tiros; trios
ripe peri; pier
ripeck picker
ripecks pickers
riped pride; pried; redip
ripens sniper
riper prier
ripes épris; peris; piers; pries; prise; speir; spire
ripest esprit; priest; Pteris; sprite; stripe; tripes
riposted diopters; dioptres; dipteros; proteids
ripostes triposes
ripped dipper
ripples slipper
ripplet tippler; tripple
ripplets stippler; tipplers; tripples
rips risp
ript trip
rise Eris; reis; sire
risen reins; resin; rinse; serin; siren
rises sires
rising siring
risk irks; kris
risked dikers
risking girkins; griskin
risp rips
risped prides; prised; redips; spider; spired
risping prising; spiring

risque quires; Quseir; squire
Riss sirs
rite Riet; tier; tire
rites reist; resit; Siret; tiers; tires; tries
rits stir
ritter territ; triter
ritters territs
riva Ravi; vair
rivage Argive; garvie
rivages Argives; garvies
rival viral
rived diver; drive; Verdi
rivel liver; livre
rivels livers; livres; silver; sliver
riven viner
Rivera arrive; varier
riveret riveter
riverets riveters
River Tees retrieves
rives siver
riveter riveret
riveters riverets
rivets stiver; strive; trevis
riving Irving; virgin
roach orach
roaches oraches
road Dora; Odra
road-end adorned
roading adoring; Gordian; gradino
roadmen Maderno
roads Doras; dorsa; Rodas; sorda
roam mora; Omar; Roma
roamed radome
roamer remora
roamers remoras
roaming Moringa
roams Maros; moras
roan Arno; Nora; Oran; Rona
roans arson; sonar
roar orra
roared adorer
roast Astor; rotas; Sarto; taros; Troas
roasted torsade
roasters assertor; oratress
roasting organist
roasts assort
rob bor; orb
robe Boer; bore; Ebro
robed bored; orbed
robes Boers; bores; brose; sober
robin inorb

robing boring; orbing
robins inorbs
robs orbs; sorb
roc cor; orc
Roca arco; Cora; Orca
rochet hector; tocher; troche
rochets hectors; tochers; torches;
  troches
rock cork
rocked corked; docker
rocker corker
rockers corkers
rocketer cork-tree
rocketers cork-trees
rockier corkier
rockiest corkiest; stockier
rocking corking
rocks corks
rocky corky
rocquet croquet
rocs cors; orcs
rod dor; ord
Rodas Doras; dorsa; roads; sorda
rode doer; Doré; Oder; re-do; roed
roded odder
Rodentia deration; ordinate;
  rationed
rodents Dorsten; snorted
rodes doers; dorse; rosed
Rodin nidor
rodless dorsels; solders
rodman random
rodmen modern
Rodney yonder
rods dors; ords; sord
rodsmen moderns
roe o'er; ore
roed doer; Doré; Oder; re-do; rode
roes Eros; ores; rose; sore
rogers groser
Roget ergot
rogue orgue; rouge
rogued drogue; gourde; rouged
rogues grouse; orgues; rouges;
  rugose
roguing rouging
roiled Del Rio
roiling ligroin
roils loris
roist riots; rosit; tiros; trios
roisted editors; rosited; sortied;
  steroid; storied; tie-rods; triodes
roister rioters

roisterer terrorise
roisterers terrorises
roisters resistor; sorriest
roists rosits
Roland Arnold; Landor; lardon;
  Ronald
role eorl; lore; Orel; orle
roles eorls; Leros; loser; orles;
  Osler; soler; Sorel
roller Orrell
Roma mora; Omar; roam
romaikas Makarios
Roman manor; Morna; Norma;
  Ramon
romance Cameron; Cremona;
  Menorca
Romanes moaners; San Remo
Romanians San Marino
Romanic Marconi; Minorca
Romanies moraines; Romanise
Romanise moraines; Romanies
Romanist Monastir
Romans manors; ramson; ransom
romantics narcotism
Romany mornay
Rome more; omer
Romeo Moore
Romeos morose
romp prom
romps proms
Ron nor
Rona Arno; Nora; Oran; roan
Ronald Arnold; Landor; lardon;
  Roland
rondache anchored
rondavel overland
ronde drone
rondes drones; snored; sorned
rondo donor; doorn
rondos donors; doorns
rondure rounder; unorder
rondures rounders; unorders
rone Nero; Nore; oner; Orne; Reno
roneos seroon; sooner
rones Norse; noser; oners; Ronse;
  Señor; seron; snore
Ronse Norse; noser; oners; rones;
  Señor; seron; snore
rood door; ordo
roods doors; Ordos; sordo
roofed foredo
rook Kroo
rooks Kroos

room moor; Moro
roomed moored
rooming mooring
rooms moors; Moros; Ormos;
  smoor
roop poor; proo
roops sopor; spoor
roost roots; stoor; torso
rooster rooters; toreros
roosts stoors; torsos
rooter torero
rooters rooster; toreros
rootiest tortoise
rootle looter; Loreto; tooler
rootles looters; toolers
roots roost; stoor; torso
rope pore
roped doper; pedro; pored
rope in orpine; Pinero
roper porer; prore
ropers porers
ropes pores; poser; prose; Soper;
  spore
ropes in orpines
ropiness pression
roping poring
roquet quoter; torque
roquets questor; quoters; torques
Rosa oars; Oras; osar; soar; sora
Rosalind ordinals
Rosaline ailerons; alerions;
  alienors
Rosas saros; soars
rose Eros; ores; roes; sore
roseate tea-rose
rose-cut scouter
rosed doers; dorse; rodes
rose-hips Seriphos
rose-hued rehoused
roses sores
roset estro; rotes; store; tores; torse
rosets sortes; stores; torses;
  tosser
Rosetta rotates; toaster; to-tears
rosety oyster; storey; Troyes;
  tyroes; Yes Tor
Rosie osier; Siero
rosiest sorites; sorties; stories
rosin inros; irons; ornis
rosined indorse; sordine
rosing girons; grison; groins;
  Signor
rosit riots; roist; tiros; trios

rosited editors; roisted; sortied;
  steroid; storied; tie-rods; triodes
rositing roisting
rosits roists
roster resort; sorter; storer
rostered Desterro; resorted;
  restored
rostering resorting; restoring
rosters resorts; sorters; storers
Rosyth shorty
rot ort; tor
rota Orta; taro; Tora
rotas Astor; roast; Sarto; taros;
  Troas
rotate to-tear
rotates Rosetta; toaster; to-tears
rote tore
rotes estro; roset; store; tores;
  torse
Rothes others; throes; tosher
roting Girton; trigon
rots orts; sort; tors
rottan ratton
rottans rattons
rotted detort
rotten Trento
rotter retort; torret
rotters retorts; torrets
rotund untrod
roué euro
roués euros; rouse
rouge orgue; rogue
rouged drogue; gourde; rogued
rouges grouse; orgues; rogues;
  rugose
rouging roguing
roulade Urodela
rounded redound; underdo
roundel lounder; roundle
roundels lounders; roundles
rounder rondure; unorder
rounders rondures; unorders
roundest tonsured; unsorted
roundle lounder; roundel
roundles lounders; roundels
roup pour
rouped poured
rouping ingroup; pouring
roups pours
rouse euros; roués
roused douser; soured
rouses serous
rousing souring

roust   routs; stour; sutor; torus; tours
rousted   detours; dourest; douters
rousts   stours; sutors
rout   tour
route   outer; outré; Touré
routed   detour; douter; outred; red out; toured
router   retour; tourer
routers   retours; tourers; trouser
routes   ouster; outers; souter; touser; trouse
routing   ring out; touring
routs   roust; stour; sutor; torus; tours
rove   over
roved   Dover; drove
roves   overs; Serov; servo; verso
rowan   Nowra
rowdily   wordily
rowdiness   windroses; wordiness
rowdy   dowry; wordy
rowed   dower
rowel   lower; owler
rowelled   well-doer
rowels   lowers; owlers; slower
rowen   owner
rowens   owners; worsen
rowers   worser
rowt   trow; wort
rowted   trowed
rowth   throw; worth; wroth
royalist   solitary
rub   bur
rubato   tabour
rubble   burble; lubber
rubella   rulable
rubied   burdie; buried
rubies   bruise; buries; busier
rubine   Brunei
ruble   bluer
rubles   Elbrus
rubs   burs
ruby   bury
ruc   cru; cur
rucked   ducker
ruckles   suckler
rucs   crus; curs; scur
rude   dure; rued; urdé
ruder   Dürer
rue   Ure
rued   dure; rude; urdé
rues   Reus; ruse; sure; ures; user

ruffed   duffer
ruffes   suffer
ruffian   funfair
ruffians   funfairs
rugged   grudge
rugose   grouse; orgues; rogues; rouges
ruin   Irun
ruinate   taurine; uranite; urinate
ruinated   daturine; indurate; urinated
ruined   inured
ruiners   insurer
ruining   inuring
rulable   rubella
rule   lure
ruled   lured
rules   lures
ruling   luring
rum   Mur
rumal   larum; mural
rumals   larums; murals
rumba   Burma; umbra
rumbas   sambur
rumble   lumber
rumbled   drumble
rumbles   Burslem; lumbers; slumber
Rumex   Murex
ruminates   misaunter
rumple   lumper; replum
rumples   lumpers
rums   smur
run   nur; urn
runch   churn
runcinate   encurtain; uncertain
rund   durn
rundale   Arundel; launder; lurdane
rundle   nurled
rundlet   trundle
rundlets   trundles
runds   durns
runed   Düren; under; urned
runes   nurse
runic   incur
runnet   unrent
runs   nurs; urns
runt   turn
runts   turns
rupee   purée
rupees   peruse; purées
rusa   sura; Ursa
ruse   Reus; rues; sure; ures; user

ruses Reuss; users
rush Rhus
rushes rhesus; ushers
rushier hurries
rusine insure; inures; ursine
rusk Krus
rusma arums; ramus; Sarum
russet estrus; tusser
russets trusses
rust ruts
rustable baluster
rusted duster
rustic citrus
rusticate urticates
rustle luster; lustre; luters; result; sutler; ulster
rustled lustred; strudel
rustles lusters; lustres; results; sutlers; ulsters
rustling lustring
rusts truss
Rute true
ruth hurt; thru; Thur

ruthful hurtful
ruthfully hurtfully
ruthless hurtless; hustlers
ruthlessly hurtlessly
ruthlessness hurtlessness
rutin Turin
ruts rust
rutter turret
rutters turrets
ryal aryl; Lyra
ryals aryls
Ryan nary; yarn
Rydal lardy; lyard
Ryde drey; dyer; yerd
Ryder Derry; dryer
rye-wolf flowery
ryot tory; troy; tyro
ryots story; tyros
rype prey; pyre
ryper perry; pryer
Ryton try on
ryve very

S

Saab abas; baas; Saba
Saadi Saida
Saar Aras; Sara
Saba abas; baas; Saab
Sabah abash
Sabal balas; balsa; basal
saber bares; baser; bears; braes; sabre
sabers sabres
sabin basin
Sabines Bassein
sabins basins
sable ables; bales; Basel; Basle; blaes; blasé
sabot basto; boast; boats; Sobat
sabots boasts
sabra Arabs; arbas; Basra
sabre bares; baser; bears; braes; saber
sabred ardebs; beards; breads; debars; serdab
sabres sabers
saccharine cane-chairs
sachem schema
sachet chaste; cheats; scathe; taches

sachets scathes
sack cask
sacked casked
sacker crakes; creaks; screak
sackers screaks
sacking casking
sacks casks
sacque casque
sacques casques
sacral lascar; rascal; scalar
sacred cadres; cedars; scared
sacrify scarify
sacring scaring
sacrist racists
sad ads; das
sadden dedans; sanded
sadder adders; dreads
saddle addles
saddled daddles
saddler ladders; raddles
Sadi aids; dais; Dias; said; Sida
Sadie aides; aside; ideas
Sado soda
sae eas; sea
saeter arêtes; easter; eaters; reates; reseat; teaser; Teresa

saeters   easters; reseats; teasers;
  tessera
safer   fares; farse; fears
safest   feasts
sag   gas
Sagar   ragas
sage   ages; gaes
sagene   senega
sager   gears; rages; sarge
sages   gases
sagest   stages
sagger   aggers; eggars; seggar
saggers   aggress; seggars
said   aids; dais; Dias; Sadi; Sida
Saida   Saadi
sail   ails; Isla; Lias; Lisa; sial
sailed   aisled; deasil; ideals; ladies
sailer   Israel; serail; serial
sailers   airless; serails; serials
sailing   nilgais
sails   Lissa; Silas; sisal
sain   anis; Isna; Nias; Nisa; Sian
sains   sasin
saint   satin; stain; Tanis
sainted   Danites; detains; instead;
  stained
Saintes   entasis; sestina; Staines;
  tansies; tisanes
saintly   nastily
saints   Säntis; satins; Sistan; stains
sair   airs; Asir; Isar; rias; sari
saith   taish; Thais
Sakai   sakia
sake   Aske; kaes; keas
saker   asker; kesar; rakes; reaks;
  skear
sakeret   retakes
sakers   askers; kesars; skears
saki   sika
sakia   Sakai
sakis   sikas
sal   als
Sala   alas
salable   Las Bela
sale   ales; Elsa; leas; seal; slae
Salem   almes; lames; leams; males;
  meals; samel; Selma
Salemi   mesail; mesial; samiel;
  Sliema
salep   Elaps; lapse; leaps; pales;
  peals; pleas; sepal; spale; speal
Salerno   loaners; orleans; reloans
salerooms   salesroom

sales   salse; seals; slaes
salesmen   lameness; maneless;
  nameless
salesroom   salerooms
Salian   lianas; salina
Salians   salinas
salient   eastlin; elastin; entails;
  slàinte; staniel
salients   eastlins; staniels
salina   lianas; Salian
salinas   Salians
saline   aliens; alines; lianes; Selina;
  silane
Salinger   aligners; engrails;
  realigns; sanglier; seal-ring
saliva   avails; salvia; Valais
salivate   aestival
sallad   Dallas
sallee   allées
sallet   Stella
sallied   dallies
sallow   allows
sallying   signally
salmi   Islam; limas; mails; malis;
  Milas; Simla
salmis   missal
salmo   loams
salmon   monals
salon   loans; sloan; solan; Solna
salons   sloans; solans
saloon   solano
salp   Alps; laps; pals; slap
salps   slaps
sals   lass
salse   sales; seals; slaes
salses   lasses
salt   last; lats; slat
Salta   atlas
saltation   stational
salted   deltas; desalt; lasted; slated;
  staled
salter   alerts; alters; artels; laster;
  ratels; slater; staler; stelar; tarsel
saltern   antlers; rentals; sternal
salters   artless; lasters; slaters;
  tarsels
saltier   Alister; realist; retails;
  saltire; slatier
saltiers   realists; saltires;
  slaister
saltiness   slatiness; stainless
salting   anglist; lasting; slating;
  staling

saltire   Alister; realist; retails;
   saltier; slatier
saltires   realists; saltiers; slaister
saltly   lastly
salt-mine   ailments; aliments;
   manliest
Salto   altos; Talos; tolas
saltpan   platans
salts   lasts; slats
saltus   saults; tussal
salty   slaty
salvage   lavages
salvages   Las Vegas
salve   Elvas; laves; selva; slave;
   vales; valse
salved   slaved; valsed
salver   lavers; ravels; serval; slaver;
   versal
salvers   servals; slavers; versals
salves   selvas; slaves; valses
Salvi   Alvis; silva; vails; valis; vials
salvia   avails; saliva; Valais
salving   slaving; valsing
salvo   ovals
Salwin   in-laws
Samar   Maras
Sambo   ambos; bomas
Sambres   ambers; breams; embars
sambur   rumbas
same   mesa; seam
samel   almes; lames; leams; males;
   meals; Salem; Selma
samely   measly
samen   amens; manes; manse;
   means; Mensa; names
Samian   animas; Maasin; manias;
   Manisa
samiel   mesail; mesial; Salemi;
   Sliema
samiels   aimless; Melissa; mesails;
   seismal
samisen   inseams
samite   tamise
samites   asteism; Matisse; tamises
samlet   lamest; metals
Samnite   inmates
Samos   Samsö
samoyed   someday
samp   amps; maps; pams; spam
sampans   passman
samphire   seraphim
sample   maples
sampler   Marples; palmers

Samsö   Samos
Samson   masons; Namsos
sanction   canonist; contains
sanctions   canonists
Sanctus   Tuscans
sand   dans
sanded   dedans; sadden
sander   redans; snared
sanders   sarsden
sandhi   Danish
San Diego   agonised; diagnose
sandier   sardine
sandiver   invaders
sane   eans; sean; Sena
saner   earns; nares; nears; snare
sanest   assent; snaste; stanes; steans
sang   nags; snag
Sanger   angers; ranges; serang
Sangir   grains; rasing
sanglier   aligners; engrails; realigns;
   Salinger; seal-ring
sangliers   seal-rings
Sangrado   Granados
sangs   snags
sanicles   laciness
sanies   sasine
sanity   satiny
sank   kans
San Marino   Romanians
San Pedro   operands; padrones;
   pandores; Sarpedon
San Remo   moaners; Romanes
sansculotterie   interosculates
sanserif   fairness
Santa   Satan; tsana
santalin   annalist
santir   instar; Sintra; strain; trains
santirs   instars; strains
Säntis   saints; satins; Sistan; stains
santon   sonant
santons   sonants
santur   Saturn
sap   asp; pas; spa
sapele   asleep; elapse; please
sapient   panties; patines; spinate
sapling   lapsing; palings
sapor   Paros; proas; psora; sopra
sapper   papers
sappers   appress
sappy   paspy
sap-rot   asport; pastor; portas
saps   asps; pass; spas
sar   ras

Sara   Aras; Saar
Sarawak   Arawaks
sarcenet   reascent
sardel   alders
sardine   sandier
sardines   aridness
sardonic   Draconis
sarge   gears; rages; sager
Sargent   garnets; Stanger; strange
sargo   Argos
sargus   sugars
sari   airs; Asir; Isar; rias; sair
saris   arsis
sark   arks; Kars
sarment   artsmen; martens;
  smarten
sarments   smartens
sarong   groans; orangs; organs;
  Sargon
saros   Rosas; soars
Sarpedon   operands; padrones;
  pandores; San Pedro
Sarre   rears; serra
sarsden   sanders
sarsen   Nasser; snares
sarsenet   assenter; earnests
Sarthe   earths; haters; hearts;
  'sheart
Sarto   Astor; roast; rotas; taros;
  Troas
Sartre   arrest; arrèts; raster; raters;
  starer; terras
Sarum   arums; ramus; rusma
sarus   suras
sashed   dashes; shades
sashes   she-ass
sasin   sains
sasine   sanies
sasse   asses
sat   Ats
Satan   Santa; Tsana
satanical   Castalian
Satanism   mantissa
Satanists   assistant
satchel   chalets; latches
sate   east; eats; seat; seta; taes; teas
sated   dates; stade; stead
sateen   ensate; senate; steane
sates   asset; seats; tasse; Tessa
sati   aits; Asti; itas; Sita
satiable   Baalites; labiates
satin   saint; stain; Tanis
satinet   instate

sating   gainst; giants
satin-paper   appertains
satins   saints; Säntis; Sistan; stains
satiny   sanity
satire   striae
satires   tirasse
satirical   racialist
Sato   oast; oats; stoa; Taos
satori   aorist
satrap   Patras; Sparta
satrapies   aspirates; parasites
Satu-Mare   amateurs
sat up   sputa
Saturn   santur
Saturnalia   Australian
Saturnian   Turanians
satyr   stray; trays
satyra   astray; tayras
satyrs   strays
sauce   cause
sauced   caused
saucer   causer; cesura; Creüsa
saucers   causers; cesuras; sucrase
sauces   causes
sauciest   suitcase
saucing   causing
sauger   argues; augers; Segura;
  usager
sault   talus; Tulsa
saults   saltus; tussal
saunter   aunters; natures; tea-urns
sauntered   denatures
saury   Surya
sausage   assuage
sausages   assuages
saut   utas
Sava   vasa
save   Aves; vaes; vase
saved   devas; vades; Vedas
saver   avers; raves; vares
saves   vases
savin   vains
saviour   various
savourily   variously
saw   was
sawder   Seward; waders
sawed   wades
sawer   sware; swear; wares; wears
sawers   swears; wrasse
sawing   aswing
sawn   awns; swan
sawpit   pit-saw
sawpits   pit-saws

sawset   sweats; tawses; wastes
sawyer   swayer
sawyers   swayers
Saxe   axes
Saxon   axons; Naxos
sayer   eyras; years
sayest   yeasts
sayst   stays
S-bend   bends
'sblood   bloods
scab   cabs
scad   cads
scalar   lascar; rascal; sacral
scalars   lascars; rascals
scale   claes; laces
scaled   decals
scalene   cleanse; elances; enlaces
scaler   Clares; clears; sclera
scales   Cassel
scall   calls
scalloped   collapsed
scalloping   collapsing
scalp   claps; clasp
scalped   clasped
scalper   carpels; clasper; parcels;
   placers
scalpers   claspers
scalping   clasping
scalps   clasps
scaly   clays
scamble   becalms
scamp   camps
scamped   decamps
scamper   campers
scan   cans
scandia   Dacians
scandium   muscadin
scanner   canners
scant   canst; cants
scanted   decants; descant
scantier   canister
scape   capes; Caspe; paces; space
scaped   spaced
scapes   spaces
scaping   spacing
scapular   capsular
scapulary   capsulary
scar   arcs; cars
scarab   barsac; Scarba
scarabs   barsacs
Scarba   barsac; scarab
scare   acers; acres; cares; carse;
   races; scrae; sérac

scared   cadres; cedars; sacred
scares   caress; carses; crases; scraes;
   séracs
scarier   carries
scarify   sacrity
scaring   sacring
scarlet   cartels; clarets; tarcels
scarp   carps; craps; scrap
scarped   redcaps; scraped
scarper   scraper
scarpers   scrapers
scarping   scraping
scarps   scraps
scarred   carders
scars   crass
scart   carts; scrat
scarth   charts; starch
scarts   scrats
Scarus   scaurs
scary   scray
scat   acts; cast; cats
scathe   chaste; cheats; sachet; taches
scathes   sachets
scatole   alecost; lactose; locates;
   talcose
scats   casts
scattier   citrates; cristate
scaurs   Scarus
scaw   caws
sceat   caste; cates
scena   canes
scenarise   increases
scenarist   canisters
scended   descend
scene   cense
scened   censed
scenes   censes
scenical   calcines
scening   censing
scent   cents
scented   descent
sceptral   spectral
sceptre   recepts; respect; spectre
sceptres   respects; spectres
Scheele   leeches
schema   sachem
schematic   catechism
schiavone   anchovies
Schlei   chesil; chiels; chiles; chisel;
   elchis
scholar   lorchas
Schubert   butchers
schwa   chaws

Schwerin   winchers
scient   incest; insect; nicest
sciential   Catilines; inelastic
Scilla   lilacs
sciolist   solicits
scion   coins; icons; sonic
Scirpus   prussic
sciurine   incisure
sclate   castle; cleats
sclates   castles
sclave   calves; cavels; claves
sclera   Clares; clears; scaler
scleral   callers; cellars; recalls
sclerite   tiercels
sclerose   coreless; recloses
scoff   coffs
scoffer   coffers
scog   cogs
scold   clods; colds
scolding   codlings
scollop   collops
scolloped   clodpoles
Scomber   combers
scone   cones; Cosne; sonce
scontion   Coniston
scoop   coops
scooper   coopers
scoot   coost; coots
scope   copes; copse; Pecos
Scopelus   close-ups; upcloses
scopes   copses
score   ceros; cores; corse
scored   Cedros; coders; credos
scorer   corers; crores
scores   corses; scorse
scorn   corns
scorned   conders; corsned
scorner   corners
scorse   corses; scores
scorsed   crossed
scorses   crosses
scorsing   crossing
scot   cost; cots
scoter   corset; Cortes; coster; escort;
   sector; Tresco
scoters   corsets; costers; escorts;
   sectors
scot-free   cost-free
Scotian   actions; cations
Scotland   cotlands
scots   costs
scour   Orcus
scoured   coursed

scourer   courser
scourers   coursers; cursores
scourge   scrouge
scourged   scrouged
scourges   scrouges
scourging   scrouging
scouring   coursing
scouter   rose-cut
scouts   custos
scow   cows
scowl   clows; cowls
scowrie   cowries
scrab   crabs
scrae   acers; acres; cares; carse;
   races; scare; sérac
scraes   caress; carses; crases; scares;
   séracs
scrag   crags
scram   crams
scramble   cambrels; clambers
scran   crans
Scranton   Cranston
scrap   carps; craps; scarp
scrape   capers; Casper; crapes;
   escarp; pacers; parsec; recaps;
   spacer
scraped   redcaps; scarped
scraper   scarper
scrapers   scarpers
scrapes   escarps; parsecs; spacers
scraping   scarping
scraps   scarps
scrat   carts; scart
scrats   scarts
scrattle   clatters
scraw   craws
scrawl   crawls
scrawler   crawlers
scray   scary
screak   crakes; creaks; sacker
screaks   sackers
scream   crames; creams; macers
screamer   creamers
scree   ceres; crees
screech   creches
screed   creeds
screen   censer; secern
screened   secerned
screening   secerning
screens   censers; secerns
screich   scriech
screiched   scrieched
screiches   scrieches

screiching screiching
screw crews
scribble cribbles
scriech screich
scrieched screiched
scrieches screiches
scrieching screiching
scried ciders; dicers
scries crises
scrieve service
scrieved serviced
scrieves services
scrieving servicing
scrike ickers; sicker
scrimp crimps
scrip crisp
scrips crisps
scripted predicts
scrod cords
scrota actors; castor; Castro; Croats;
    tarocs
scrotal crotals
scrouge scourge
scrouged scourged
scrouges scourges
scrouging scourging
scrow crows
scrub curbs
scruto courts; Turcos
scrutoire courtiers
scud cuds
scuddle cuddles
scudler curdles
scuff cuffs
scull culls
sculler cruells; cullers
sculling cullings
scullion cullions
sculpin insculp; unclips
sculpins insculps
scumber cumbers
scup cups; cusp
scupper cuppers
scur crus; curs; rucs
scurries cruisers
scut cuts
scutcher crutches
scutter cutters
scuttle cutlets; cuttles
scye syce
scyes syces
scyphi physic
scythe chesty

'sdeath deaths; hasted; tashed
sdeign deigns; design; signed;
    singed
sdeigned designed
sdeigning designing
sdeigns designs
sea eas; sae
sea-bat abates
sea-bed debase
seabird air-beds; braised; darbies
sea-cat acates
sea-dog dagoes; dosage; sea-god
sea-dogs dosages; sea-gods
sea-fir fraise
sea-fire arefies; faeries; freesia
sea-firs fraises
sea-fret afreets; feaster
sea-girt agister; gaiters; stagier;
    strigae; triages
sea-god dagoes; dosage; sea-dog
sea-gods dosages; sea-dogs
seagull ullages
seahorse seashore
seahorses seashores
seal ales; Elsa; leas; sale; slae
sealed leased
sea-legs ageless
sealer leaser; resale; Searle
sealers earless; leasers
sealing leasing; linages
sea-lord loaders; ordeals; reloads
seal-ring aligners; engrails;
    realigns; Salinger; sanglier
seal-rings sangliers
seals sales; salse; slaes
seam mesa; same
seamed adeems
seamen enemas; enseam
seamer ameers; Mersea
seamers Rameses
seaming enigmas; gamines
seams massé; mesas
Seamus amuses; assume
sean eans; sane; Sena
seance Cesena; encase; Seneca
seances encases
sea-perch peachers; preaches
seaport proteas
sear Ares; arse; ears; eras; rase;
    sera
searce crease
searced creased
searces creases

search   arches; chares; chaser; eschar; raches
searcher   reachers; research
searchers   archeress
searcing   creasing; Grecians
seared   aredes; deares; erased; Red Sea; reseda
searing   earings; erasing; gainers; regains; seraing; seringa
Searle   leaser; resale; sealer
sears   arses; rases; rasse
seashore   seahorse
seashores   seahorses
seaside   disease
seat   east; eats; sate; seta; taes; teas
sea-term   steamer
sea-terms   masseter; steamers
seating   easting; Gastein; genista; ingates; ingesta; tangies; teasing; tsigane
Seaton   atones; Easton
seats   asset; sates; tasse; Tessa
Sebat   abets; baste; bates; beast; beats; besat; tabes
secant   ascent; enacts; stance
secants   ascents; stances
secco   cosec
seceder   decrees; recedes
seceders   recessed
secern   censer; screen
secerned   screened
secernent   sentencer
secerning   screening
secerns   censers; screens
seckel   cleeks
seclude   Culdees
seconde   encodes
seconder   seed-corn
seconding   consigned
secondly   condyles
secret   certes; erects; resect
secreta   cerates; creates
secreted   resected
secretes   sesterce
secreting   resecting
secretion   erections; resection
secretions   resections
secrets   cresset; resects
sectarian   ascertain; Cartesian
sectarians   ascertains; Cartesians
section   notices
sectional   coastline

sector   corset; Cortes; coster; escort; scoter; Tresco
sectorial   loricates
sectors   corsets; costers; escorts; scoters
secund   dunces
securable   rescuable
secure   Cereus; ceruse; Creuse; recuse; rescue
secured   recused; reduces; rescued; seducer
securer   recures; rescuer
securers   rescuers
secures   recuses; rescues
securing   recusing; rescuing
sedan   Andes; Danes; deans; Desna; snead
sedans   sneads
sedate   easted; seated; teased
sedated   dead-set; steaded
sedating   d'Estaing; steading
sedative   deviates
sedent   nested; tensed
Seder   deres; drees; redes; reeds
sederunt   dentures; underset; undesert
sederunts   undersets
sedes   seeds
sedge   edges
sedile   diesel; elides; seiled
sedilia   dailies
sedition   editions
seduce   deuces; educes
seduced   deduces
seducer   recused; reduces; rescued; secured
seduction   eductions
seductor   eductors
sedum   mused
seed-corn   seconder
seedily   eyelids
seedings   edginess
seeds   sedes
seedsmen   demesnes
seeing   eignes; genies
seek   ekes; skee
seeker   kreese
seekers   kreeses
seeking   skeeing
seeks   skees
seel   eels; else; lees; sele; slee
seels   seles

seem   emes; Esme; mese; semé;
  smee
seen   esne
seep   pees
seer   Erse; sere
seers   seres
sees   esse
seethed   sheeted
seething   sheeting
Sefton   soften
seggar   aggers; eggars; sagger
seggars   aggress; saggers
segni   singe
segno   Sogne
sego   goes
segol   loges; ogles
Segre   egers; grees; grese; serge
segreant   estrange; grantees;
  greatens; reagents; sergeant
segregate   Easter egg
segregates   Easter eggs
Segura   argues; augers; sauger;
  usager
seil   Elis; isle; leis; lies; sile
seiled   diesel; elides; sedile
seils   isles; siles
Seim   mise; semi
seined   denies
seiner   serein; serine
seines   in esse; Neisse
seining   insigne
seism   mises; semis
seismal   aimless; Melissa; mesails;
  samiels
seisms   misses
seizable   sizeable
sekos   skeos; sokes
selah   hales; halse; heals; leash;
  shale; sheal
seld   sled
seldom   models
sele   eels; else; lees; seel; slee
select   elects
selection   elections
selector   corselet; electors
selectors   corselets
seled   deles; Edsel; Leeds
Selenga   Senegal
selenic   license; silence
seles   seels
self-same   fameless
Selina   aliens; alines; lianes; saline;
  silane

seling   ingles; lignes; single
Selk   elks; leks
sell   ells
seller   resell
sellers   resells
sell-out   outsell
sell-outs   outsells
Selma   almes; lames; leams; males;
  meals; Salem; samel
selva   Elvas; laves; salve; slave;
  vales; valse
selvas   salves; slaves; valses
selves   vessel
Semarang   managers
semé   emes; Esme; mese; seem;
  smee
Semele   mêlées
semen   menes; mense; mesne
semi   mise; Seim
seminal   isleman; malines; menials
seminar   marines; remains; sirname
seminars   sirnames
seminate   matinées
seminates   amnesties; meatiness
semiotic   comities
semi-pro   imposer; promise
semi-pros   imposers; promises
semis   mises; seism
semitar   Artemis; imarets; maestri;
  maister; misrate; St. Marie
semitars   asterism; maisters;
  misrates
Semlin   limens; simnel
sen   ens
Sena   eans; sane; sean
senary   renays; yearns
senate   ensate; sateen; steane
senates   steanes
senator   treason
senatorial   alienators
senators   assentor; star-nose;
  treasons
send   dens; ends; sned
Sendai   Adenis
sendal   Landes
sender   denser
senders   redness
sends   sneds
send-up   up-ends; upsend
send-ups   upsends
Seneca   Cesena; encase; seance
senega   sagene
Senegal   Selenga

senescent sentences
senga Agnes; geans; genas
Senhor herons; rhones
Senhora Hornsea
Senhorita Hortensia
senile enisle; ensile; nelies; Silene
senior nosier; soneri
Senlac cleans; lances
sennit sinnet; tennis
sennits sinnets
Señor Norse; noser; oners; rones;
   Ronse; seron; snore
Señora reason
Señoras reasons
Señorita notaries
Señoritas assertion
Señors nosers; sensor; serons;
   snores
Sens ness
sense esnes; Essen
sensing ensigns
sensor nosers; Señors; serons;
   snores
sensual unseals
sent nest; nets; sten; tens
Senta antes; etnas; nates; Nesta;
   stane; stean; Teans
sentencer secernent
sentencers recentness
sentences senescent
sentries trenises
Senusis Senussi
Senussi Senusis
senza nazes
Seoul louse; ousel
sepad spade; spaed
sepads passed; spades
sepal Elaps; lapse; leaps; pales;
   peals; pleas; salep; spale; speal
sepalous espousal
sepals lapses; spales;
   speals
sepoy poesy
sepsis pisses; speiss
sept pest; pets; step
septa paste; pates; spate; speat;
   tapes
septal palest; palets; pastel; petals;
   plates; pleats; staple
septaria aspirate; parasite
septimal implates; palmiest;
   palmiets; petalism
septs pests; steps

septuor petrous; posture; pouters;
   Proteus; spouter; troupes
sera Ares; arse; ears; eras; rase; sear
sérac acers; acres; cares; carse;
   races; scare; scrae
séracs caress; carses; crases; scares;
   scraes
seraglio girasole
serai aesir; Aries; arise; raise; Riesa;
   Seria
serail Israel; sailer; serial
serails airless; sailers; serials
Seraing earings; erasing; gainers;
   regains; searing; seringa
serais arises; raises
serang angers; ranges; Sanger
seraph phares; phrase; raphes;
   shaper; Sherpa; sphaer
seraphic parchesi
seraphim samphire
seraphs phrases; shapers; Sherpas;
   sphaers
Serapic Epacris
Serapis aspires; paresis; praises
Serbia braise; rabies
serdab ardebs; beards; breads;
   debars; sabred
sere Erse; seer
serein seiner; serine
serenata arsenate
seres seers
Sereth Esther; Hester; threes
serfish fishers; sherifs
serge egers; grees; grese; Segre
sergeant estrange; grantees;
   greatens; reagents; segreant
sergeants estranges; greatness
Sergo goers; gores; gorse; ogres;
   soger
Seria aesir; Aries; arise; raise; Riesa;
   serai
serial Israel; sailer; serail
serialised idealisers
serialized idealizers
serials airless; sailers; serails
seric cries; erics; icers
sericon coiners; crinose; cronies
serif fires; fries
serin reins; resin; rinse; risen; siren
serine seiner; serein
seringa earings; erasing; gainers;
   regains; searing; Seraing
serins resins; rinses; sirens

seriph perish; reship
Seriphos rose-hips
seriphs reships
serk erks; sker
serks skers
Serlio elisor; lories; oilers; oriels
sermon mornes
sermonic incomers
seron Norse; noser; oners; rones;
  Ronse; Señor; snore
serons nosers; Señors; sensor;
  snores
seroon roneos; sooner
serous rouses
Serov overs; roves; servo; verso
serow owers; sower; swore; worse
serows sowers
serpent present; repents
serpented presented
serpenting presenting
serpents pertness; presents
serpigo porgies
serpula perusal
serr errs
serra rears; Sarre
Sérrai airers; raiser; sierra
serranid drainers
serrate re-rates; tearers
serrated retreads; treaders
serrates asserter; reassert
serrature treasurer
serried desirer; Dreiser
serum mures; muser; Remus;
  Sumer
serval lavers; ravels; salver; slaver;
  versal
servals salvers; slavers; versals
servant taverns; versant
servants St. Servan
serve sever; veers; verse
served versed
server revers; verser
servers versers
serves severs; Sèvres; verses
Servia varies
Servian ravines
service scrieve
serviced scrieved
services scrieves
servicing scrieving
servient nerviest; reinvest; sirvente
servile Liévres; relives; reviles
serving versing

Servite restive
servo overs; roves; Serov; verso
session essoins
sesterce secretes
sestet testes; tsetse
sestets tsetses
sestina entasis; Saintes; Staines;
  tansies; tisanes
Sestos tosses
seta east; eats; sate; seat; taes; teas
setae tease
setback backets; backset
setbacks backsets
Sète Este; tees
Seth Esth; hest; shet
Sethon honest; Stheno
set in inset; neist; stein; tines
set-off offset
set-offs offsets
seton Eston; notes; onset; stone;
  Tenos; tones
setons Nestos; onsets; sets on;
  stones
sets Tess
sets in insets; steins; Tessin
sets on Nestos; onsets; setons;
  stones
sett stet; test
setter street; tester
setters streets; tersest; testers
setting testing
settle ettles
settler letters; sterlet; trestle
settlers sterlets; trestles
set-to totes
setts tests
set-up stupe; upset
setwall wallets
Seurat Atreus; Auster
Sevan avens; Evans; naves; vanes
seven evens; Neves
seventy-nine ninety-seven
seventy-six sixty-seven
sever serve; veers; verse
several laveers; leavers; reveals
severe reeves
severed deserve
Severn nerves; Nevers
severs serves; Sèvres; verses
Sèvres serves; severs; verses
sewan wanes; weans
Seward sawder; waders
sewed swede; sweed; weeds

sewel   Lewes; sweel; weels; Wesel
sewels   sweels
sewen   enews; weens
sewer   ewers; sweer; Weser
sewers   sweers
sewin   sinew; swine; wines
sewing   swinge; winges
sewn   news; wens
sexes   Essex
sexist   exists
sexpartite   extirpates
sextan   Texans
sey   sye; yes
shack   hacks
shackle   hackles
Shackleton   shecklaton
shad   dahs; dash
shaddock   haddocks
shade   Hades; heads
shaded   dashed
shades   dashes; sashed
shading   dashing
shady   Hyads
shaft   hafts
shafter   fathers
shag   gash; hags
shah   hash
Shairp   Hispar; parish; raphis
shaker   kasher
shaking   Kashing
Shakti   skaith
shale   hales; halse; heals; leash;
   selah; sheal
shales   halses; hassle; lashes; sheals
shall   halls
shallow   hallows
shalt   halts; laths; Stahl
sham   hams; mash
shamble   hambles
shame   hames; Shema
shamed   mashed
shamer   harems; masher
shamers   mashers; smasher
shames   mashes
shaming   mashing
shammer   hammers
shams   smash
shan   Hans; Nash
shand   hands
Shane   ashen; Hanse
shank   ankhs; hanks; khans
shans   snash
shan't   Hants.; snath

shanties   anthesis
Shap   haps; hasp; pash
shape   heaps; Pesah; phase
shaped   hasped; pashed; phased
shaper   phares; phrase; raphes;
   seraph; Sherpa; sphaer
shapers   phrases; seraphs; Sherpas;
   sphaers
shapes   pashes; phases
shaping   hasping; pashing; phasing
shard   hards
share   hares; hears; rheas; shear
shared   dasher
share-outs   authoress
sharer   rasher
sharers   rashers
shares   rashes; shears
Shari   arish; hairs
sharing   garnish
shark   harks
sharp   harps
sharped   phrased
sharper   harpers; phraser
sharpers   phrasers
sharpest   sharp-set
sharping   phrasing
sharp-set   sharpest
shatter   hatters; rathest; threats
shattering   straighten
shave   haves; sheva
shaven   havens; Hesvan
shaver   havers
shaw   haws; wash
shawling   whalings
shawm   hawms
shaws   swash
shay   ashy; hays
sheading   headings
sheal   hales; halse; heals; leash;
   selah; shale
shealing   leashing
sheals   halses; hassle; lashes; shales
shear   hares; hears; rheas; share
sheared   adheres; headers
shearer   hearers; rehears
shearing   hearings
shears   rashes; shares
'sheart   earths; haters; hearts;
   Sarthe
she-ass   sashes
sheath   heaths
sheave   heaves
Shebat   bathes

shecklaton Shackleton
she-devil dishevel
she-devils dishevels
sheel heels; heles
sheen Esneh
sheens Hessen; sneesh
sheep phese
sheer Esher; herse
sheering greenish
sheers herses
sheet thees; these
sheeted seethed
sheeting seething
sheets theses
sheik hikes
Sheila Ilesha
sheiling shieling
shelf flesh
sheify fleshy
shell hells
sheller hellers
Shelta haslet; lathes; Thales
shelve helves
Shem hems; mesh
Shema hames; shame
Shensi shines
She'ol holes
Sheraton North Sea
sherd herds; shred
sherds shreds
sheriat hastier
sherif fisher
sherifs fishers; serfish
Sherpa phares; phrase; raphes;
  seraph; shaper; sphaer
Sherpas phrases; seraphs; shapers;
  sphaers
shes Hess
shet Esth; hest; Seth
Shetland Stendhal
shets hests
sheugh Hughes
sheva haves; shave
shew hews
shewel wheels
shewing hewings; whinges
shicker skriech
shied hides
shieling sheiling
shier heirs; hires; shire
shiers shires
shiest heists; shites; sithes; Theiss;
  thesis

shikar rakish
shill hills
shin hisn; sinh
shindig dishing; hidings
shiner rhines; shrine
shiners shrines
shines Shensi
shingle English
shingled hind legs
ship hips; pish
shipmates steamship
shippo hippos; popish
shir Shri
shire heirs; hires; shier
shires shiers
shirra arrish; Harris; sirrah
shirty Irtysh; thyrsi
shit hist; hits; sith; this; Tshi
shite heist; sithe; Thiès
shites heists; shiest; sithes; Theiss;
  thesis
shiting insight
shits hists
shive hives
shiver hivers; shrive
shivered shrieved
shivering shrieving
shivers shrives
shoal halos; shola; solah
shoals sholas; solahs
shoat Athos; hoast; hosta; oaths
shoats hoasts; hostas; Thasos
shock hocks
shocker chokers; hockers
shod hods
shoder hordes; horsed; Rhodes;
  shored
shoe hoes; hose
shoed doseh; hosed
shoer hoers; horse; shore
shoers horses; shores
shoes hoses
shog gosh; hogs
shola halos; shoal; solah
sholas shoals; solahs
shone hones; hosen
shoo Soho
shook hooks
shoot hoots; sooth; Sotho
shooter hooters; soother
shooters soothers
shooting soothing
shoots Sothos

shop hops; posh; soph
shopper hoppers
shopping hoppings
shops sophs; sposh
shore hoers; horse; shoer
shore-crab broachers
shored hordes; horsed; Rhodes; shoder
shores horses; shoers
shore up Orpheus
shoring horsing
shorn horns
short horst
shorted dehorts
shorten hornets; thrones
shortened dethrones
shortie hoister
shorts horsts
shorty Rosyth
shot host; hots; tosh
shote ethos; those
shotgun gunshot; noughts
shotguns gunshots
shout south; thous
shouted southed
shouter souther
shouters southers
shouting southing
shouts souths
shove hoves
shovel hovels
shover hovers; shrove
shovers shroves
show band bow-hands
shower whores
shred herds; sherd
shred-pie hesperid; perished
shred-pies hesperids
shreds sherds
shrew wersh
Shri shir
shriek hikers; shrike
shrieks shrikes
shrieval lavisher
shrieved shivered
shrieving shivering
shrift firths; friths
shrike hikers; shriek
shrikes shrieks
shrine rhines; shiner
shrined hinders
shrines shiners
shrive hivers; shiver

shrived dervish
shrives shivers
shroudy hydrous
shrove hovers; shover
shroves shovers
shrub brush
shul lush; Suhl
shun Huns
shuns snush
shunt hunts
shunter hunters
shunters huntress
shut huts; thus; tush
shut up Pushtu
si is
sial ails; Isla; Lias; Lisa; sail
Siam aims; Amis; Mais; sima
siamang Magians
siamangs amassing
Siamese misease
Sian anis; Isna; Nias; Nisa; sain
sib bis
Siberian Iberians
Sican Canis; Incas
sice ices
Sicel ceils; ciels; Leics.; slice
Sicels slices
sicker ickers; scrike
Sickert rickets; sticker; tickers
sickled slicked
Sid Dis
Sida aids; dais; Dias; Sadi; said
Sidcup cupids; cuspid
side dies; Ides
sidearms misreads
sideboard broadside
sideboards broadsides
sidecar radices
sidecars Cressida
sideman demains; maidens; medians
side-on donsie; Edison; noised; onside
side-post deposits; topsides
sider dries; rides; sired
sideral derails
sidereal realised
side-step despites
sidle deils; idles; slide
sidles slides
sidling sliding
Sidney Disney
Sidra raids

siemens   Meissen; misseen; nemesis
Siena   Aisne; anise
sienna   insane
Siero   osier; Rosie
sierra   airers; raiser; Sérrai
sierras   raisers
siesta   tassie
siestas   tassies
sieved   devise; viséed
sieves   essive
sift   fist; fits
sifted   fisted
sifter   refits; strife
sifting   fisting
sifts   fists
sight   thigs
sigmatron   Montargis; stroaming
sign   gins; sing; snig
Signac   casing
signal   aligns
signally   sallying
signatory   gyrations
signature   gauntries
signboard   boardings
signed   deigns; design; sdeign; singed
signer   Ingres; reigns; renigs; resign; singer
signers   ingress; resigns; singers
signet   ingest; tinges
signets   ingests
Signor   girons; grison; groins; rosing
Signora   ignaros; soaring
Signoras   assignor
Signore   ignores; regions
signpost   postings; stopings
signs   sings; snigs
sika   saki
sikas   sakis
sike   Eisk
Sikel   likes
sikes   skies
silane   aliens; alines; lianes; saline; Selina
Silas   Lissa; sails; sisal
sild   lids; slid
sile   Elis; isle; leis; lies; seil
silen   elsin; lenis; liens; lines; nelis; Niles
silence   license; selenic
silenced   declines; licensed

silencer   licenser; reclines
silencers   licensers
silences   licenses
silencing   licensing
Silene   enisle; ensile; nelies; senile
silens   elsins
silent   enlist; inlets; listen; tinsel
siler   leirs; liers; riels; riles
siles   isles; seils
silhouette   hotel suite
silhouettes   hotel suites
silken   inkles; likens
sill   ills
silly   slily
silo   Lois; oils; soil; soli
silo'd   idols; Isold; lidos; sloid; soldi; solid
siloed   Isolde; soiled
siloing   soiling
Silone   eloins; esloin; insole; lesion
silos   soils
silt   list; slit
silted   idlest; listed; tildes
silting   listing
silts   lists; slits
silva   Alvis; Salvi; vails; valis; vials
silvan   anvils
silver   livers; livres; rivels; sliver
silvered   delivers; desilver; slivered
silvering   slivering
silvers   slivers
sima   aims; Amis; Mais; Siam
simar   ramis
simarre   marries
Simeon   eonism; Miseno; monies; Simone
similes   missile
Simla   Islam; limas; mails; malis; Milas; salmi
simmer   merism; mimers
simmered   immersed
simmering   immersing
simnel   limens; Semlin
Simon   Minos
Simone   eonism; Miseno; monies; Simeon
simoons   monosis
simp   imps
simper   primes
simpered   demireps; premised
simperer   premiers
simpering   premising
simpers   impress; Persism; premiss

simple   impels; Milspe
simpler   limpers; prelims
sin   ins; nis
since   Cenis
sincere   ceresin
sind   dins
Sindara   radians
sine   Ines
sinecure   insecure
sines   nisse
sinew   sewin; swine; wines
sinewed   endwise
sinews   swines
sinewy   winsey
sing   gins; sign; snig
singable   Belgians; Bengalis
singe   segni
singed   deigns; design; sdeign;
   signed
singer   Ingres; reigns; renigs;
   resign; signer
singers   ingress; resigns; signers
singes   gneiss
single   ingles; lignes; seling
singled   dingles; engilds
singles   Lessing
singlet   glisten; tingles
singlets   glistens
singling   gin-sling; slinging
singly   Glynis; lysing
sings   signs; snigs
singult   lusting
sinh   hisn; shin
sink   inks; kins; skin
sinker   inkers
sinks   skins
sinned   Dennis
sinner   inners
sinnet   sennit; tennis
sinnets   sennits
sinning   innings; inn-sign
sinter   insert; inters; Strine; trines
sintered   Dneister; inserted;
   resident
sintering   inserting
sinters   inserts
Sintra   instar; santir; strain; trains
sinuate   aunties
Sion   ions
sip   psi
sipe   pies; pisé
siped   spied
sipes   spies

siphons   sonship
Siporex   proxies
sipper   pipers
sippled   slipped
sippling   slipping
sips   piss
sir   Sri
sire   Eris; reis; rise
sired   dries; rides; sider
siren   reins; resin; rinse; risen; serin
sirenians   raininess
sirens   resins; rinses; serins
sires   rises
Siret   reist; resit; rites; tiers; tires;
   tries
siring   rising
sirname   marines; remains; seminar
sirnames   seminars
sirrah   arrish; Harris; shirra
sirred   derris; driers; reirds; riders
sirs   Riss
sirvente   nerviest; reinvest; servient
sirventes   reinvests
sisal   Lissa; sails; Silas
Sistan   saints; Säntis; satins; stains
sisted   deists; desist
sister   reists; resist; resits
sisters   resists
sistra   sitars; stairs
sistrum   trismus; truisms
sit   its; tis
Sita   aits; Asti; itas; sati
sitar   airts; astir; raits; Sitra; stair;
   stria; tarsi; Trias
sitars   sistra; stairs
site   stie; ties
sited   deist; diets; dites; edits; id est;
   St. Dié; stied; tides
sites   sties
sith   hist; hits; shit; this; Tshi
sithe   heist; shite; Thiès
Sithes   heists; shiest; shites; Theiss;
   thesis
Sitra   airts; astir; raits; sitar; stair;
   stria; tarsi; Trias
Sittang   stating; tasting
sittar   artist; strait; strati; traits
sittars   artists; straits; tsarist
sitter   titres; trites
situs   suits
Siva   Avis; visa
Sivan   vinas
Sivas   visas

siver rives
sixte exist; exits
sixty xysti
sixty-nine ninety-six
sixty-seven seventy-six
sizeable seizable
skail kails; kalis; laiks; Laski
skaith Shakti
Skåne skean; snake; sneak
skart karst; karts; stark; strak
skat kats; taks; task
skate Keats; Skeat; stake; steak;
   takes; teaks
skated staked; tasked
skater strake; streak; takers; tasker
skaters strakes; streaks; taskers
skates stakes; steaks
skating staking; takings; tasking
skean Skåne; snake; sneak
skeans snakes; sneaks
skear asker; kesar; rakes; reaks
   saker
skears askers; kesars; sakers
Skeat Keats; skate; stake; steak;
   takes; teaks
skee ekes; seek
skeeing seeking
skeer esker; reeks
skeers eskers
skees seeks
skeet skete
skeg kegs
skein Skien
skeletal lakelets
skene keens; knees
skeo Keos; okes; soke
skeos sekos; sokes
skep keps
skeptic pickets
sker erks; serk
skerry skryer
skers serks
skete skeet
skewer Wesker
skid disk; kids
skids disks
skied dikes
Skien skein
skier keirs; kiers
skiers kisser
skies sikes
skiey Yeisk
skill kills

skin inks; kins; sink
skink kinks
skins sinks
skint knits; stink; tinks
skip kips
skipper kippers
skirret striker
skirrets strikers
skirt stirk
skirting striking
skirts stirks
skis kiss
skit kist; kits
skite kites; tikes
skittle kittles
skiving Vikings
sklim milks
skran knars; krans; narks; ranks;
   snark
skreigh skriegh
skreighed skrieghed
skreighing skrieghing
skreighs skrieghs
skriech shicker
skriegh skreigh
skrieghed skreighed
skrieghing skreighing
skrieghs skreighs
skryer skerry
skua auks
Skye keys; syke; yesk
skyey Yeysk
skyte kytes; tykes
slab albs; labs
slabbed dabbles
slabber barbels; rabbles
slack calks; lacks
slacker calkers; lackers
slade dales; deals; lades; leads
slae ales; Elsa; leas; sale; seal
slaes sales; salse; seals
slag gals; lags
slagged daggles
slaid Aldis; dalis; dials
slain nails; snail
slàinte eastlin; elastin; entails;
   salient; staniel
slaister realists; saltiers; saltires
slake kales; lakes; leaks
slakes Kassel
slam alms; lams
slander enlards; landers; snarled
slane lanes; leans

slang glans
slanged dangles
slangish slashing
slap Alps; laps; pals; salp
slapped dapples
slapper lappers; rapples
slaps salps
slap-up palpus
slashed hassled
slasher ashlers; lashers
slashes hassles
slashing hassling; lashings; slangish
slat last; lats; salt
slate least; leats; Stael; stale; steal; stela; taels; tales; teals; tesla
slated deltas; desalt; lasted; salted; staled
slater alerts; alters; artels; laster; ratels; salter; staler; stelar; tarsel
slaters artless; lasters; salters; tarsels
slates stales; steals; tassel; teslas
slather halters; harslet; Herstal; lathers
slatier Alister; realist; retails; saltier; saltire
slatiness saltiness; stainless
slating anglist; lasting; salting; staling
slats lasts; salts
slatter rattles; starlet; startle; tatlers; Telstar
slattern trentals
slatters starlets; startles
slaty salty
slave Elvas; laves; salve; selva; vales; valse
slaved salved; valsed
slaver lavers; ravels; salver; serval; versal
slaverer reversal
slaverers reversals
slavers salvers; servals; versals
slaves salves; selvas; valses
Slavic cavils; clavis
slaving salving; valsing
slaw awls; laws
slay lays
slayer layers; relays
slayers rayless
sleave leaves
sled seld

sledge gledes; gleeds; ledges
sledger gelders; ledgers
slee eels; else; lees; seel; sele
sleek keels; leeks
sleeker keelers
sleep peels; speel
sleeper peelers; speeler
sleepers peerless; speelers
sleeping peelings; speeling
sleeps speels
sleet leets; steel; stele
sleeted deletes; steeled
sleeting gentiles; steeling
sleets steels; steles
sleety steely
sleeve levees
slender lenders
slept pelts; spelt
sleuth hustle
sleuths hustles
slew Wels
slewing swingle
sley leys; lyes; lyse
sleys lyses; Yssel
slice ceils; ciels; Leics.; Sicel
slicer relics
slices Sicels
slick licks
slicked sickled
slicken nickels
slicker lickers; rickles
slid lids; sild
slidden dindles
slidder riddles
slide deils; idles; sidle
slider idlers
slides sidles
sliding sidling
Sliema mesail; mesial; Salemi; samiel
'slife Felis; files; flies
slight lights
slighted delights
slighter lighters; relights
slily silly
slime limes; miles; smile
slimed misled; smiled
slimes missel; smiles
slimier milreis
sliming smiling
sling lings
slinger lingers
slingers ringless**

slinging   gin-sling; singling
sling ink   inklings; slinking
slink   kilns; links
slinking   inklings; sling ink
slip   lips; lisp
slipe   piles; plies; spiel; spile
slipes   plissé; spiels; spiles
slipped   sippled
slipper   ripples
slipping   sippling
slips   lisps
slipt   spilt; split
slip up   pupils
slit   list; silt
slits   lists; silts
slitter   litters; stilter; testril; tilters; titlers
slitting   stilting; Tlingits
slive   Elvis; evils; levis; lives; veils; vleis
slived   devils
Sliven   livens; snivel
sliver   livers; livres; rivels; silver
slivered   delivers; desilver; silvered
slivering   silvering
slivers   silvers
sloan   loans; salon; solan; Solna
sloans   salons; solans
slob   Bols; lobs
sloe   lose; Ösel; sole
sloes   loess; loses; soles
slog   Glos.; logs
slogged   dog-legs
slogger   loggers
slogs   gloss
sloid   idols; Isold; lidos; silo'd; soldi; solid
sloom   looms; mools
sloop   loops; pools; spool
sloops   spools
slop   lops
slope   elops; lopes; olpes; poles
sloppy   polyps
slopy   ploys; Pylos
slot   lost; lots; St. Lô
sloth   Holst; holts
slotted   dottles
slough   ghouls; loughs
slove   loves; solve; voles
sloven   novels
slow   lows; owls; sowl
slowed   dowels; sowled
slower   lowers; owlers; rowels

slowing   sowling
slowness   snowless
slows   sowls
slubber   burbles; lubbers
slued   duels; dulse
slug   lugs
slugger   gurgles; luggers
sluices   Celsius
slum   lums
slumber   Burslem; lumbers; rumbles
slump   lumps; plums
slumped   dumples
slung   lungs
slurb   blurs; burls
slut   lust
sluts   lusts
sly   Lys
slyer   lyres
slyest   styles
smack   macks
smaik   kaims; kamis; maiks
small   malls
smalt   malts
smart   marts; trams
smarten   artsmen; martens; sarment
smartened   tradesmen
smartens   sarments
smarter   armrest
smartest   mattress; smatters
smarting   migrants
smash   shams
smasher   mashers; shamers
smatter   matters
smatters   mattress; smartest
smear   mares; maser; reams
smears   masers; Ramses
smeath   Thames
smee   emes; Esme; mese; seem; semé
smeeth   themes
smell   mells
smelt   melts
smelter   melters
smelters   termless
smew   mews
smile   limes; miles; slime
smiled   misled; slimed
smiler   merils; milers
smilers   rimless
smiles   missel; slimes
smiling   sliming

smir mirs; rims
smirch chrism
smit mist
smite emits; items; metis; mites;
  stime; times
smiter merits; mister; mitres;
  remits; timers
smites misset; stimes; tmesis
smiting misting; stiming; timings
smitten mittens
smock mocks
smoke mokes
smolder molders
smoor moors; Moros; Ormos;
  rooms
smooring moorings
smoot moots; tooms
smore Moers; mores; morse; omers
smored dromes
smores morses
smote mesto; motes; tomes
smother mothers; thermos
smoulder moulders; remoulds
smouse mousse
smouser mousers
smouses mousses
smug gums; mugs
smugger muggers
smur rums
smurred murders
smut must; stum; tums
smuts stums
smytrie mistery
snab bans; nabs
snafu fauns; Fusan
snag nags; sang
snags sangs
snail nails; slain
snailed denails; lead-ins
snake Skåne; skean; sneak
snakes skeans; sneaks
snap naps; pans; span
snapped appends
snapper nappers; parpens;
  parsnep
snappered end-papers
snappers parsneps
snaps spans
snare earns; nares; nears; saner
snared redans; sander
snares Nasser; sarsen
snark knars; krans; narks; ranks;
  skran

snarled enlards; landers; slander
snary yarns
snash shans
snaste assent; sanest; stanes; steans
snastes assents
snatch chants; stanch
snatched stanched
snatcher chanters; stancher;
  tranches
snatchers stanchers
snatches stanches
snatching stanching
snath Hants.; shan't
snathe Athens; hasten; sneath;
  thanes
snathes hastens; sneaths
snead Andes; Danes; deans;
  Desna; sedan
sneads sedans
sneak Skåne; skean; snake
sneaks skeans; snakes
sneap aspen; napes; neaps; panes;
  peans; spane; spean
sneaped speaned
sneaping speaning
sneaps aspens; spanes; speans
sneath Athens; hasten; snathe;
  thanes
sneaths hastens; snathes
sneb bens; nebs
sneck necks
sned dens; ends; send
sneds sends
Sneek knees
sneer ernes
sneered needers
sneesh Hessen; sheens
snib bins; nibs
snick nicks
snicked dickens
snicker nickers
snide Denis; dines
sniff niffs
snig gins; sign; sing
snigger gingers; niggers
sniggle gingles; niggles
sniggled geldings
snigs signs; sings
snip nips; pins; spin
snipe penis; pines; spine
sniped piends; spined
sniper ripens
snipes spines

snipper nippers
snips spins
snivel livens; Sliven
snob bos'n; nobs
snobs bos'ns
snod dons; nods
snoep opens; peons; pones; Posen
snog nogs; song
snogs songs
snook nooks
snool loons; Solon
snoop spoon
snooped spooned
snooper Spooner
snooping spooning
snoops spoons
snore Norse; noser; oners; rones;
  Ronse; Señor; seron
snored drones; rondes; sorned
snorer sorner
snorers sorners
snores nosers; Señors; sensor;
  serons
snoring sorning
snorted Dorsten; rodents
snot onst; tons
snotter stentor
snotters stentors
snow owns; sown
snowed endows
snowk knows
snowless slowness
snub buns; nubs
snudge nudges
snug gnus; guns; sung
snush shuns
snuzzle nuzzles
so os
soak koas; oaks; okas
soaker arkose
soap apso
soaped apodes
soaps apsos; psoas
soar oars; Oras; osar; Rosa; sora
soare arose
soared adores; oreads
soaring ignaros; Signora
soars Rosas; saros
Sobat basto; boast; boats; sabot
sobbing gibbons
sober boers; bores; broes; robes
sobered bedsore
sobole lobose

sobs boss
soc cos
socager cargoes; corsage
socagers corsages
soccer escroc
Soche chose
social Licosa
societal alootico
Socinus cousins
socle close; coles
socles closes
socman mascon
Socrates coarsest; coasters
Socratic acrostic
sod dso
soda Sado
Sodom dooms; dsomo; moods
sods doss; dsos
sofa oafs
softa fatso
soften Sefton
softener enforest
softeners enforests
soger goers; gores; gorse; ogres;
  Sergo
sogers ogress
Sogne segno
Soho shoo
soil Lois; oils; silo; soli
soiled Isolde; siloed
soiling siloing
soils silos
soke Keos; okes; skeo
sokes sekos; skeos
Sokol kolos; looks
sola also; Laos
solacer escolar; oracles
solacers escolars; lacrosse
solah halos; shoal; shola
solahs shoals; sholas
solan loans; salon; sloan; Solna
solano saloon
solans salons; sloans
solas lasso
solder dorsel; drôles; resold
solderers orderless
solders dorsels; rodless
soldi idols; Isold; lidos; silo'd; sloid;
  solid
sole lose; Ösel; sloe
solecises isosceles
solecist solstice
solecists solstices

soled Delos; doles; lodes
solemn Lemnos; lemons; melons
soieness noseless
Solent stolen; telson
soler eorls; Leros; loser; orles; Osler; roles; Sorel
solers lessor; losers
soles loess; loses; sloes
soleus louses; ousels
sol-fa foals; loafs
soli Lois; oils; silo; soil
solicit colitis
solicitation coalitionist
solicitations coalitionists
solicits sciolist
solid idols; Isold; lidos; silo'd; sloid; soldi
solids dossil
Soliman malison; Osmanli
soling losing
soliped despoil; diploes; dipoles; peloids; spoiled
solipeds despoils
solitary royalist
solitudes dissolute
solive olives
Solly lysol
Solna loans; salon; sloan; solan
solo loos; Oslo
Solon loons; snool
sols loss
solstice solecist
solstices solecists
Solti Isolt; toils
soluble lobules
solus souls
solve loves; slove; voles
solver lovers
solves Lesvos
soma Amos; moas
somatist atomists
Sombor brooms
someday samoyed
Somme memos; momes
son nos.
sonance ancones
sonances canoness
sonant santon
sonants santons
sonar arson; roans
sonce cones; Cosne; scone
sonde nodes; nosed
sondeli dolines; Leonids

Sondrio indoors; sordino
sone Enos; eons; noes; nose; ones
soneri nosier; senior
sones noses; sonse
song nogs; snog
songs snogs
sonic coins; icons; scion
sonless lessons
sonnet Neston; nonets; stonen; tenons; tenson; tonnes
sonnets Stenson; tensons
Sonnite intones; tension
sonse noses; sones
sonship siphons
sonsie enosis; essoin; noesis; noises; ossein
sontag Gaston; tangos; tongas
soole loose; oleos
sooled loosed; oodles
sooles looses
sooling loosing; olingos
soom moos
soon oons
sooner roneos; seroon
sooth hoots; shoot; Sotho
soother hooters; shooter
soothers shooters
soothing shooting
sootiest tootsies
sop ops; pos
Soper pores; poser; prose; ropes; spore
soph hops; posh; shop
sophister prothesis; store-ship
sophisters store-ships
sophs shops; sposh
sopor roops; spoor
Sopot stoop
soppy popsy
sopra Paros; proas; psora; sapor
sops poss
sora oars; Oras; osar; Rosa; soar
soral orals
sorb orbs; robs
sorbet Osbert; strobe
sord dors; ords; rods
sorda Doras; dorsa; roads; Rodas
sordes dorses; dosser
sordine indorse; rosined
sordino indoors; Sondrio
sordo doors; Ordos; roods
sords dross
sore Eros; ores; roes; rose

soredium dimerous
Sorel eorls; Leros; loser; orles; Osler; roles; soler
sores roses
Sorex oxers
sorites rosiest; sorties; stories
sorned drones; rondes; snored
sorner snorer
sorners snorers
sorning snoring
soroche chooser
sorriest resistor; roisters
sort orts; rots; tors
sortable bloaters; storable
sorted Dorset; stored; strode
sorter resort; roster; storer
sorters resorts; rosters; storers
sortes rosets; stores; torses; tosser
sortie tiroes; tories
sortied editors; roisted; rosited; steroid; storied; tie-rods; triodes
sorties rosiest; sorites; stories
sorting storing; trigons
sortment torments
sortments sternmost
sorus sours
Sotho hoots; shoot; sooth
Sothos shoots
sots toss
sought toughs
souled loused
souls solus
Soult lotus; louts
soumed moused; Usedom
souming mousing
sound nodus
sounder Öresund; resound; undoers
sounders dourness; resounds
soup opus
souple poules
sour ours
source cerous; course; crouse; Crusoe
sources courses; Croesus; sucrose
soured douser; roused
sourest estrous; oestrus; ousters; souters; tousers; trouses; tussore
souring rousing
sours sorus
souses Sousse
Sousse souses

souter ouster; outers; routes; touser; trouse
souters estrous; oestrus; ousters; sourest; tousers; trouses; tussore
south shout; thous
southed shouted
souther shouter
southers shouters
southing shouting
souths shouts
soviets stovies
sowed dowse
sower owers; serow; swore; worse
sowers serows
sowl lows; owls; slow
sowled dowels; slowed
sowling slowing
sowls slows
sowm mows
sown owns; snow
sowp pows; swop; wops
sowps swops
sowter stower; stowre; towers; towser; twoers
sowters stowers; stowres; towsers
spa asp; pas; sap
space capes; Caspe; paces; scape
spaced scaped
spacer capers; Casper; crapes; escarp; pacers; parsec; recaps; scrape
spacers escarps; parsecs; scrapes
spaces scapes
spacing scaping
spade sepad; spaed
spades sepads; passed
spadroon pandoors
spae apes; apse; peas
spaed sepad; spade
spaer asper; pares; parse; pears; prase; presa; rapes; reaps; spare; spear
spaers aspers; parses; passer; repass; spares; sparse; spears
spaes apses; passé
spahi aphis; apish
Spain pains; piñas; spina
spake peaks; speak
spale Elaps; lapse; leaps; pales; peals; pleas; salep; sepal; speal
spales lapses; sepals; speals
spall palls
spalt plats; splat

spalts splats
spam amps; maps; pams; samp
span naps; pans; snap
spancel enclasp
spancels enclasps
spane aspen; napes; neaps; panes;
  peans; sneap; spean
spanes aspens; sneaps; speans
spang pangs
spangler sprangle
spanglers sprangles
spaniel alpines
spaniels painless
spank knaps
spans snaps
spar raps; rasp
sparable parables
spare asper; pares; parse; pears;
  prase; presa; rapes; reaps; spaer;
  spear
spared drapes; padres; parsed;
  rasped; repads; spread
sparely parleys; parsley; players;
  replays
sparer parers; parser; rasper
sparers parsers; raspers; sparser
spares aspers; parses; passer;
  repass; spaers; sparse; spears
sparge gapers; gasper; grapes;
  parges
sparged grasped
sparger grasper
spargers graspers
sparges gaspers
sparging grasping
Sparidae paradise
sparing parings; parsing; rasping
sparingly raspingly
spark parks
sparred drapers
spars rasps
sparse aspers; parses; passer;
  repass; spaers; spares; spears
sparser parsers; raspers; sparers
sparsest trespass
spart parts; prats; sprat; strap;
  traps
Sparta Patras; satrap
Spartan tarpans; trapans
Spartel palters; per-salt; plaster;
  platers; psalter; stapler
spas asps; pass; saps
spat past; pats; stap; taps

spate paste; pates; septa; speat;
  tapes
spates pastes; speats; stapes
spathed heptads
spats pasts; staps
spatter patters; tapster
spatters tapsters
spavie pavise
spaw paws; swap; waps; wasp
spawl pawls
spawling lapwings
spawn pawns
spawner enwraps; pawners
spaws swaps; wasps
spay pays; yaps
speak peaks; spake
speal Elaps; lapse; leaps; pales;
  peals; pleas; salep; sepal; spale
speals lapses; sepals; spales
spean aspen; napes; neaps; panes;
  peans; sneap; spane
speaned sneaped
speaning sneaping
speans aspens; sneaps; spanes
spear asper; pares; parse; pears;
  prase; presa; rapes; reaps; spaer;
  spare
spearman Parmesan
spears aspers; parses; passer;
  repass; spaers; spares; sparse
speary payers; repays
speat paste; pates; septa; spate;
  tapes
speats pastes; spates; stapes
spec pecs
specie pieces
speck pecks
spectra carpets; precast
spectral sceptral
spectre recepts; respect; sceptre
spectres respects; sceptres
spectrum crumpets
specula capsule
speculate peculates
speculation peculations
speculator peculators
sped peds
speech cheeps; peches
speed deeps
speeder speered
speedo epodes; depose
speedos deposes
speel peels; sleep

speeler peelers; sleeper
speelers peerless; sleepers
speeling peelings; sleeping
speels sleeps
speer peers; perse; prees; prese;
  spree
speered speeder
speers preses; sperse; sprees
speir épris; peris; piers; pries; prise;
  ripes; spire
speired Perseid; predies; preside
speirs prises; spires
speiss pisses; sepsis
Speke keeps; peeks; pekes
speldin spindle
speldins spindles
spell pells
speller respell
spellers respells
spelt pelts; slept
spelter pelters; petrels
spend pends
speos pesos; poses; posse
sperling springle
sperm perms
spermaceti imprecates
sperm-oil implores; pelorism
sperse preses; speers; sprees
spersed depress; pressed
spersing pressing; springes
spew pews
Spey espy; sype
sphaer phares; phrase; raphes;
  seraph; shaper; Sherpa
sphaere reshape
sphaeres reshapes
sphaers phrases; seraphs; shapers;
  Sherpas
sphenic pinches
sphere herpes; Hesper; pheers
spheric ceriphs; ciphers
spial lapis; pails
spica aspic; Capis; picas
spicae apices
spice epics
spicer cripes; Persic; precis; prices
spices pisces
spick picks
spider prides; prised; redips;
  risped; spired
spider-crab crispbread
spied siped
spiel piles; plies; slipe; spile

spieler replies
spiels plissé; slipes; spiles
spies sipes
spignel pingles; pin-legs
spike kepis; kipes; pikes; Pisek
spikelet pikelets
spiking pigskin
spile piles; plies; slipe; spiel
spiled dispel; lisped
spiles plissé; slipes; spiels
spiling lisping
spill pills
spillage pillages
spilt slipt; split
spin nips; pins; snip
spina pains; piñas; Spain
spinal plains
spinate panties; patines; sapient
spindle speldin
spindled splendid
spindles speldins
spine penis; pines; snipe
spined piends; sniped
spinel pensil; Pilsen; spline
spinels pensils; splines
spines snipes
spinet instep; step-in
spinets insteps; step-ins
spinier inspire; pirnies
spink pinks; Pinsk
spinner pinners
spinnet tenpins
spinode dispone
spinodes dispones
spins snips
spinule line-ups; lupines; up-lines
spiracle calipers; replicas
spiral prials
spirant spraint
spire épris; peris; piers; pries; prise;
  ripes; speir
spired prides; prised; redips;
  risped; spider
spireme empires; emprise;
  epimers; imprese; premise
spiremes emprises; impreses;
  premises
spires prises; speirs
spiring prising; risping
spirited tide-rips
spirits tripsis
spirt sprit; stirp; strip; trips
spirted striped

spirting   striping
spirts   sprits; stirps; strips
spit   pits; tips
spital   plaits
spitcher   pitchers
spite   piets; piste; stipe
spites   pistes; stipes
spitter   pitters; tipster
spitters   tipsters
splat   plats; spalt
splats   spalts
splatter   partlets; platters; prattles;
   sprattle
splatters   sprattles
splay   palsy; plays
splaying   palsying
splendid   spindled
splenic   pencils
splice   clipes
spline   pensil; Pilsen; spinel
splines   pensils; spinels
splinters   printless
split   slipt; spilt
split ring   stripling; triplings
splitter   triplets
splore   polers; proles
sploshing   longships
Spock   pocks
spode   dopes; posed
spoiled   despoil; diploes; dipoles;
   peloids; soliped
spoilers   oil-press
spoilt   pilots; pistol; postil
spoke   pokes
spoliation   positional
spoliator   troopials
spondee   depones
spongier   reposing
spontoon   pontoons
spoof   poofs
spool   loops; pools; sloop
spooled   poodles
spooler   loopers
spools   sloops
spoon   snoop
spooned   snooped
Spooner   snooper
spooning   snooping
spoons   snoops
spoor   roops; sopor
sporadic   picadors
spore   pores; poser; prose; ropes;
   Soper

spores   posers; proses
sport   ports; strop
sported   deports
sporter   porters; pretors; reports
sporters   portress
sports   strops
sporule   leprous
sposh   shops; sophs
spot   opts; post; pots; stop;
   tops
spots   posts; stops
spotter   potters; protest
spotters   protests
spotty   typtos
spout   pouts; stoup
spouter   petrous; posture; pouters;
   Proteus; septuor; troupes
spouters   postures
spouts   toss-up
sprag   grasp
sprags   grasps
spraid   rapids
spraint   spirant
sprang   prangs
sprangle   spangler
sprangles   spanglers
sprat   parts; prats; spart; strap; traps
sprats   straps
sprattle   partlets; platters; prattles;
   splatter
sprattles   splatters
spray   prays; raspy
sprayer   prayers; respray
sprayers   resprays
spread   drapes; padres; parsed;
   rasped; repads; spared
spreads   adpress
spreathing   strap-hinge
spree   peers; perse; prees; prese;
   speer
sprees   preses; speers; sperse
sprig   grips; prigs
springe   pingers
springes   pressing; spersing
springier   reprising; respiring
springiest   persisting
springle   sperling
sprint   prints
sprinter   printers; reprints
sprit   spirt; stirp; strip; trips
sprite   esprit; priest; Pteris; ripest;
   stripe; tripes
spritely   priestly

sprites   persist; priests; stirpes; stripes
sprits   spirts; stirps; strips
sprod   dorps; drops; prods
sprout   Proust; stroup; stupor
sprouted   postured; proudest
sprouting   outspring; posturing
sprouts   stroups; stupors
spruces   percuss
sprue   puers; pures; purse; super
sprues   purses; supers
spruit   purist; stir up; uprist
spruits   purists; stirs up
spud   puds
spued   dupes; pseud
spule   pules; pulse
spules   pulses
spuming   impugns
spun   puns
spunk   punks
spur   purs
spuriae   Piraeus; upraise
spurner   pruners
spurt   turps
sputa   sat up
sputter   putters
spying   pigsny
squad   quads
squail   quails
squatter   quartets
squeak   quakes
squeal   equals
squid   quids
squill   quills
squire   quires; Quseir; risqué
squireen   enquires
squit   quits
Sri   sir
stab   bast; bats; tabs
stabbed   tebbads
stabber   barbets; rabbets
stabile   astilbe; bestial
stable   ablest; ablets; bleats; tables
stabled   blasted
stabler   alberts; blaster; labrets; tablers
stablers   blasters
stabling   blasting
staccato   toccatas
stack   tacks
stacker   rackets; tackers
stacket   tackets
stade   dates; sated; stead

stades   steads
Stael   least; leats; slate; stale; steal; stela; taels; tales; teals; tesla
stag   gats; tags
stage   gates; geats
stager   grates; greats; targes
stages   sagest
stagey   gayest
stagged   gadgets
stagger   taggers
stagier   agister; gaiters; sea-girt; strigae; triages
stagnation   antagonist
Stahl   halts; laths; shalt
staid   adits; ditas
stain   saint; satin; Tanis
stained   Danites; detains; instead; sainted
stainer   nastier; ratines; resiant; retains; retinas; retsina; starnie; stearin
stainers   starnies; stearins
Staines   entasis; Saintes; sestina; tansies; tisanes
stainless   saltiness; slatiness
stains   saints; Säntis; satins; Sistan
stair   airts; astir; raits; sitar; Sitra; stria; tarsi; Trias
staired   asterid; astride; diaster; disrate; tirades
stairs   sistra; sitars
staithe   atheist
staithes   atheists
stake   Keats; skate; Skeat; steak; takes; teaks
staked   skated; tasked
stakes   skates; steaks
staking   skating; takings; tasking
stale   least; leats; slate; Stael; steal; stela; taels; tales; teals; tesla
staled   deltas; desalt; lasted; salted; slated
staler   alerts; alters; artels; laster; ratels; salter; slater; stelar; tarsel
stales   slates; steals; tassel; teslas
Stalin   instal; Latins
staling   anglist; lasting; salting; slating
stalk   talks
stalker   talkers
stamen   aments; mantes
staminal   talisman
stamp   tamps

stampede stepdame
stampedes stepdames
stamper tampers
Stan ants; tans
stance ascent; enacts; secant
stances ascents; secants
stanch chants; snatch
stanched snatched
stancher chanters; snatcher;
  tranches
stanchers snatchers
stanches snatches
stanching snatching
stander endarts; red ants
stane antes; etnas; nates; Nesta;
  Senta; stean; Teans
stanes assent; sanest; snaste; steans
stang angst; gants; gnats; tangs
Stanger garnets; Sargent; strange
Stanhope phaetons; Stephano
staniel eastlin; elastin; entails;
  salient; slàinte
staniels eastlins; salients
stank kants; tanks
stannate tannates
stannic tin cans
stap past; pats; spat; taps
stapes pastes; spates; speats
staple palest; palets; pastel; petals;
  plates; pleats; septal
stapler palters; per-salt; plaster;
  platers; psalter; spartel
staplers per-salts; plasters; psalters
staples pastels
staps pasts; spats
star arts; rats; tars; tsar
starch charts; scarth
starcher charters; Chartres
stardom tsardom
stare arets; aster; astre; earst; rates;
  reast; resat; strae; tares; tears; teras
stared adrets; daters; trades; treads
starer arrest; arrêts; raster; raters;
  Sartre; terras
starers arrests; rasters
stares assert; asters; astres; reasts;
  Stresa
staring ratings
stark karst; karts; skart; strak
starlet rattles; slatter; startle;
  tatlers; Telstar
starlets slatters; startles
starling ratlings

starn rants; tarns
starnie nastier; ratines; resiant;
  retains; retinas; retsina; stainer;
  stearin
starnies stainers; stearins
star-nose assentor; senators;
  treasons
star-noses assentors
starred darters; retards; traders
stars tsars; trass
starshine tarnishes
start tarts
started tetrads
starter ratters; restart
starters restarts
startle rattles; slatter; starlet;
  tatlers; Telstar
startler rattlers
startles slatters; starlets
startling rattlings
starve averts; tavers; traves; vaster
starved adverts
stashing Hastings
stasis assist
state taste; tates; teats; testa
stated tasted
stateless tasteless
statement testament
statements testaments
stater aretts; taster; taters; tetras;
  treats
staters tasters
states tastes
stateside steadiest
static attics
statical cat's-tail
stating Sittang; tasting
stational saltation
stator tarots
statue astute
stature Steuart
staunch canthus; chaunts
stauncher chaunters
stave vesta
staves vestas
staw swat; taws; twas; wast
stawed wadset; wasted
stawing wasting
staws swats
stayed steady
stayer estray; reasty; yarest
stayers estrays
staying Stygian

196

St. Clair Carlist
St. Dié deist; diets; dites; edits; id est; sited; stied; tides
stead dates; sated; stade
steaded dead-set; sedated
steadier readiest
steadiest stateside
steadily diastyle
steading d'Estaing; sedating
steads stades
steady stayed
steak Keats; skate; Skeat; stake; takes; teaks
steaks skates; stakes
steal least; leats; slate; Stael; stale; stela; taels; tales; teals; tesla
steale elates; stelae; teasel
stealer elaters; Laertes; relates
stealers tearless; tesseral
steales teasels
stealing eastling; Galenist; genitals
steals slates; stales; tassel; teslas
stealt latest
steam mates; meats; Mesta; tames; teams
steamer sea-term
steamers sea-terms
steamier emirates
steaming mintages
steamship shipmates
steamy mayest
stean antes; etnas; nates; Nesta; Senta; stane; Teans
steane ensate; sateen; senate
steanes senates
steans assent; sanest; snaste; stanes
stearin nastier; ratines; resiant; retains; retinas; retsina; stainer; starnie
stearine arsenite
stearins stainers; starnies
steel leets; sleet; stele
Steele eel-set
steeled deletes; sleeted
steelier leeriest
steeling gentiles; sleeting
steels sleets; steles
steely sleety
steen etens; teens; tense
steens tenses
steeped deepest
steeper estrepe
steepled depletes

steer ester; reest; reset; retes; stere; teers; terse; trees
steered reested
steering integers; reesting; streigne
steers esters; reets; resets; steres
Stefan fasten; nefast
steil islet; istle; stile; teils; tiles
steils islets; stiles
stein inset; neist; set in; tines
Steiner entires; entries; Teniers; trenise
steins insets; sets in; Tessin
stela least; leats; slate; Stael; stale; steal; taels; tales; teals; tesla
stelae elates; steale; teasel
stelar alerts; alters; artels; laster; ratels; salter; slater; staler; tarsel
stele leets; sleet; steel
steles sleets; steels
stell tells
Stella sallet
stellar tellars
St. Elmo molest; motels
stem tems
stempel pelmets; stemple; temples
stempels stemples
stemple pelmets; stempel; temples
stemples stempels
sten nest; nets; sent; tens
stencil clients
stend dents; tends
Stendhal Shetland
stens nests
Stenson sonnets; tensons
stent tents
stentor snotter
stentors snotters
step pest; pets; sept
stepdame stampede
stepdames stampedes
Stephano phaetons; Stanhope
step-in instep; spinet
step-ins insteps; spinets
steps pests; septs
stere ester; reest; reset; retes; steer; teers; terse; trees
steres esters; reests; resets; steers
steric trices
sterical articles; recitals
sterigma magister; migrates
sterile leister
sterlet letters; settler; trestle
sterlets settlers; trestles

sterling   ringlets; tinglers; tringles
stern   Ernst; rents; terns
sterna   antres; astern
sternal   antlers; rentals; saltern
Sterne   enters; Ernest; nester;
   rentes; resent; tenser; ternes
sterned   tenders
sternmost   sortments
sternum   Munster
steroid   editors; roisted; rosited;
   sortied; storied; tie-rods; triodes
sterol   ostler
sterols   ostlers
stet   sett; test
stetson   ostents; St. Neots
Steuart   stature
Steve   evets
Steven   events
stew   ewts; tews; west; wets
steward   strawed
Stewart   swatter; tewarts
stewed   tweeds; wested
stewer   sweert; tweers; wester
stewers   westers
stewing   twinges; westing
stews   wests
stey   stye; tyes
Steyr   resty; treys; tyres
St. Germain   emigrants; mastering;
   streaming
sthenic   ethnics
Stheno   honest; Sethon
stibbler   tribbles
stich   chits
stick   ticks
sticker   rickets; Sickert; tickers
stickle   tickles
stickler   strickle; ticklers; trickles
sticklers   strickles
stie   site; ties
stied   deist; diets; dites; edits; id est;
   St. Dié; sited; tides
sties   sites
stieve   evites
stiff   tiffs
stiffen   infefts
stiffer   restiff
stifle   filets; itself
stifler   filters; lifters; trifles
stile   islet; istle; steil; teils; tiles
stiles   islets; steils
stilet   titles
still   lilts; tills

stillage   legalist; tillages
stillages   legalists
stiller   rillets; tillers; trellis
stilt   tilts
stilter   litters; slitter; testril; tilters;
   titlers
stilting   slitting; Tlingits
stime   emits; items; metis; mites;
   smite; times
stimed   demits; misted
stimes   misset; smites; tmesis
stiming   misting; smiting; timings
Stimson   monists
stimulate   mutilates
stimulator   mutilators
sting   tings
stingaree   reseating
stinger   resting
stingo   ingots; tigons; tosing
stingray   straying
stink   knits; skint; tinks
stinker   Inkster; tinkers
stint   tints; 'tisn't
stinted   dentist
stinter   tinters
stipe   piets; piste; spite
stipes   pistes; spites
stipple   tipples
stippler   ripplets; tipplers; tripples
stir   rits
stirk   skirt
stirks   skirts
stirp   spirt; sprit; strip; trips
stirpes   persist; priests; sprites;
   stripes
stirps   spirts; sprits; strips
stirred   strider
stirs up   purists; spruits
stir up   purist; spruit; uprist
stitcher   chitters
stiver   rivets; strive; trevis
stivers   strives; treviss
St. Lô   lost; lots
St. Marie   Artemis; imarets;
   maestri; maister; misrate; semitar
St. Michael   alchemist
St. Neots   ostents; stetson
stoa   oast; oats; Sato; Taos
stoas   assot; oasts; Tasso
stoat   toast
stoats   toasts
stob   bots
stocked   dockets

stockier   corkiest; rockiest
stockinger   restocking
stodge   godets
stoep   estop; poets; potes; stope;
  topes
stoeps   estops; posset; stopes
stoically   callosity
stoker   stroke
stokers   strokes
stolen   Solent; telson
Stolp   plots; polts
stoma   atoms; moats
stomacher   chromates
stomatic   masticot
stone   Eston; notes; onset; seton;
  Tenos; tones
stone-coal   consolate
stoned   doesn't; Donets; Ostend
stone-mill   millstone
stonen   Neston; nonets; sonnet;
  tenons; tenson; tonnes
stone-pine   Penistone
stone-pits   pottiness
stoner   noters; Reston; tenors;
  tensor; Terson; trones
stoners   tensors
stones   Nestos; onsets; setons; sets
  on
stonier   in store; orients; triones
stonk   knots
stook   kotos
stool   loots; lotos; tools
stoop   Sopot
stoor   roost; roots; torso
stoors   roosts; torsos
stop   opts; post; pots; spot; tops
stope   estop; poets; potes; stoep;
  topes
stoped   depots; despot; posted
stopes   estops; posset; stoeps
stoping   posting
stopings   postings; signpost
stopper   toppers
stopping   toppings
stopple   topples
stops   posts; spots
storable   bloaters; sortable
storax   taxors
store   estro; roset; rotes; tores; torse
stored   Dorset; sorted; strode
storer   resort; roster; sorter
storers   resorts; rosters; sorters
stores   rosets; sortes; torses; tosser

store-ship   prothesis; sophister
store-ships   sophisters
storey   oyster; rosety; Troyes;
  tyroes; Yes Tor
storeys   oysters
storied   editors; roisted; rosited;
  sortied; steroid; tie-rods; triodes
stories   rosiest; sorites; sorties
storing   sorting; trigons
storm   morts; Troms
story   ryots; tyros
stot   tost; tots
stotter   stretto; totters
stound   donuts
stoup   pouts; spout
stoups   spouts
stour   roust; routs; sutor; torus;
  tours
stours   rousts; sutors
stout   touts
stove   votes
stover   strove; voters
stovies   soviets
stow   swot; tows; twos
stowed   towsed
stower   sowter; stowre; towers;
  towser; twoers
stowers   sowters; stowres; towsers
stowing   towsing; Wigston
stown   towns; wonts
stowre   sowter; stower; towers;
  towser; twoers
stowres   sowters; stowers; towsers
stows   swots
Strabo   aborts; boarts; tabors
strack   tracks
strad   darts; drats
strae   arets; aster; astre; earst; rates;
  reast; resat; stare; tares; tears; teras
strafe   afters; faster
strafing   ingrafts
straighten   shattering
straik   traiks
strain   instar; santir; Sintra; trains
strained   detrains; tan-rides
strainer   restrain; terrains; trainers;
  transire
strainers   restrains; transires
strains   instars; santirs
strait   artist; sittar; strati; traits
straiten   intreats; nitrates; tartines
straitens   resistant
straits   artists; sittars; tsarist

strak   karst; karts; skart; stark
strakes   skaters; streaks; taskers
stramp   tramps
strange   garnets; Sargent; Stanger
stranger   granters; regrants
strangle   tanglers; trangles
strap   parts; prats; spart; sprat; traps
strap-hinge   spreathing
strapless   psaltress
strapper   trappers
strapping   trappings
straps   sprats
strata   Tatars
strati   artist; sittar; strait; traits
Straus   Rastus; sutras; Tarsus
straw   swart; warst; warts; wrast
strawed   steward
strawy   swarty
stray   satyr; trays
strayed   rest-day
straying   stingray
strays   satyrs
streak   skater; strake; takers; tasker
streaks   skaters; strakes; taskers
stream   armets; master; maters; tamers
streamed   mastered
streaming   emigrants; mastering; St. Germain
streamless   masterless
streams   masters
stream-tin   martinets
streamy   mastery
streel   Lester; relets
street   setter; tester
streets   setters; tersest; testers
streigne   integers; reesting; steering
strelitz   streltzi
streltzi   strelitz
Stresa   assert; asters; astres; reasts; stares
stressed   desserts
stretta   tatters
stretto   stotter; totters
strew   trews; wrest
strewed   wrested
strewer   wrester
strewers   wresters
strewing   wresting
strews   wrests
stria   airts; astir; raits; sitar; Sitra; stair; tarsi; Trias
striae   satire

striate   artiste; attires; tastier
striated   tardiest
strickle   stickler; ticklers; trickles
strickles   sticklers
stricter   critters; restrict
strid   dirts
striddle   tiddlers
stride   direst; driest
strident   tridents
strider   stirred
strife   refits; sifter
strig   girts; grist; grits; trigs
striga   gratis
strigae   agister; gaiters; sea-girt; stagier; triages
Striges   tigress
strigine   igniters; resiting
strike   trikes
striker   skirret
strikers   skirrets
striking   skirting
Strine   insert; inters; sinter; trines
string-bean   banterings
strinkle   tinklers
strip   spirt; sprit; stirp; trips
stripe   esprit; priest; Pteris; ripest; sprite; tripes
striped   spirted
stripes   persist; priests; sprites; stirpes
striping   spirting
stripling   split ring; triplings
stripper   trippers
strips   spirts; sprits; stirps
striptease   tapestries
strive   rivets; stiver; trevis
strived   diverts
striven   inverts; Ventris
strives   stivers; treviss
stroam   Martos; Mostar; stroma
stroaming   Montargis; sigmatron
stroams   matross
strobe   Osbert; sorbet
stroddle   strodled; toddlers
Stroheim   isotherm; moithers
stroke   stoker
strokes   stokers
stroma   Martos; Mostar; stroam
strongarm   Armstrong
strop   ports; sport
strophe   pothers; thorpes
strops   sports
Stroud   Tudors

stroup Proust; sprout; stupor
stroups sprouts; stupors
strout trouts; tutors
strove stover; voters
strow trows; worst; worts
strowed worsted
strowing worsting
strows worsts
struck trucks
strudel lustred; rustled
strum turms
strumae matures
strumpet trumpets
strung grunts
strut sturt; trust
struts sturts; trusts
St. Servan servants
stub bust; buts; tubs
stubs busts
stuck tucks
stud dust
student stunted
studs dusts
study dusty
stum must; smut; tums
stumble tumbles
stumbler tumblers; tumbrels
stumbling tumblings
stumer estrum; muster
stumers musters
stumper sumpter
stumpers sumpters
stums smuts
stun nuts; tuns; Unst
stunted student
stupe set-up; upset
stupes upsets
stupor Proust; sprout; stroup
stupors sprouts; stroups
sturt strut; trust
sturted trusted
sturting trusting
sturts struts; trusts
stye stey; tyes
Stygian staying
style yelts
styles slyest
stylite testily
styrene yestern
Styx xyst
suable usable
sub bus
subedar daubers

suber burse; rebus
sublet bluest; bustle; subtle
subman busman
suborn bourns
suborned bounders; rebounds
subpoena bean soup
subs buss
substation bus station
substations bus stations
substract subtracts
substraction subtractions
substractor subtractors
subtle bluest; bustle; sublet
subtler bluster; bustler;
   butlers
subtractions substraction
subtractors substractor
subtracts substract
succade accused
succor crocus
such Cush
suck cusk
suckler ruckles
sucks cusks
sucrase causers; cesuras; saucers
sucre cruse; cures; curse
sucrose courses; Croesus; sources
sudd duds
sudder udders
sue use
sued deus; dues; Duse; used
sues uses
suet Utes
Suez Zeus
suffer ruffes
sugar Argus; gaurs
sugars Sargus
Suhl lush; shul
suing using
suint inust; Tunis; units
Suisse issues
suit Uist
suitcase sauciest
suite etuis
suites tissue
suits situs
sulcal callus
sullied illudes; ill-used
sullies ill-uses
sulphured desulphur
sultanic lunatics
sum Mus
sumac Camus; caums; Musca

Sumer mures; muser; Remus; serum
sumless mussels
summae Emmaus
summist summits
summits summist
sumph humps
sumpter stumper
sumpters stumpers
sums muss
Sunay unsay
sunburned unburdens
sun-cured uncursed
sunder nursed
sundering undersign
sunders undress
sun-dog sungod; ungods
sun-dogs sungods
sung gnus; guns; snug
sungod sun-dog; ungods
sungods sun-dogs
sunhat haunts; unhats; Ushant
sunlight hustling
sunlit insult
sunn nuns
sunrise insures
sunset unsets
sunspot unstops
sup pus; ups
super puers; pures; purse; sprue
supernal purslane
supers purses; sprues
supersonic percussion
supine puisne
supper uppers
supple peplus
supplier periplus
supposer purposes
supreme presume
sups puss
sura rusa; Ursa
sural Larus; Urals
suras sarus
surat sutra
surbase abusers
sure Reus; rues; ruse; ures; user
sureness Suresnes
Suresnes sureness
surf furs
surfeits surfiest
surfier friseur; frisure
surfiest surfeits
surge urges

Surinam uranism
surmise misuser; mussier
surmises misusers
surname manures
surnamed maunders
surreined reinsured
Surya saury
Susie issue
suspire uprises
suspiring uprisings
sustain issuant
sutler luster; lustre; luters; result; rustle; ulster
sutlers lusters; lustres; results; rustles; ulsters
sutor roust; routs; stour; torus; tours
sutors rousts; stours
sutra surat
sutras Rastus; Straus; Tarsus
suture uterus
Svengali leavings
swad daws; wads
swaddle dawdles; waddles
swaddler dawdlers; waddlers
swag wags
swage wages
swain wains
swale Lawes; sweal; wales; weals
swaled dwales
swales sweals
swallow wallows
swaly swayl; yawls
swam maws
swami aswim
swan awns; sawn
swang gnaws; wangs
swank wanks
swanker wankers
swap paws; spaw; waps; wasp
swaps spaws; wasps
sward draws; wards
sware sawer; swear; wares; wears
swarm mawrs; warms
swarmer warmers
swart straw; warst; warts; wrast
swarty strawy
swarve wavers
swash shaws
swasher hawsers; washers
swat staw; taws; twas; wast
swath thaws
swathe wheats

swats   staws
swatter   Stewart; tewarts
sway   ways; yaws
swayer   sawyer
swayers   sawyers
swayl   swaly; yawls
sweal   Lawes; swale; wales; weals
sweals   swales
swear   sawer; sware; wares; wears
swearer   wearers
swears   sawers; wrasse
sweat   tawse; waste
sweatier   weariest
sweats   sawset; tawses; wastes
swede   sewed; sweed; weeds
Sweden   endews
Swedish   swished; whissed
swee   ewes; wees
sweed   sewed; swede; weeds
sweel   Lewes; sewel; weels; Wesel
sweels   sewels
sweep   weeps
sweeper   weepers
sweer   ewers; sewer; Weser
sweered   weeders
sweers   sewers
sweert   stewer; tweers; wester
sweet   ewest
sweir   swire; weirs; wires; wiser
sweirt   twiers; twires; writes
swell   wells
swelt   welts
swelter   welters; wrestle
swelters   wrestles
swig   wigs
swill   wills
swindles   wildness; windless
swine   sewin; sinew; wines
swines   sinews
swing   wings
swinge   sewing; winges

swinger   wingers
swingle   slewing
swingles   wingless
swingtree   westering
swink   winks
swinker   winkers
swipe   wipes
swiper   wipers
swire   sweir; weirs; wires; wiser
swished   Swedish; whissed
swisher   wishers
swishes   whisses
swishing   whissing
swith   whist; whits
swither   withers; writhes
swive   views; wives
swob   bows
swop   pows; sowp; wops
swops   sowps
sword   drows; words
sworder   rewords
swore   owers; serow; sower; worse
swot   stow; tows; twos
swots   stows
swound   wounds
sybarite   bestiary
sybo   boys; yobs
syboe   obeys
syce   scye
syces   scyes
sye   sey; yes
syed   deys; dyes
syke   keys; Skye; yesk
Sykes   yesks
syndicate   asyndetic
syne   yens
synod   Dyson
sype   espy; Spey
Syra   rays
syrtes   tressy
syrup   pursy; Pyrus

T

ta   at
tab   bat
tabards   bastard
tabbed   tebbad
tabes   abets; baste; bates; beast;
   beats; besat; Sebat
Tabitha   habitat
table   ablet; blate; bleat

tableau   tabulae
tabler   albert; labret
tablers   alberts; blaster; labrets;
   stabler
tables   ablest; ablets; bleats; stable
tablet   battle
tablets   batteis; battles
tabor   abort; boart; Rabot

tabored aborted; borated	**taigling** ligating
taboring aborting; borating	**tail** alit; Atli; Lita; tali
tabors aborts; boarts; Strabo	**tailed** detail; dilate
tabour rubato	**tailles** Liestal; tallies
taboured obdurate	**tailor** Rialto
tabouret obturate	**tailored** idolater
tabourets obturates	**Tain** ain't; Tina
tabret batter	**Taine** entia; tinea
tabrets batters	**taint** tanti; titan
tabs bast; bats; stab	**taints** tanist; titans
tabu abut; buat; tuba	**taish** saith; Thais
tabula ablaut	**taj** Jat
tabulae tableau	**tak** kat
tabus abuts; buats; tubas	**take** Kate; keta; teak
tach Cath; chat	**take-in** intake
tache cheat; teach; theca	**take-ins** intakes
taches chaste; cheats; sachet; scathe	**takers** skater; strake; streak; tasker
tachisme misteach	**takes** Keats; skate; Skeat; stake;
tacit attic	steak; teaks
tacker racket	**takings** skating; staking; tasking
tackers rackets; stacker	**taks** kats; skat; task
tackets stacket	**talar** altar; ratal
tackled talcked	**talars** altars; astral; tarsal
tackling talcking	**talc** clat
tacks stack	**talcked** tackled
tactic tic-tac	**talcking** tackling
tactics tic-tacs	**talcose** alecost; lactose; locates;
tactile lattice	scatole
Tadcaster castrated	**tale** et al.; late; leat; tael; teal; tela
tae ate; eat; eta; tea	**talent** Lanett; latent; latten
tael et al.; late; leat; tale; teal; tela	**taler** alert; alter; artel; later; ratel
taels least; leats; slate; Stael; stale;	**tales** least; leats; slate; Stael; stale;
steal; stela; tales; teals; tesla	steal; stela; taels; teals; tesla
taenioid ideation	**tali** alit; Atli; Lita; tail
taes east; eats; sate; seat; seta; teas	**talisman** staminal
tag gat	**talkers** stalker
tagged gadget	**talks** stalk
tagger garget	**taller** tellar
taggers stagger	**tallies** Liestal; tailles
taglioni intaglio; ligation	**tally-ho** loathly
taglionis ligations	**tallymen** mentally
Tagore orgeat	**talon** notal; tolan; tonal
tag-rag rag-tag	**Talos** altos; Salto; tolas
tags gats; stag	**talus** sault; Tulsa
Tagus Tsuga	**tam** mat
tahr hart; rath; thar	**tamal** Malta
tahrs harts; raths; thars; trash	**tamale** malate
tahsil latish	**tamales** malates
tai ait; ita	**Tamar** Marat
Taiden Danite; detain	**tamarin** martian
taigle aiglet; ligate	**tamarins** martians
taigled ligated	**tame** mate; meat; Meta; team; Tema
taigles aiglets; ligates	**tamed** mated

tameless mateless; meatless
tameness Massenet
tamer armet; mater; trema
tamers armets; master; maters; stream
tames mates; meats; Mesta; steam; teams
tamin matin
tamine inmate
taming mating
tamise samite
tamises asteism; Matisse; samites
tammies mismate
Tampere tempera
tampers stamper
Tampico potamic
tampion ptomain
tampon potman
tampons postman
tamps stamp
tams mast; mats
tan ant; Nat
Tancred tranced
tang gant; gnat
tanged ganted
tangerine Argentine
tangi giant
tangible belating; bleating
tangie eating; ingate
Tangier Geraint; granite; ingrate; tearing
tangies easting; Gastein; genista; ingates; ingesta; seating; teasing; tsigane
tangiest estating
tanging ganting
tangle Anglet
tangler trangle
tanglers strangle; trangles
tango tonga
tangos Gaston; Sontag; tongas
tangs angst; gants; gnats; stang
tanh than
Tanis saint; satin; stain
tanist taints; titans
tank kant
tanks kants; stank
tannates stannate
tannic tin can
tanrec canter; carnet; creant; Cretan; nectar; recant; trance
tanrecs canters; carnets; Cretans; recants; trances

tan-ride detrain; trade-in; trained
tan-rides detrains; strained
tans ants; Stan
tansies entasis; Saintes; sestina; Staines; tisanes
tansy nasty
tanti taint; titan
Tantra rattan; tartan
Tantras rattans; tartans
Tao oat
Taoism Maoist
Taos oast; oats; Sato; stoa
tap apt; pat
tape pate; peat
taped adept; pated
tapeline petaline
tapen paten
taper apert; pater; peart; Petra; prate; trape
tapered predate; red tape
tapers paster; paters; Praest; prates; repast; trapes
tapes paste; pates; septa; spate; speat
tapestries striptease
tapir atrip; parti
tapirs rapist
taplash asphalt
taps past; pats; spat; stap
tapster patters; spatter
tapsters spatters
tar art; rat
tara rata
Tarbes barest; baster; bestar; breast
tarcel cartel; claret; rectal
tarcels cartels; clarets; scarlet
tardier tarried
tardiest striated
tare aret; rate; tear
tared adret; dater; rated; trade; tread
Taree arête; eater; reate
tares arets; aster; astre; earst; rates; reast; resat; stare; strae; tears; teras
targe grate; great; Greta; terga
targed der Tag; grated
targes grates; Greats; stager
targing grating
tar-heel leather
tar-heels leathers
taring rating
tarn rant
tarnishes starshine

tarns   rants; starn
taro   Orta; rota; Tora
taroc   actor; Crato; Croat
tarocs   actors; castor; Castro; Croats;
    scrota
taros   Astor; roast; rotas; Sarto;
    Troas
tarot   ottar
tarots   stator
tarpan   trapan
tarpans   Spartan; trapans
Tarpeian   Patarine
tarpon   patron
tarred   darter; dartre; retard; trader
tarried   tardier
tarries   tarsier
tars   arts; rats; star; tsar
tarsal   altars; astral; talars
tarsel   alerts; alters; artels; laster;
    ratels; salter; slater; staler; stelar
tarsels   artless; lasters; salters;
    slaters
tarsi   airts; astir; raits; sitar; Sitra;
    stair; stria; Trias
tarsia   arista; tiaras
tarsier   tarries
Tarsipes   pastries; piastres;
    raspiest; traipses
Tarsus   Rastus; Straus; sutras
tartan   rattan; Tantra
tartans   rattans; Tantras
tarted   ratted; tetrad
tartine   intreat; iterant; nattier;
    nitrate; tertian
tartines   intreats; nitrates; straiten
tartish   athirst
tartlet   tattler
tartlets   tattlers
tarts   start
tarty   ratty
tarweed   watered
tasar   ratas
tash   hast; hats
tashed   deaths; hasted; 'sdeath
tashes   ashets; hastes
tashing   hasting
task   kats; skat; taks
tasked   skated; staked
tasker   skater; strake; streak; takers
taskers   skaters; strakes; streaks
tasking   skating; staking; takings
Tasman   mantas
tasse   asset; sates; seats; Tessa

tassel   slates; stales; steals; teslas
tasses   assets
tassie   siesta
tassies   siestas
Tasso   assot; oasts; stoas
taste   state; tates; teats; testa
tasted   stated
tasteless   stateless
taster   aretts; stater; taters; tetras;
    treats
tasters   staters
tastes   states
tastier   artiste; attires; striate
tasting   Sittang; stating
Tatar   attar
Tatars   strata
tate   Etta; teat
tater   arett; tetra; treat
taters   aretts; stater; taster; tetras;
    treats
tates   state; taste; teats; testa
tath   that
tatler   latter; rattle
tatlers   rattles; slatter; starlet;
    startle; Telstar
tatters   stretta
tattier   attrite; titrate
tattler   tartlet
tattlers   tartlets
tatu   taut
tatus   tauts
taube   beaut; Butea; tubae
Tauber   arbute
taubes   beauts
taunted   attuned
taunting   attuning
taunts   tutsan
taurine   ruinate; uranite; urinate
taut   tatu
tauts   tatus
taver   avert; trave
tavered   averted
tavering   averting; vintager
taverns   servant; versant
tavers   averts; starve; traves; vaster
taw   twa; wat
tawer   water; wrate
tawers   waster; waters
tawery   watery
tawnier   tinware
tawny   wanty
taws   staw; swat; twas; wast
tawse   sweat; waste

tawses   sawset; sweats; wastes
taxer   extra
taxers   astrex; extras
taxes   Texas
taxors   storax
tayras   astray; satyra
tea   ate; eat; eta; tae
tea-bag   atabeg
tea-bags   atabegs
teach   cheat; tache; theca
teacher   cheater; hectare
teachers   cheaters; hectares
teaches   escheat
teaching   cheating
teacups   cuspate
teagle   eaglet; Galtee; gelate; legate;
  telega
teagles   eaglets; legates; telegas
teak   Kate; keta; take
teaks   Keats; skate; Skeat; stake;
  steak; takes
teal   et al.; late; leat; tael; tale;
  tela
teals   least; leats; slate; Stael; stale;
  steal; stela; taels; tales; tesla
team   mate; meat; Meta; tame; Tema
teaming   mintage; tegmina
teams   mates; meats; Mesta; steam;
  tames
teamwork   workmate
Tean   ante; Aten; etna; neat
Teans   antes; etnas; nates; Nesta;
  Senta; stane; stean
teapot   aptote
teapots   aptotes
tear   aret; rate; tare
tear-drop   parroted; predator;
  prorated
tear-drops   predators
tearer   re-rate
tearers   re-rates; serrate
tearing   Geraint; granite; ingrate;
  Tangier
tearless   stealers; tesseral
tea-rose   roseate
tear-pit   partite
tears   arets; aster; astre; earst; rates;
  reast; resat; stare; strae; tares; teras
teas   east; eats; sate; seat; seta; taes
tease   setae
teased   easted; seated; sedate
teasel   elates; steale; stelae
teasels   steales

teaser   arêtes; easter; eaters; reates;
  reseat; saeter; Teresa
teasers   easters; reseats; saeters;
  tessera
tea-set   estate; testae
tea-sets   estates
teasing   easting; Gastein; genista;
  ingates; ingesta; seating; tangies;
  tsigane
teat   Etta; tate
teats   state; taste; tates; testa
tea-urn   aunter; nature; Neutra
tea-urns   aunters; natures; saunter
tebbad   tabbed
tebbads   stabbed
Tebet   Bette
tec   etc.
tech   echt; etch
techs   chest
tectonic   concetti
tedious   outside
teem   meet; mete; Teme
teeming   meeting
teems   meets; metes; Temes; temse
teen   eten; nete; tene
teenager   generate; green tea;
  renegate
teenagers   generates; renegates
teens   etens; steen; tense
teer   rete; tree
teering   integer; treeing
teers   ester; reest; reset; retes; steer;
  stere; terse; trees
tees   Este; Sète
teeter   terete
teeth   thete
teg   get
tegmina   mintage; teaming
tegs   gest; gets
Teheran   earthen; hearten
Tehran   anther; thenar
tehrs   Herts.; Resht
teil   tile
teils   islet; istle; steil; stile; tiles
teind   tined
tel   elt; let
tela   et al.; late; leat; tael; tale; teal
telae   elate
telega   eaglet; Galtee; gelate; legate;
  teagle
telegas   eaglets; legates; teagles
telephony   polythene
teleran   eternal

telesis tieless
tellar taller
tellars stellar
teller retell
tellers retells
tells stell
tellurian ill-nature
tels elts; lest; lets
telson Solent; stolen
Telstar rattles; slatter; starlet;
 startle; tatlers
Tema mate; meat; Meta; tame; team
Teme meet; mete; teem
Temes meets; metes; teems;
 temse
tempera Tampere
temperated attempered
temperating attempering
Templar trample
Templars tramples
template palmette
templates palmettes
temple pelmet
temples pelmets; stempel; stemple
temporise peristome
temporises peristomes
tems stem
temse meets; metes; teems; Temes
ten net
tenable Beltane
tenace cetane
tend dent
tended dented
tender rented; terned
tenderising ingredients
tenders sterned
tending denting
tendon Denton
tends dents; stend
tene eten; nete; teen
Tenebrae bean tree
Tenedos denotes
tenesmus muteness
Teniers entires; entries; Steiner;
 trenise
tenioid edition
tenner rennet
tenners rennets
tennis sennit; sinnet
tenon nonet; tonne
tenoned Edenton
tenons Neston; nonets; sonnet;
 stonen; tenson; tonnes

tenor noter; trone
tenors noters; Reston; stoner;
 tensor; Terson; trones
Tenos Eston; notes; onset, seton;
 stone; tones
tenpins spinnet
tenrec center; centre; recent
tenrecs centers; centres
tens nest; nets; sent; sten
tense etens; steen; teens
tensed nested; sedent
tenser enters; Ernest; nester;
 rentes; resent; Sterne; ternes
tenses steens
tensing nesting
tension intones; Sonnite
tenson Neston; nonets; sonnet;
 stonen; tenons; tonnes
tensons sonnets; Stenson
tensor noters; Reston; stoner;
 tenors; Terson; trones
tensors stoners
tent nett
tentative attentive
tented detent; netted
tenters testern
tenting netting
tents stent
tenty netty
tenuis unites; unties
tenure neuter; retune; tureen
tenures neuters; retunes; tureens
Teos toes; tose
tequila liquate
terai irate
teraph threap
teras arets; aster; astre; earst; rates;
 reast; resat; stare; strae; tares; tears
terbia baiter; barite
terce Crete; erect
terefah feather
Teresa arêtes; easter; eaters; reates;
 reseat; saeter; teaser
Teresina trainees
terete teeter
terga grate; great; Greta; targe
tergiversation interrogatives
Termes merest; Mestre; meters;
 metres
terminal tramline
terminals tramlines
terminates martensite
termini interim; mintier

termless smelters
termly myrtle
termor tremor
termors tremors
tern rent
ternal altern; antler; learnt; rental
ternaries Eritreans; rain-trees;
  retainers
ternate entreat; ratteen
terne enter; rente; treen
terned rented; tender
ternes enters; Ernest; nester;
  rentes; resent; Sterne; tenser
Terni inert; inter; nitre; trine
terning renting; ringent
ternion intoner
ternions intoners
terns Ernst; rents; stern
terpenes pretense
terpsichorean cheiropterans
terra arrêt; rater
terrace caterer; retrace
terraced retraced
terraces caterers; retraces
terracing retracing
terrain trainer
terrains restrain; strainer; trainers;
  transire
terrapins transpire
terras arrest; arrêts; raster; raters;
  Sartre; starer
terrene enterer; re-enter
terrenes enterers; re-enters;
  resenter
terries étriers; reiters; retires;
  retries
terrine reinter; rentier
terrines reinsert; reinters;
  rentiers
territ ritter; triter
territs ritters
terrorise roisterer
terrorises roisterers
terry retry; tryer
terse ester; reest; reset; retes; steer;
  stere; teers; trees
tersely restyle
terser rester
tersest setters; streets; testers
Terson noters; Reston; stoner;
  tenors; tensor; trones
tertian intreat; iterant; nattier;
  nitrate; tartine

tesla least; leats; slate; Stael; stale;
  steal; stela; taels; tales; teals
teslas slates; stales; steals; tassel
Tess sets
Tessa asset; sates; seats; tasse
tessera easters; reseats; saeters;
  teasers
tesseral stealers; tearless
Tessin insets; sets in; steins
test sett; stet
testa state; taste; tates; teats
testae estate; tea-set
testament statement
testaments statements
test-ban battens
test-case cassette
test-cases cassettes
tested detest
tester setter; street
testern tenters
testers setters; streets; tersest
testes sestet; tsetse
testicular trisulcate
testier Trieste
testily stylite
testing setting
testril litters; slitter; stilter; tilters;
  titlers
test run entrust; nutters
test runs entrusts
tests setts
tetanic nictate
tetanus attunes
tetra arett; tater; treat
tetrad ratted; tarted
tetrads started
tetras aretts; stater; taster; taters;
  treats
Tetuán attune
tew ewt; wet
tewarts Stewart; swatter
tewing twinge
tewit twite
tewits twites
tews ewts; stew; west; wets
Texans sextan
Texas taxes
thae eath; hate; heat; Thea
Thais saith; taish
thaler halter; lather
Thales haslet; lathes; Shelta
Thame Meath
Thames smeath

than tanh
thane neath
thanes Athens; hasten; snathe; sneath
thar hart; rath; tahr
thars harts; raths; tahrs; trash
Thasos hoasts; hostas; shoats
that tath
thaw Wath; what
thawer wreath
thawers wreaths
thaws swath
the eth; het
Thea eath; hate; heat; thae
theater theatre; thereat
theaters theatres
theatre theater; thereat
theatres theaters
Thebaid habited
Thebes behest
theca cheat; tache; teach
thecal chalet; Thecla
Thecla chalet; thecal
thee ethe
thees sheet; these
theics itches
thein thine
their Erith
theirs Thiers
theism Themis
Theiss heists; shiest; shites; sithes; thesis
theist Thetis; tithes
theistic ethicist; itchiest
the Lamb Lambeth
Thelma Eltham; hamlet
themes smeeth
Themis theism
then hent
thenar anther; Tehran
thenars anthers
theologic ethologic
theological ethological
theologist ethologist
theologists ethologists
theology ethology
Thera earth; Harte; hater; heart; Herat; rathe; thrae
there ether; three
thereat theater; theatre
therein neither
Theresa heaters; reheats
thermos mothers; smother

these sheet; thees
theses sheets
thesis heists; shiest; shites; sithes; Theiss
thete teeth
Thetis theist; tithes
thew whet
thews whets
thible blithe
thicken kitchen
thickened kitchened
thickener kitchener
thickeners kitcheners
thickening kitchening
thickens kitchens
thickest thickets; thickset
thickets thickest; thickset
thicks kitsch
thickset thickest; thickets
Thiers theirs
Thiès heist; shite; sithe
thigh hight
thighs hights
thigs sight
thin hint; Nith
thine thein
thing night
things nights
thinker rethink
thinkers rethinks
thins hints
third thrid
thirds thrids
this hist; hits; shit; sith; Tshi
thistle Lettish; lithest
tho' hot
thole helot; hotel
tholes helots; hostel; hotels
tholi litho
Thor thro'
Thora Horta; Torah
thoracic trochaic
thorn north
thorned northed; throned
thorning northing; throning
thorns norths
thorny rhyton
thorpe pother
thorpes pothers; strophe
those ethos; shote
thous shout; south
thousand hand-outs
thowel howlet

thowels howlets
thrae earth; Harte; hater; heart;
  Herat; rathe; Thera
thrashes harshest
thraves harvest
thraw wrath
thread dearth; hatred; red-hat
threads dearths; hardest; hatreds;
  red-hats; trashed
thready hydrate
threap teraph
threat hatter
threats hatters; rathest; shatter
three ether; there
threes Esther; ethers; Hester
threne nether
thrice cither
thrid third
thrids thirds
thripses hipsters
thro' Thor
throb broth
throbs broths
throe other
throes others; Rothes; tosher
throne hornet; Horten
throned northed; thorned
thrones hornets; shorten
throning northing; thorning
throw worth; wroth
throwing ingrowth; Worthing
thru hurt; ruth; Thur
thrust truths
Thun hunt
Thur hurt; ruth; thru
Thurles hurtles; hustler
thus huts; shut; tush
thyrsi Irtysh; shirty
ti it
tiaraed radiate
tiaras arista; tarsia
Tiaret attire; ratite
Tib bit
Tiber biter; rebit; tribe
Tibet Betti
Tibur bruit
tic cit
tice Ceti; cite
tices cites
tickers rickets; Sickert; sticker
tickle Keltic
tickler trickle
ticklers stickler; strickle; trickles

tickles stickle
ticks stick
tics cist; cits
tic-tac tactic
tic-tacs tactics
tiddlers striddle
tide diet; dite; edit; tied
tided dited
tide-rips spirited
tides deist; diets; dites; edits; id est;
  sited; St. Dié; stied
tidiness insisted
tidying dignity
tied diet; dite; edit; tide
tieless telesis
tier Riet; rite; tire
tierce cerite; recite
tiercels sclerite
tierces recites
tiering igniter; tigrine
tie-rod editor; rioted; triode
tie-rods editors; roisted; rosited;
  sortied; steroid; storied; triodes
tiers reist; resit; rites; Siret; tires;
  tries
ties site; stie
tiffs stiff
tige gite
tiger Tigre
tiger-nut uttering
tiges gites
tigon ingot
tigons ingots; stingo; tosing
Tigre tiger
tigress Striges
tigrine igniter; tiering
tigs gist
Tijuana Juanita
tike kite
tikes kites; skite
til lit
tilde tiled
tildes idlest; listed; silted
tile teil
tiled tilde
tiler litre; relit
tilers lister; litres
tiles islet; istle; steil; stile; teils
till lilt
tillages legalist; stillage
tilled lilted
tiller rillet
tillered tredille

tillers   rillets; stiller; trellis
tilling   lilting
tills   lilts; still
tilted   titled
tilter   litter; titler
tilters   litters; slitter; stilter; testril;
    titlers
tilting   titling
tilts   stilt
timbale   limbate
timbales   balmiest
timber   betrim; timbre
timbers   betrims; timbres
timbre   betrim; timber
timbres   betrims; timbers
time   emit; item; mite
timed   demit
timer   merit; mitre; remit
timers   merits; mister; mitres;
    remits; smiter
times   emits; items; metis; mites;
    smite; stime
time-saving   negativism
timings   misting; smiting; stiming
Timon   Minot
Timor Sea   amortise; atomiser
tin   nit
Tina   ain't; Tain
tin can   tannic
tin cans   stannic
tind   dint
tinded   dinted
tinder   rident; trined
tinding   dinting
tinds   dints
tinea   entia; Taine
tinean   innate
tineas   tisane
tined   teind
tineid   indite
tines   inset; neist; set in; stein
tinged   nidget
tinges   ingest; signet
tingled   glinted
tingler   ringlet; tringle
tinglers   ringlets; sterling; tringles
tingles   glisten; singlet
tingling   glinting
tin god   doting
tings   sting
tink   knit
tinkers   Inkster; stinker
tinklers   strinkle

tinkles   lentisk
tinks   knits; skint; stink
tinned   indent; intend
tinner   intern
tinners   interns
tins   nits
tinsel   enlist; inlets; listen; silent
tinsels   enlists; listens
tinters   stinter
tints   stint; 'tisn't
tinware   tawnier
tip   pit
tipper   Pripet
tippler   ripplet; tripple
tipplers   ripplets; stippler; tripples
tipples   stipple
tips   pits; spit
tipster   pitters; spitter
tipsters   spitters
tiptoes   potties
tirade   airted; raited
tirades   asterid; astride; diaster;
    disrate; staired
Tiranë   Nerita; ratine; retain; retina
tirasse   satires
tire   Riet; rite; tier
tired   tried
tiredness   dissenter; residents
tireless   leisters
tires   reist; resit; rites; Siret; tiers;
    tries
Tir na n-Og   ignorant
tiro   riot; tori; trio
tiroes   sortie; tories
tiros   riots; roist; rosit; trios
tis   its; sit
tisane   tineas
tisanes   entasis; Saintes; sestina;
    Staines; tansies
'tisn't   stint; tints
tissue   suites
titan   taint; tanti
titans   taints; tanist
titfer   fitter
titfers   fitters
tither   hitter
tithers   hitters
tithes   theist; Thetis
titled   tilted
titler   litter; tilter
titlers   litters; slitter; stilter; testril;
    tilters
titles   stilet

titling   tilting
titrate   attrite; tattier
titration   attrition
titre   trite
titres   sitter; trites
titters   tritest
titup   putti
Tiw   Twi; wit
Tlemcen   clement
Tlingits   slitting; stilting
tmesis   misset; smites; stimes
toad   dato
toads   datos
toady   today
toast   stoat
toaster   Rosetta; rotates; to-tears
toasting   Tsingtao
toasts   stoats
Tobago   Bogota
toccatas   staccato
tocher   hector; rochet; troche
tochered   hectored
tochering   hectoring
tochers   hectors; rochets; torches;
   troches
toco   coot
tocsin   tonics
tocsins   consist
tod   dot
today   toady
toddlers   stroddle; strodled
tods   dost; dots
toecap   Capote
toenail   elation
toes   Teos; tose
tofore   foetor; footer; refoot
tog   got
toga   goat; Göta
togaed   dogate; dotage
togas   goats; SOGAT
toggle   goglet
toggles   goglets
toho   hoot; Otho
to-hunga   hang-out
toil   Loti
toile   Eliot
toiler   Loiret; loiter
toilers   Estoril; estriol; loiters
toilet   Lottie
toilets   litotes; T. S. Eliot
toils   Isolt; Solti
toko   koto; took
Tokyo   Kyoto

tola   alto; lota
tolan   notal; talon; tonal
tolas   altos; Salto; Talos
told   dolt
tole   lote
Toledo   looted; tooled
tolerance   coeternal
toles   lotes
tolu   lout; Toul
tom   mot
tombac   combat
tome   mote
tomes   mesto; motes; smote
toms   most; mots
tomtom   motmot
tomtoms   motmots
ton   not
tonal   notal; talon; tolan
Tonbridge   Bridgeton
tone   Eton; note
toned   Donet; noted
toneless   noteless
tones   Eston; notes; onset; seton;
   stone; Tenos
tonga   tango
tongas   Gaston; Sontag; tangos
tonic   Cinto
tonics   tocsin
tonight   hotting
toning   noting
tonne   nonet; tenon
tonnes   Neston; nonets; sonnet;
   stonen; tenons; tenson
tons   onst; snot
tonsorial   torsional
tonsured   roundest; unsorted
took   koto; toko
tool   loot
tooled   looted; Toledo
tooler   looter; Loreto; rootle
toolers   looters; rootles
tooling   looting
tools   loots; lotos; stool
toom   moot
toomed   mooted
tooming   mooting
tooms   moots; smoot
toon   Noto; onto; oont
toot   Otto
tootsies   sootiest
top   opt; pot
tope   poet; pote
toped   depot; opted; poted

toper Porte; repot; trope
topers poster; presto; repost; repots; tropes
topes estop; poets; stoep; stope;
top hat hot tap
top hats hot taps
topic optic; picot
topical Capitol; coal-pit; optical; pit-coal
topically optically
topics optics; picots
toping opting; poting
topis posit
top-line pointel; pontile
topology optology
toppers stopper
toppings stopping
topples stopple
tops opts; post; pots; spot; stop
topside deposit; dopiest; posited
topsides deposits; side-post
tor ort; rot
Tora rota; Orta; taro
Torah Horta; Thora
toran orant; trona
torches hectors; rochets; tochers; troches
tore rote
torero rooter
toreros rooster; rooters
tores estro; roset; rotes; store; torse
tori riot; tiro; trio
tories sortie; tiroes
torments sortment
torn tron
tornado donator; odorant
torpedo trooped
torpid tripod
torque quoter; roquet
torques questor; quoters; roquets
torret retort; rotter
torrets retorts; rotters
tors orts; rots; sort
torsade roasted
torse estro; roset; rotes; store; tores
torses rosets; sortes; stores; tosser
torsional tonsorial
torso roost; roots; stoor
torsos roosts; stoors
tort trot
tortile triolet
tortilla littoral

tortillas littorals
tortoise rootiest
torts trots
torus roust; routs; stour; sutor; tours
tory ryot; troy; tyro
Tosca Ascot; coast; coats; costa
tose Teos; toes
tosed dotes
tosh host; hots; shot
toshed hosted
tosher others; Rothes; throes
toshing hosting
tosing ingots; stingo; tigons
toss sots
tosser rosets; sortes; stores; torses
tosses Sestos
toss-up spouts
tost stot; tots
to-tear rotate
to-tears Rosetta; rotates; toaster
totem motet; motte
totems motets; mottes
totes set-to
tother hotter
Totnes ostent
tots stot; tost
totters stotter; stretto
touch chout; couth
toucher retouch
tough ought
toughs sought
Toul lout; tolu
toupets outstep
tour rout
Touré outer; outré; route
toured detour; douter; outred; red out; routed
tourer retour; router
tourers retours; routers; trouser
touring ring out; routing
tours roust; routs; stour; sutor; torus
toused ousted
touser ouster; outers; routes; souter; trouse
tousers estrous; oestrus; ousters; sourest; souters; trouses; tussore
tousing ousting; outings
tousled loudest
touted duetto
touts stout
tow two; wot

towel owlet
towels Elstow; lowest; owlets
tower twoer; wrote
towers sowter; stower; stowre;
  towser; twoers
towing Wigton
towline two-line
town nowt; wont
towns stown; wonts
tows stow; swot; twos
towsed stowed
towser sowter; stower; stowre;
  towers; twoers
towsers sowters; stowers; stowres
towsing stowing; Wigston
trace caret; carte; cater; crate; react;
  recta
traceable creatable
traced carted; crated; Dectra; redact
tracer arrect; carter; crater
tracers carters; craters
traces carets; cartes; caster; caters;
  crates; Cresta; reacts; recast
tracing carting
tracks strack
trad dart; drat
trade adret; dater; rated; tared;
  tread
trade counters unstercorated
traded darted
trade-in detrain; tan-ride; trained
trader darter; dartre; retard; tarred
traders darters; retards; starred
trades adrets; daters; stared; treads
tradesmen smartened
trading darting
traduce Decatur
tragedy gyrated
tragion orating
traiks straik
trail liart; trial
trailer retiral; retrial
trailers retrials
trailing ringtail
trails trials
train intra; Nitra; riant; Trani
trained detrain; tan-ride; trade-in
trainee Aintree; retinae
trainees Teresina
trainer terrain
trainers restrain; strainer; terrains;
  transire
trains instar; santir; Sintra; strain

traipse parties; piastre; pirates;
  praties
traipses pastries; piastres; raspiest;
  Tarsipes
traits artist; sittar; strait; strati
Tralee relate
tram mart
tramline terminal
tramlines terminals
trample Templar
tramples Templars
tramps stramp
trams marts; smart
trance canter; carnet; creant;
  Cretan; nectar; recant; tanrec
tranced Tancred
trances canters; carnets; Cretans;
  recants; tanrecs
tranche chanter
tranches chanters; snatcher;
  stancher
trangle tangler
trangles strangle; tanglers
Trani intra; Nitra; riant; train
transept patterns
tranships transship
transience nectarines
transient instanter
transire restrain; strainer; terrains;
  trainers
transires restrains; strainers
transom Marston; matrons
transpire terrapins
transpose patroness
transship tranships
trap part; prat; rapt
trapan tarpan
trapans Spartan; tarpans
trape apert; pater; peart; Petra;
  prate; taper
traped depart; parted; petard;
  prated
trapes paster; paters; Praest; prates;
  repast; tapers
trapesed pederast; predates
traping gin trap; parting; prating
trappean apparent
trappers strapper
trappings strapping
traps parts; prats; spart; sprat; strap
trash harts; raths; tahrs; thars
trashed dearths; hardest; hatreds;
  red-hats; threads

trass   stars; tsars
trave   avert; taver
travel   varlet
traveled   Arteveld
travels   varlets; vestral
traves   averts; starve; tavers; vaster
tray   arty
trays   satyr; stray
treacle   Electra
treacles   clearest
tread   adret; dater; rated; tared;
    trade
treader   retread
treaders   retreads; serrated
treading   derating; gradient; red
    giant
treadle   alerted; altered; related
treads   adrets; daters; stared; trades
treason   senator
treasons   assentor; senators;
    star-nose
treasurer   serrature
treat   arett; tater; tetra
treated   aretted
treater   retreat
treaters   retreats
treaties   ariettes; iterates; treatise
treating   aretting
treatise   ariettes; iterates; treaties
treats   aretts; stater; taster; taters;
    tetras
treaty   yatter
Tredegar   garreted; gartered;
    regrated
tredille   tillered
tree   rete; teer
treed   deter
treeing   integer; teering
treen   enter; rente; terne
treenail   elaterin; entailer
treenails   entailers
trees   ester; reest; reset; retes; steer;
    stere; teers; terse
trefoil   loftier
trellis   rillets; stiller; tillers
trema   armet; mater; tamer
tremor   termor
tremors   termors
trenail   entrail; Latiner; latrine;
    ratline; reliant; retinal
trenails   entrails; Latiners; latrines;
    ratlines
trencher   retrench

trenise   entires; entries; Steiner;
    Teniers
trenises   sentries
trentals   slattern
Trento   rotten
trepan   arpent; enrapt; entrap;
    panter; parent
trepans   arpents; entraps; panters;
    parents; pastern
trephine   nephrite
trepidation   partitioned
Tresco   corset; Cortes; coster;
    escort; scoter; sector
trespass   sparsest
tress   rests
tressed   deserts; dessert
tressels   restless
tressing   trigness
tressy   syrtes
trestle   letters; settler; sterlet
trestles   settlers; sterlets
trevis   rivets; stiver; strive
treviss   stivers; strives
trews   strew; wrest
trey   tyre
treys   resty; Steyr; tyres
triable   Alberti; librate
triacid   triadic
triadic   triacid
triads   Astrid
triage   gaiter
triages   agister; gaiters; sea-girt;
    stagier; strigae
trial   liart; trail
trials   trails
triangle   alerting; altering; integral;
    relating
triangles   integrals
Trias   airts; astir; raits; sitar; Sitra;
    stair; stria; tarsi
tribbles   stibbler
tribe   biter; rebit; Tiber
tribes   bestir; bister; bistre; biters
tribunal   turbinal
tribunate   turbinate
tribune   turbine
tribunes   turbines
trice   recti
triced   credit; direct
Tricel   relict
trices   steric
Tricia   iatric
trickle   tickler

trickles   stickler; strickle; ticklers
tridents   strident
tried   tired
tries   reist; resit; rites; Siret; tiers; tires
Trieste   testier
trifle   filter; lifter
trifled   flirted
trifles   filters; lifters; stifler
trifling   flirting
trig   girt; grit
trigness   tressing
trigon   Girton; roting
trigons   sorting; storing
trigs   girts; grist; grits; strig
trikes   strike
trimester   remitters; trimeters
trimeter   remitter
trimeters   remitters; trimester
trimmed   midterm
trimness   minsters
trinal   ratlin
trine   inert; inter; nitre; Terni
trined   rident; tinder
trines   insert; inters; sinter; Strine
tringle   ringlet; tingler
tringles   ringlets; sterling; tinglers
trinket   knitter
trinkets   knitters
trio   riot; tiro; tori
triode   editor; rioted; tie-rod
triodes   editors; roisted; rosited; sortied; steroid; storied; tie-rods
triolet   tortile
triones   in store; orients; stonier
trios   riots; roist; rosit; tiros
trip   ript
tripe   petri; piert
tripes   esprit; priest; Pteris; ripest; sprite; stripe
triple   let rip
triplets   splitter
triplings   split ring; stripling
tripod   torpid
tripodic   dioptric
tripods   disport
tripos   prosit
triposes   ripostes
trippers   stripper
tripple   ripplet; tippler
tripples   ripplets; stippler; tipplers
trips   sprit; stirp; strip
tripsis   spirits

triremes   merriest; rimester
trismus   sistrum; truisms
trisulcate   testicular
trite   titre
triteness   interests; resistent
triter   ritter; territ
trites   sitter; titres
tritest   titters
triune   uniter
triunes   uniters
Troas   Astor; roast; rotas; Sarto; taros
trocar   carrot
trocars   carrots
trochaic   thoracic
troche   hector; rochet; tocher
troches   hectors; rochets; tochers; torches
trod   dort
trolls   stroll
Troms   morts; storm
Tromsö   motors
tron   torn
trona   orant; toran
trone   noter; tenor
trones   noters; Reston; stoner; tenors; tensor; Terson
Troon   Orton
troop   poort; Porto
trooped   torpedo
troopials   spoliator
troops   poorts
trope   Porte; repot; toper
tropes   poster; presto; repost; repots; topers
tropine   pointer; protein; pterion
tropism   imports
tropist   protist
tropists   protists
Troste   otters
trot   tort
trots   torts
trouble   blue-rot; boulter
troubles   boulters
trounce   cornute; counter; recount
trounced   cornuted
trounces   construe; cornutes; counters; recounts
trouncing   cornuting
troupe   pouter
troupes   petrous; posture; pouters; Proteus; septuor; spouter
trouse   ouster; outers; routes; souter; touser

trouser retours; routers; tourers
trouses estrous; oestrus; ousters; sourest; souters; tousers; tussore
trout tutor
trouts strout; tutors
trouvère overture
trouvères overtures
trove overt; voter
trow wort
trowed rowted
trowel wortle
trowels wortles
trows strow; worst; worts
troy ryot; tory; tyro
Troyes oyster; rosety; storey; tyroes; Yes Tor
truce cruet; cuter; eruct
truces cruets; cruset; Custer; eructs; rectus
trucial curtail
trucks struck
trudgen grunted
true Rute
true-love revolute
truest utters
truffle fretful
truisms sistrum; trismus
Truman antrum
trumpets strumpet
trundle rundlet
trundles rundlets
truss rusts
trussed dusters
trusses russets
trust strut; sturt
trusted sturted
trusting sturting
trusts struts; sturts
truths thrust
try Tyr
tryer retry; terry
try on Ryton
Tsabian abstain
Tsabians abstains
Tsana Santa; Satan
tsar arts; rats; star; tars
tsardom stardom
tsarina artisan
tsarinas artisans
tsarism Marists; Ramists
tsarist artists; sittars; straits
tsars stars; trass
T. S. Eliot litotes; toilets

tsetse sestet; testes
tsetses sestets
Tshi hist; hits; shit; sith; this
tsigane easting; Gastein; genista; ingates; ingesta; seating; tangies; teasing
Tsingtao toasting
Tsuga Tagus
tuan aunt; tuna
tub but
tuba abut; buat; tabu
tubae beaut; Butea; taube
tubas abuts; buats; tabus
tube Bute
tubed debut
tuber brute; rebut
tubers brutes; buster; rebuts
tubs bust; buts; stub
tucks stuck
Tucson counts
Tudors Stroud
tug gut
tugs gust; guts
tule lute
tules lutes
Tulsa sault; talus
tumbler tumbrel
tumblers stumbler; tumbrels
tumbles stumble
tumblings stumbling
tumbrel tumbler
tumbrels stumbler; tumblers
tums must; smut; stum
tun nut
tuna aunt; tuan
tunas aunts
tuner urent
tuners unrest
tunes unset; usen't
tungstic cuttings
tunic cut in; incut
tunics cuts in
Tunis inust; suint; units
Tunja jaunt; junta
tuns nuts; stun; Unst
tup put
tups puts
turacin curtain
Turanians Saturnian
turbaned breadnut
turbinal tribunal
turbinate tribunate
turbine tribune

turbines   tribunes
Turco   court
Turcos   courts; scruto
turdine   intrude; untired; untried
turds   durst
tureen   neuter; retune; tenure
tureens   neuters; retunes; tenures
Turin   rutin
Turk   kurt
Turkess   tuskers
turms   strum
turn   runt
turned   retund
turner   return
turners   returns
turnings   unstring
turnips   unstrip
turnover   overturn
turnovers   overturns
turns   runts
turps   spurt
turret   rutter
turrets   rutters
Tuscan   cantus
Tuscans   Sanctus
tush   huts; shut; thus
tuskers   Turkess
tussal   saltus; saults
tusser   estrus; russet
tussore   estrous; oestrus; ousters;
   sourest; souters; tousers; trouses
tutor   trout
tutors   strout; trouts
tutsan   taunts
Tver   vert
twa   taw; wat
twain   witan
twas   staw; swat; taws; wast
twat   watt
twats   watts

tweed   De Wet
tweeds   stewed; wested
tweers   stewer; sweert; wester
Twi   Tiw; wit
twier   twire; write
twiers   sweirt; twires; writes
twiner   winter
twiners   winters
twinge   tewing
twinges   stewing; westing
twire   twier; write
twires   sweirt; twiers; writes
twist   twits
twite   tewit
twites   tewits
twits   twist
two   tow; wot
twoer   tower; wrote
twoers   sowter; stower; stowre;
   towers; towser
two-line   towline
twos   stow; swot; tows
tye   yet
tyes   stey; stye
tyke   kyte
tykes   kytes; skyte
typical   clay-pit
typographer   petrography
typto   potty
typtos   spotty
Tyr   try
tyre   trey
tyres   resty; Steyr; treys
Tyrian   in-tray
Tyrians   in-trays
tyro   ryot; tory; troy
tyroes   oyster; rosety; storey;
   Troyes; Yes Tor
tyros   ryots; story

U

U-boat   about
U-boats   Basuto
U-bolt   boult
U-bolts   boults
udal   auld; dual; laud
udaller   allured
udals   Aldus; lauds
udder   dured
udders   sudder

udo   duo; Oud
ugh   hug
ugly   guly
Uhlans   unlash
Uist   suit
ulan   Luna; ulna
ulcer   cruel; lucre
ulcerous   urceolus
ulcers   cruels

ullages seagull
ulna Luna; ulan
ulnar lunar; urnal
ulnare neural; unreal
ulnares Laurens
ulster luster; lustre; luters; result;
  rustle; sutler
ulstered resulted
ulsters lusters; lustres; results;
  rustles; sutlers
ultimate mutilate
Ultonian Lutonian
Ultonians Lutonians
ultraism altruism
ultraist altruist
ultraistic altruistic
ultraists altruists
umbels umbles
umber brume; umbre
umbers umbres
umbles umbels
umbo ombú
umbos ombús
umbra Burma; rumba
umbral brumal; labrum; lumbar
umbrated drumbeat
umbre brume; umber
umbres umbers
Umbria barium
umlaut mutual
umph hump
umpire impure
umpired dumpier
unable Nabeul; nebula
unaired uranide
unaltered unrelated
unarm Namur
unarmed duramen; manured;
  maunder
unbar buran; urban
unbare unbear; urbane
unbares unbears
unbars burans
unbear unbare; urbane
unbears unbares
unboding bounding
unboiled unilobed
unbred burden; burned
unburden unburned
unburdens sunburned
uncage cangue
uncages cangues
uncarted underact; untraced

uncase usance
uncate Canute
uncertain encurtain; runcinate
unchal launch; nuchal
unchosen nonesuch
uncial Alcuin; Lucian; Lucina
unclaimed undecimal
unclear lucarne; nuclear
uncles Clunes
unclips insculp; sculpin
unclose counsel
unclosed enclouds
uncloses counsels
uncoil Culion
uncope pounce
uncoped pounced
uncopes pounces
uncoping pouncing
uncursed sun-cured
undam maund; Munda
undams maunds; Mundas
undated daunted
unde dune; nude
undecimal unclaimed
undelight unlighted
under Düren; runed; urned
underact uncarted; untraced
underacts undercast
underage dungaree; ungeared
underarm unmarred
underbrush undershrub
undercast underacts
underdo redound; rounded
underdog grounded
underdoing redounding
underfed refunded
underfur unfurred
undergo guerdon; ungored
underleased undersealed
underleasing undersealing
underlying enduringly
undernote undertone
undernotes undertones
undersealed underleased
undersealing underleasing
underset dentures; sederunt;
  undesert
undersets sederunts
undershrub underbrush
underside undesired
undersign sundering
undersigns undressing
undertone undernote

undertones undernotes
undesert dentures; sederunt; underset
undeserve unsevered
undesired underside
undies indues
undoers Öresund; resound; sounder
undrape unpared
undrapes unspared
undreamed maundered
undreaming maundering
undress sunders
undressing undersigns
unearth haunter
unearths haunters
unfelt fluent
unfolder flounder
unfolders flounders
unfolding foundling
unforced frounced
unforested unfostered
unfostered unforested
unfurred underfur
ungainly unlaying
ungeared dungaree; underage
ungilded deluding; indulged
ungird during
ungirth hurting; unright
ungirths unrights
ungods sun-dog; sungod
ungored guerdon; undergo
ungual ungula
ungula ungual
unhalsed unlashed
unhasting hauntings
unhat haunt
unhats haunts; sunhat; Ushant
unhorsed enshroud
uniate auntie
unilobed unboiled
unions unison
unison unions
unite untie
united untied
uniter triune
uniters triunes
unites tenuis; unties
units inust; suint; Tunis
unlace cuneal; launce; Lucena
unlaces censual; launces; unscale
unlaid Lindau
unlash Uhlans

unlashed unhalsed
unlay yulan
unlaying ungainly
unleased unsealed
unleash unshale
unlighted undelight
unlisted insulted
unlit until
unloaded duodenal
unmarred underarm
unmastered unstreamed
unmated untamed
unmined minuend
unnamed mundane
unnoticed continued
unorder rondure; rounder
unorders rondures; rounders
unpaired unrepaid
unpared undrape
unpent punnet
unperch puncher
unpoetical peculation
unqueen Neuquen
unraised denarius; Eridanus
unreal neural; ulnare
unrelated unaltered
unrent runnet
unrepaid unpaired
unreserved unreversed
unrest tuners
unresting insurgent
unreversed unreserved
unright hurting; ungirth
unrights ungirths
unripe punier; purine
unrobe bourne
unrobed bounder; rebound
unrobes bournes
unsainted inundates; unstained
unsay Sunay
unscale censual; launces; unlaces
unscored crunodes
unsealed unleased
unseals sensual
unseat nasute
unseats nasutes
unseeing ingénues
unseens unsense
unsense unseens
unset tunes; usen't
unsets sunset
unsettle lunettes
unsevered undeserve**

unshale unleash
unship punish
unshod hounds; Hudson
unsliced includes; nuclides
unsocial Alcinoüs
unsoiled delusion; insouled
unsorted roundest; tonsured
unspared undrapes
unspent punnets
unspoilt Plotinus
Unst nuts; stun; tuns
unstained inundates; unsainted
unstated Neustadt; untasted
unstayed unsteady
unsteady unstayed
unstercorated trade counters
unstirred intruders
unstop puntos
unstops sunspot
unstreamed unmastered
unstring turnings
unstrip turnips
untame unteam
untamed unmated
untames unteams
untasted Neustadt; unstated
unteach Chanute
unteam untame
unteams untames
untidy nudity
untie unite
untied united
unties tenuis; unites
until unlit
untiled diluent
untimely minutely
untired intrude; turdine; untried
untrace centaur
untraced uncarted; underact
untraces centaurs; Etruscan;
  recusant
untried intrude; turdine; untired
untrod rotund
upbreak break-up
upcast catsup
upcasts catsups
upclose close-up; couples; opuscle
upcloses close-ups; Scopelus
up-ends send-up; upsend
uphold hold-up
upholds hold-ups
uplander pendular
upled duple; puled

up-line line-up; lupine
up-lines line-ups; lupines; spinule
upon noup; Puno
uppers supper
upraise Piraeus; spuriae
uprear parure
uprears parures
uprise Epirus
uprises suspire
uprisings suspiring
uprist purist; spruit; stir up
ups pus; sup
upsend send-up; up-ends
upsends send-ups
upset set-up; stupe
upsets stupes
uptrain puritan
uptrains puritans; Rasputin
uptrend prudent
uracil curial; Uralic
Uralic curial; uracil
Urals Larus; sural
uranide unaired
uranism Surinam
uranite ruinate; taurine; urinate
urban buran; unbar
urbane unbare; unbear
urceolus ulcerous
urdé dure; rude; rued
ure rue
urent tuner
ures Reus; rues; ruse; sure; user
uresis issuer
urgent gunter; gurnet
urges surge
urinals insular
urinate ruinate; taurine; uranite
urinated daturine; indurate;
  ruinated
urinates Neustria
urine inure
urn nur; run
urnal lunar; ulnar
urned Düren; runed; under
urns nurs; runs
Urodela roulade
Ursa rusa; sura
ursine insure; inures; rusine
urticates rusticate
usable suable
usager argues; augers; sauger;
  Segura
usance uncase

use sue
used deus; dues; Duse; sued
used cars crusades
Usedom moused; soumed
usen't tunes; unset
user Reus; rues; ruse; sure; ures
users Reuss; ruses
uses sues
Ushant haunts; sunhat; unhats
usher huers
ushers rhesus; rushes
using suing
usurped pursued
usurper pursuer
usurpers pursuers

usurping pursuing
Utah haut
utas saut
utensil luniest
uterine retinue; reunite
uterus suture
Utes suet
Utopian Opuntia
utterer reutter
utterers reutters
uttering tiger-nut
utters truest
uva vau
uveal Le Vau; value

V

Vaal Alva; aval; lava
vacate caveat
vacates caveats
vade Dave; deva; Veda
vaded Vedda
vades devas; saved; Vedas
vae ave; Eva
vaes Aves; save; vase
vaginate navigate
vaguest Gustave
vail vali; vial
vails Alvis; Salvi; silva; valis; vials
vain Ivan; vina
vainer Erivan; ravine; Vanier
vains savin
vair Ravi; riva
Valais avails; saliva; salvia
vale lave; leva; veal; vela
valence enclave
valences enclaves
valentine Levantine
vales Elvas; laves; salve; selva;
    slave; valse
valets vestal
vali vail; vial
valiant Latvian
valis Alvis; Salvi; silva; vails; vials
valise Aviles; Leavis
vallar larval
Valona Avalon; Avlona
valse Elvas; laves; salve; selva;
    slave; vales
valsed salved; slaved
valses salves; selvas; slaves

valsing salving; slaving
value Le Vau; uveal
vamose amoves
vamper revamp
vampers revamps
vane Evan; nave; Neva; vena
vanes avens; Evans; naves; Sevan
vaneless enslaves
Vanier Erivan; ravine; vainer
vanishers varnishes
vapid pavid
Varde drave; raved; Revda
vare Arve; aver; rave; Vera
varec carve; caver; crave
vares avers; raves; saver
Varese averse; reaves
varices viscera
varier arrive; Rivera
variers arrives
varies Servia
various saviour
variously savourily
varlet travel
varlets travels; vestral
varnishes vanishers
vasa Sava
vasal lavas
vase Aves; save; vaes
vases saves
vast vats
vaster averts; starve; tavers; traves
vaticide cavitied
vats vast
vau uva

vaulters vestural
veal lave; leva; vale; vela
Vectis civets; evicts
vector corvet; covert
vectors corvets; coverts
Veda Dave; deva; vade
Vedantic ci-devant
Vedas devas; saved; vades
Vedda vaded
Vedic viced
vee eve
veer ever
veered reeved
veering reeving
veers serve; sever; verse
vees eves
Vega gave
veil evil; Levi; live; vile; vlei
veils Elvis; evils; levis; lives; slive
vein vine
veined endive; envied
veinous envious; niveous
veins Nevis; vines; visne
vela lave; leva; vale; veal
velar laver; ravel; Reval
Veles elves
velour louver; louvre
velours louvers; louvres
vena Evan; nave; Neva; vane
venal elvan; levan; navel
venality natively
venation innovate
vender Denver; nerved; Verden
veneer enerve
veneers enerves
Vener erven; nerve; never; Verne
venerate enervate
venerated enervated
venerates enervates
venerating enervating
veneration enervation
venge Negev
venial alevin; alvine
Venice evince
Venlo novel; Vlonë
Ventris inverts; striven
Vera Arve; aver; rave; vare
verbose observe; obverse
Verden Denver; nerved; vender
Verdi diver; drive; rived
veriest restive
verifiers versifier
verily livery

veritable avertible
vermian Minerva
vernal nerval
vernation nervation
Verne erven; nerve; never; Vener
Verona Averno
Veronica Corvinae
versal lavers; ravels; salver; serval;
    slaver
versals salvers; servals; slavers
versant servant; taverns
versatile relatives
verse serve; sever; veers
versed served
verser revers; server
versers servers
verses serves; severs; Sèvres
versifier verifiers
versine enviers; inverse; Viersen
versines inverses
versing serving
version renvois
verso overs; roves; Serov; servo
verst verts
vert Tver
verticals cat-silver
verts verst
very ryve
Vespa paves
vespertine presentive
vest vets
vesta stave
vestal valets
vestas staves
vested devest
vestral travels; varlets
vestural vaulters
veto vote
vetoed devote
vets vest
vial vail; vali
vials Alvis; Salvi; silva; vails; valis
viand divan; Dvina
viands divans
vibes Bevis
vice cive
viced Vedic
vicegerent viceregent
vicegerents viceregents
vice-presidents predictiveness
viceregent vicegerent
viceregents vicegerents
vices cives

Vichy chivy
Vida avid; diva
vied Devi; dive
Viersen enviers; inverse; versine
vies Ives; vise
Viet-Cong coveting
view wive
viewer review
viewers reviews
views swive; wives
vigilante genitival
vikings skiving
vilde devil; lived
vile evil; Levi; live; veil; vlei
vilely evilly; lively
vileness evilness
Vilna Alvin; anvil; nival
vina Ivan; vain
vinas Sivan
vine vein
vinegar reaving
viner riven
vines Nevis; veins; visne
vintager averting; tavering
viola Oliva
violaceous olivaceous
violated dovetail
violet olivet
violets olivets
viperous pervious; previous
viral rival
virent invert
virgin Irving; riving
visa Avis; siva
visaed advise; Davies
visas Sivas
viscera varices
visceral calivers; claviers

vise Ives; vies
vised dives
viséed devise; sieved
visitant nativist
visitants nativists
visne Nevis; veins; vines
visored devisor; devoirs; voiders
vitrine inviter
vitrines inviters
vivers vivres
vivres vivers
vlei evil; Levi; live; veil; vile
vleis Elvis; evils; levis; lives; slive; veils
Vlonë novel; Venlo
void Ovid
voided devoid
voider devoir
voiders devisor; devoirs; visored
voile olive
vola Olav; oval
vole love
voled loved
voles loves; slove; solve
voling Gonvil; loving
volley lovely
Volsci Clovis
volt VTOL
vomer mover
vomers movers
vote veto
voter overt; trove
voters stover; strove
votes stove
vowels wolves
Vratca cravat
VTOL volt

W

wabble bawble
wabbles bawbles
wad daw
wadd dawd
wadded dawded
waddle dawdle
waddled dawdled
waddler dawdler; drawled
waddlers dawdlers; swaddler
waddles dawdles; swaddle
waddling dawdling

wade awed
wade in dewani; wained
wader Dewar; wared
waders sawder; Seward
wades sawed
wads daws; swad
wadset stawed; wasted
wae awe
waesome awesome
wafters fretsaw
wagered Edgware; ragweed

wages swage
wags swag
wail wali
wailed Dewali
wained dewani; wade in
wains swain
waist waits
waisted dawties
waister waiters; wariest
waisters waitress
waited dawtie
waiters waister; wariest
waitress waisters
waits waist
wake weak; weka
waker wreak
wakers wreaks
wakes askew; wekas
Walden lawned
wale weal
waled dwale; lawed; weald
wales Lawes; swale; sweal; weals
wali wail
waling lawing
walk lawk
walks lawks
wallets setwall
wallows swallow
waly yawl
wan awn
wand dawn
wander Andrew; Darwen; dawner;
    warden; warned
wandered dawnered
wandering dawnering
wanders dawners; wardens
wands dawns
wane anew; Ewan; wean
waned awned; dewan
wanes sewan; weans
wang gnaw
wangler Wrangel; wrangle
wanglers wrangles
wangs gnaws; swang
waning awning
wanker Newark
wankers swanker
wankle knawel
wanks swank
wanty tawny
wap paw
waps paws; spaw; swap; wasp
war raw

warble bawler
warbled brawled
warbler brawler
warblers brawlers
warbles bawlers
warbling brawling
ward draw
warded Edward
warden Andrew; Darwen; dawner;
    wander; warned
wardens dawners; wanders
warder drawer; redraw; reward;
    warred
warders drawers; redraws;
    rewards
warding drawing
wards draws; sward
ware Rewa; wear
wared Dewar; wader
warely lawyer
wares sawer; sware; swear; wears
warier Rewari
wariest waister; waiters
waring rawing
warm mawr
warmers swarmer
warms mawrs; swarm
warn rawn
warned Andrew; Darwen; dawner;
    wander; warden
warner warren
warners warrens
warns rawns
warp wrap
warper prewar
warps wraps
warred drawer; redraw; reward;
    warder
warren warner
warrens warners
warst straw; swart; warts; wrast
warts straw; swart; warst; wrast
wary awry
was saw
wase awes
wash haws; shaw
washer hawser; whares
washers hawsers; swasher
wasp paws; spaw; swap; waps
wasps swaps
wast staw; swat; taws; twas
waste sweat; tawse
wasted stawed; wadset

226

waster tawers; waters
wastes sawset; sweats; tawses
wasting stawing
wat taw; twa
watch-dog dog-watch
water tawer; wrate
watered tarweed
waterfalls Fats Waller
water-hen wreathen
wateriness earwitness
waters tawers; waster
watery tawery
Wath thaw; what
watt twat
watts twats
wavers swarve
way yaw
wayboard broadway
wayboards broadways
ways sway
weak wake; weka
weal wale
weald dwale; lawed; waled
weals Lawes; swale; sweal; wales
wean anew; Ewan; wane
weans sewan; wanes
wear Rewa; ware
Weardale Delaware
wearers swearer
weariest sweatier
wears sawer; sware; swear; wares
weasels aweless
weather whereat; wreathe
weathers wreathes
webster bestrew
websters bestrews
wed dew
weds dews
wee ewe
weeders sweered
weeds sewed; swede; sweed
weedy Dewey
weels Lewes; sewel; sweel; Wesel
ween enew
weened enewed
weening enewing
weens enews; sewen
weepers sweeper
weeps sweep
wees ewes; swee
weid wide
weil wiel; wile
weils lewis; wiels; wiles

weir wire
weird wider; wired
weirs sweir; swire; wires; wiser
weka wake; weak
wekas askew; wakes
weld lewd
welder lewder
welkin winkle
well-doer rowelled
well-doing dowelling
wells swell
Wels slew
welters swelter; wrestle
welting winglet
welts swelt
Wem mew
wen new
Wendic winced
wens news; sewn
went newt
were ewer
wersh shrew
Werther wherret
Wesel Lewes; sewel; sweel; weels
Weser ewers; sewer; sweer
Wesker skewer
west ewts; stew; tews; wets
wested stewed; tweeds
wester stewer; sweert; tweers
westering swingtree
westers stewers
westing stewing; twinges
wests stews
wet ewt; tew
wets ewts; stew; tews; west
wettish whitest
wey wye; yew
weys wyes; yews
whale wheal
whales wheals
whalings shawling
wham hawm
whams hawms; shawm
whares hawser; washer
what thaw; Wath
wheal whale
wheals whales
wheatear a-weather
wheats swathe
wheedle wheeled
wheeled wheedle
wheels shewel
when hewn

where hewer
whereat weather; wreathe
whereon Erewhon; nowhere
wherret Werther
whet thew
whets thews
whines newish
whinge hewing
whinges hewings; shewing
whirtles whistler
whissed Swedish; swished
whisses swishes
whissing swishing
whist swith; whits
whistler whirtles
whit with
white withe
whiter wither; writhe
white rose otherwise
whites withes
whitest wettish
whits swith; whist
whity withy
who how
whoever however
whom Mhow
whores shower
wide weid
widely wieldy
widen dwine; Edwin; wined
wideness dewiness
widens dwines; Widnes
wider weird; wired
Widnes dwines; widens
wiel weil; wile
wield Wilde; wiled
wieldy widely
wiels lewis; weils; wiles
wigan awing
wiggler wriggle
wigglers wriggles
Wigner winger
wigs swig
Wigston stowing; towsing
Wigton towing
Wilde wield; wiled
wildness swindles; windless
wile weil; wiel
wiled wield; Wilde
wiles lewis; weils; wiels
willer Irwell
wills swill
wilting witling

winced Wendic
wincher new rich
winchers Schwerin
winded dwined
winder rewind
winders rewinds
winding dwining
windless swindles; wildness
windroses rowdiness; wordiness
wined dwine; Edwin; widen
wines sewin; sinew; swine
winge Ewing
winger Wigner
wingers swinger
winges sewing; swinge
wingless swingles
winglet welting
wings swing
winker Wrekin
winkers swinker
winkle welkin
winks swink
winsey sinewy
winter twiner
winters twiners
winze wizen
winzes wizens
wipers swiper
wipes swipe
wire weir
wired weird; wider
wires sweir; swire; weirs; wiser
wiser sweir; swire; weirs; wires
wishers swisher
wist wits
wit Tiw; Twi
witan twain
with whit
withe white
wither whiter; writhe
withers swither; writhes
withes whites
within inwith
without outwith
withy whity
witling wilting
wits wist
wive view
wives swive; views
wizen winze
wizens winzes
woalds dowlas
wobbly by-blow

Woden endow; nowed; owned
woe owe
woes owes
wolf flow; fowl
wolfed flowed; fowled
wolfer flower; fowler; reflow
wolfers flowers; fowlers; reflows
wolfing flowing; fowling
wolves vowels
won now; own
wont nowt; town
wonts stown; towns
wop pow
wops pows; sowp; swop
wordier worried
wordily rowdily
wordiness rowdiness; windroses
words drows; sword
wordy dowry; rowdy
wore ower; owre
work-basket basketwork
worker rework
workers reworks
workhouse housework
work-master master-work
work-mate team-work
work-out outwork
workpiece piece-work
worried wordier
worse owers; serow; sower; swore
worsed dowers; dowser; drowse
worsen owners; rowens
worsens New Ross
worser rowers
worst strow; trows; worts
worsted strowed
worsting strowing
worsts strows
wort rowt; trow
worth rowth; throw; worth
Worthing ingrowth; throwing
wortle trowel
wortles trowels
worts strow; trows; worst

wot tow
wounder rewound
wounds swound
Wrangel wangler; wrangle
wrangle wangler; Wrangel
wrangles wanglers
wrap warp
wraps warps
wrasse sawers; swears
wrast straw; swart; warst; warts
wrate tawer; water
wrath thraw
wreak waker
wreaks wakers
wreath thawer
wreathe weather; whereat
wreathen water-hen
wreathes weathers
wreaths thawers
Wrekin winker
wrest strew; trews
wrested strewed
wrester strewer
wresters strewers
wresting strewing
wrestle swelter; welters
wrestles swelters
wrests strews
wriggle wiggler
wriggles wigglers
wringed redwing
wrist writs
write twier; twire
writes sweirt; twiers; twires
writhe whiter; wither
writhes swither; withers
writs wrist
wroken knower
wrong grown
wrote tower; twoer
wroth rowth; throw; worth
wye wey; yew
wyes weys; yews

X

xanthein xanthine
xanthine xanthein
Xema exam
xenial alexin

xerotic excitor
xylic cylix
xyst Styx
xysti sixty

Y

yacht Cathy
yager gayer
yah hay
Yahve heavy
yak Kay
yald lady
y'all ally
yam Amy; may; Mya
Yamal Malay
yamen Mayen; meany
yamens yes-man
yams mays
yanker Kearny
yap pay; pya
yaps pays; spay
yard adry; dray
yards drays
yare aery; Ayer; eyra; year
yarely yearly
yarest estray; reasty; stayer
yarn nary; Ryan
yarned denary
yarns snary
yarrow arrowy
yatter treaty
yaw way
yawl waly
yawled Dawley
yawls swaly; swayl
yaws sway; ways
ybet byte
ydred reddy
yea aye
yead Eday
year aery; Ayer; eyra; yare
yeard deary; deray; rayed; ready
yearded derayed
yearding deraying; readying
yeards derays
yearling layering; relaying
yearly yarely
yearn renay
yearned deanery; renayed
yearning renaying
yearns renays; senary
years eyras; sayer
yeas easy; eyas
yeast Yeats
yeasts sayest

Yeats yeast
Yecla lacey
yede eyed; yeed
yeed eyed; yede
yegg eggy
Yeisk skiey
yell Lely
yelts style
Yemen enemy
yen Ney
yens syne
yep Pye
yerd drey; dyer; Ryde
yerds dreys; dyers
yes sey; sye
yesk keys; Skye; syke
yesks Sykes
yes-man yamens
yestern styrene
Yes Tor oyster; rosety; storey;
  Troyes; tyroes
yet tye
yew wey; wye
yews weys; wyes
Yeysk skyey
Yezo oyez
Ygerne energy; greeny
yielder reedily
yill illy; lily
ylem elmy; Lyme
Ymir miry; rimy
yob boy
yobbo booby
yobs boys; sybo
yodel odyle; yodle
yodels yodles
yodle odyle; yodel
yodles yodels
yoga Goya
yogurt grouty
yon noy
yonder Rodney
Yonkers Orkneys
yore oyer
Ypres preys; pyres
Yssel lyses; sleys
yug guy
yulan unlay

Z

Zabian banzai
zabra bazar
zabras bazars
zaffer zaffre
zaffre zaffer
Zahle hazel
zeal laze
zebra braze

zebras brazes
zein Inez
Zelda lazed
zerda razed
zeriba braize
Zeus Suez
zo Oz
zoned dozen

Cognate Anagrams

A cognate anagram is a special variety of anagram in which the letters of a word or phrase are transposed to form another word or phrase which redefines, or is closely related in meaning to, the original. Listed here are some outstanding examples, both ancient and modern, of this most impressive aspect of the anagrammatic art.

ABANDON HOPE ALL YE WHO ENTER HERE
    Hear Dante! Oh, beware yon open hell
ABSENCE MAKES THE HEART GROW FONDER
    He wants back dearest gone from here
ACTIONS SPEAK LOUDER THAN WORDS
    Talk or airs can not show up deeds
ACTORS
    Or cast
ADELINA PATTI
    Italian adept
ADOLF HITLER
    Hated for ill
ADVERTISEMENTS
    i.e. tradesman's TV
AFTERMATH
    At the farm

AIRFIELDS
    Aid fliers
ALEC GUINNESS
    Genuine class
ALFRED TENNYSON, POET LAUREATE
    Neat sonnet or deep tearful lay
ALISON STEADMAN
    A main lass noted
ALLEGORIES
    Lies galore
ALPHABETICALLY
    I play all the ABC
AMENITY
    Any time
AMERICAN
    Main race
AMERICAN INDIAN
    I red man, I an Inca
ANAGRAMS
    Ars Magna
AND WHEN DID YOU LAST SEE YOUR FATHER?
    A roundhead: "Thy sire flew on Tuesday?"
ANGERED
    Enraged
ANIMOSITY
    Is no amity
ARABIAN DESERT
    A date is barren
THE ARCTIC CIRCLE
    Chart ice circlet
THE ARISTOCRACY
    A rich Tory caste
ASININE
    Is inane
ASPERITY
    Yet I rasp
ASPERSION
    No praises
ASSEVERATION
    As one avers it

ASTHENIC
  Thin case
ASTRONAUT
  Unto a star
ASTRONOMER
  Moon-starer
ASTRONOMERS
  On! More stars!
ATHLETICS
  Lithe acts
AYE
  Yea
BALANCE SHEETS
  Cash table seen
BALLESTEROS
  Balls or tees
BARBARA WINDSOR
  A bird, a bra's worn
BARGAIN SALE
  An aisle grab
BASTARD
  Sad brat
BATHING GIRLS
  In slight garb
THE BEATLES
  These bleat
BELLIGERENTS
  Rebelling set
BENEATH THE SOD
  Death – then be so
BENEDICTIONS
  Cited benison
THE BEST THINGS IN LIFE ARE FREE
  Nail-biting refreshes the feet
BLANDISHMENT
  Blinds the man
THE BLARNEY STONE
  Blather sent on ye
THE BOARDING HOUSE
  This abode o' hunger

BONE IDLE
    Lie on bed
BOYFRIEND
    Yen of bird
BRIGANDAGE
    A big danger
BROADCASTER
    Bred as actor
BURNISHING
    Shining rub
BUTTERFLY
    Flutter by
CARRIER PIGEONS
    Racing o'er spire
CHAPELMASTER
    Psalm teacher
CHARISMA
    Is a charm
CHARITABLENESS
    I can bless earth
CHARLES, PRINCE OF WALES
    Flaws license reproach
CHOIRMAN
    Harmonic
CHRISTIAN
    Rich saint
CHRISTIANITY
    (i) Charity's in it   (ii) I cry that I sin
CIDER WITH ROSIE
    (i) Dire erotic wish   (ii) Is rhetoric wide?
CIRCUMSTANTIAL EVIDENCE
    Actual crime isn't evinced
CLACTON-ON-SEA
    On clean coast
CLEANLINESS
    All niceness
CLINT EASTWOOD
    Old West action
COMBINE HARVESTERS
    Betrim corn sheaves

COMPASSIONATENESS
Stamps one as so nice
COMPOUND INTEREST
Sum to do in per cent
CONIFER
Fir cone
CONSERVATIVE
Not vice versa
THE CONSERVATIVE PARTY
Teacher in vast poverty
CONSIDERATE
Care is noted
CONSTRAINT
Can not stir
CONTEMPLATION
  (i) On mental topic   (ii) Time to con plan
CONTRADICTION
Accord not in it
CONVERSATION
Voices rant on
THE COUNTRYSIDE
No city dust here
COUPLES
Up close
CROCODILE TEARS
Cries do act role
CURTAILMENT
Terminal cut
CUSTOMS AND EXCISE
Cussed 'incomes' tax
DANTE GABRIEL ROSSETTI
Greatest idealist born
THE DAWNING
Night waned
DEBENTURES
Ensure debt
THE DECAMERON
Read them once
DECIMAL POINT
I'm dot in place

DECLARATION
   An oral edict
DELICATESSEN
   Ensliced eats
DENNIS WATERMAN
   Warm and intense
DESEGREGATION
   Negroes get aid
DESIGNATION
   Is a denoting
THE DETECTIVES
   Detect thieves
DEVOTIONAL SONGS
   God loves not a sin
DISCONSOLATE
   Is not solaced
DISCOUNTER
   Reductions
DISCRETION
   Consider it
DISEMBARKATION
   Drake's ambition
DISRAELI
   I lead, sir
DISTILLATION
   Do it in a still
DOCTOR FAUSTUS
   Crafts outdo us
DOLCE FAR NIENTE
   After indolence
A DOMESTICATED ANIMAL
   Docile, as man tamed it
DORMITORY
   Dirty room
DYNAMITE
   May end it
EARNESTNESS
   A stern sense
THE ECONOMIST
   He tots income

THE EIFFEL TOWER
  Flew flit o'er thee
ELEVEN PLUS TWO
  Twelve plus one
ENDEARMENT
  Tender name
THE END OF THE WORLD IS NIGH
  Down this hole, frightened
EPISCOPALIANISM
  Claim a pope is sin
ETERNAL DEVOTION
  I note ardent love
ETERNITY
  Entirety
THE EYES
  They see
FAINT-HEARTED
  Hinted at fear
FAITHLESSNESS
  This falseness
FAMILIES
  Life's aim
A FAREWELL TO ARMS
  Tale of war's realm
FELICITY KENDAL
  Liked act finely
FLIRTING
  Trifling
FLOAT
  Aloft
FLORENCE NIGHTINGALE
  Flit on, cheering angel!
FLYING BOAT
  Floating by
FOOL'S PARADISE
  So ideal for sap
FORESTER
  For trees
FOR MANY ARE CALLED BUT FEW ARE CHOSEN
  Half of a crowd? Nay, e'er a select number!

FRENCH REVOLUTION
  Violence run forth
FRIENDS AND NEIGHBOURS
  Abhor finding rudeness
GARAGE MECHANICS
  Change car's image
GENERAL PINOCHET
  (i) Chile parent gone   (ii)The replacing one
A GENTLEMAN
  Elegant man
GERARD MANLEY HOPKINS
  A lord-hymner speaking
GOLDEN WEDDINGS
  Sign long wedded
GRACE DARLING
  Ace, grand girl
GRAND FINALE
  A flaring end
THE GUARDIAN
  Naught I read
HAM SANDWICHES
  Dish a man chews
HAROLD WILSON
  (i) Who's'n old liar?   (ii) All show or din
HENRY WADSWORTH LONGFELLOW
  Won half the New World's glory
HERMAPHRODITE
  Adept him or her
HIBERNATED
  Bed in earth
HMS PINAFORE
  Name for ship
HORATIO NELSON
  (i) Lo! Nation's hero   (ii) Honor est a Nilo
HOUSES OF PARLIAMENT
  A pile for us on Thames
IDENTIFIED
  I defined it
IMPERSONATION
  Apers in motion

IMPETUS
    Time's up!
INCOME TAXES
    Exact monies
INCOMPREHENSIBLE
    Problem in Chinese
INDIRA GANDHI
    Had Indian rig
INDOMITABLENESS
    Endless ambition
INNOMINATE
    No name in it
INSURANCE POLICIES
    Coin is in sure place
INSURGENT
    Unresting
INTEGRAL CALCULUS
    Calculating rules
IN THE GLOAMING
    Main light gone
INTOXICATE
    Excitation
INTRUSION
    Is to run in
THE IRISH NATION
    Oh, that is in Erin
IVANHOE BY SIR WALTER SCOTT
    A novel by a Scottish writer
JAMES STUART
    A just master
JEANNE D'ARC, MAID OF ORLEANS
    As a man, rejoined old France
THE KINSEY REPORT
    Try pokes in there
KINGSLEY AMIS
    Slimy ink sage
KYLIE MINOGUE
    I like me young
LADY CHATTERLEY'S LOVER
    (i) Act really served hot

(ii) Hero, varlet, acted slyly
(iii) Hey! tart served locally
(iv) Loved lechery, salty art
(v) The clearly loved satyr
LANZAROTE
Laze or tan
LAURENCE OLIVIER
(i) A virile cruel one   (ii) I value a nicer role
THE LAW OF SELF-PRESERVATION
What a preventer of life loss!
THE LEAGUE OF NATIONS
Ah, late foes get union
THE LEANING TOWER OF PISA
What a foreign stone pile!
THE LEGAL PROFESSION
Sole great help of sin
A LIBEL SUIT
I'll sue a bit
LIFE INSURANCE
I rule finances
LIKENESS
Ilk's seen
LONG-DISTANCE
STD line can go
LOOK BACK IN ANGER
Bleak croaking on
LORD PETER WIMSEY
Mostly weird peer
THE LORD'S PRAYER
Thy errors plead
THE LOST PARADISE
Earth's ideal spot
LOWSPIRITEDNESS
Depressed wilts
LUBRICATION
Act, rub oil in
MADAM CURIE
Radium came
MANDELA
Lead, man

MANY A TRUE WORD IS SPOKEN IN JEST
  Men joke and so win trusty praise
MARCEL PROUST
  (i) Corrupt males   (ii) Oral spectrum
MARGARET THATCHER
  (i) That great charmer
  (ii) Great charm threat
  (iii) Meg, the arch tartar
MARRIAGE
  A grim era
MARTIN AMIS
  Art's minima
MARTIN SCORSESE
  Screen is a storm
MARY WHITEHOUSE
  (i) I may rue the show
  (ii) Is mouthy, we hear
  (iii) The wise harm you
A MASTERPIECE
  See me, I cap art
MATERNITY HOSPITAL
  I pity natal mothers
MEADOWS
  As mowed
MEASURED
  Made sure
MEASUREMENTS
  Man uses meter
MEAT BALLS
  Stale lamb
MEDICATION
  I made tonic
MELTON MOWBRAY
  Town, memorably
MEPHISTOPHELES
  The hopeless imp
METAPHYSICIANS
  Mystics in a heap
METHODIST CHURCH
  Christ doeth much

MICHAEL CURL
    I recall much
MICHAEL JACKSON
    (i) He can mock jails   (ii) Jail can shock me
MIDWINTER WEATHER
    Wind, rime, wet earth
MIGUEL CERVANTES DE SAAVEDRA
    Gave us a damned clever satire
MINCE PIES
    Spice in 'em
MISANTHROPE
    Spare him not
MISCHIEF-MAKER
    Mark if I scheme
MISFORTUNE
    Oft ruins me
MISREPRESENTATION
    Interpret one amiss
MODULATION
    I am not loud
THE MONA LISA
    Ah, not a smile?
MOONLIGHT
    Thin gloom
MOONLIGHT SERENADE
    An old-time song here
THE MORSE CODE
    Here come dots
MOUNTEBANK
    Meant bunko
MOUSTACHE
    Mouth case
MUTTERING
    Emit grunt
NESSITERAS RHOMBOPTERYX
(Scientific name for the Loch Ness Monster, coined by Sir Peter Scott)
    Monster hoax by Sir Peter S.
NOMINATE
    A mention

THE NUDIST COLONY
    No untidy clothes
NUMERALS
    Mensural
NUMISMATIST
    Mint is a must
OLD ENGLAND
    Golden land
OLD-FASHIONED WINTER
    I folded earth in snow
OLD MASTERS
    Art's models
OLIVER WENDELL HOLMES
    He'll do in mellow verse
ONE-ARMED BANDIT
    A damned iron bet
ONE GOOD TURN DESERVES ANOTHER
    No rogues never do endorse that!
ORATOR
    To roar
OUR FATHER WHO ART IN HEAVEN
    In woe, haven for a hurt heart
OUTSIDE BROADCAST
    Be sad, studio actors
PARISHIONER
    I hire parson
PARISH PRIEST
    Spirit shaper
PARLIAMENT
    Partial men
PATENIR
    Painter
PATERNAL
    (i) Parental   (ii) Pre-natal
PATRICK MOORE
    I'm a rocket pro
PAYMENT RECEIVED
    Every cent paid me
PETER ABELARD
    Bleeder apart

PETER OOSTERHUIS
  See pro hit so true
PETER SCUDAMORE
  Presumed to race
PIETRO ANNIGONI
  I ignore no paint
PIRATES
  Sea trip
PITTANCE
  A cent tip
POACHERS
  Cop hares
POCKET HANDKERCHIEF
  Oft reach'd pink cheek
POINT
  On tip
POLICEMAN
  Menial cop
POLICE PROTECTION
  Let cop cope in riot
POSTMAN
  No stamp?
THE POSTMASTER-GENERAL
  He's top letters manager
PREDESTINATION
  I pertain to ends
PREMEDITATION
  I ponder it, mate
PRESBYTERIAN
  Best in prayer
PRODUCE
  Due crop
PROSECUTOR
  Court poser
THE PUBLIC ART GALLERIES
  Large picture halls, I bet
PUNISHMENT
  Nine thumps
RADICAL REFORM
  Rare mad frolic

RAIDERS OF THE LOST ARK
 Ford, the real star, is OK
RALPH WALDO EMERSON
 Person whom all read
REALISTIC
 It is clear
REGINALD MAUDLING
 In a glaring muddle
REMUNERATION
 Our men earn it
REQUIESCAT
 (i) Quiet acres   (ii) 'e quits care
RESTRAINT
 Start rein
RETRACTIONS
 To recant, sir
REVOLUTION
 Love to ruin
RHAPSODY IN BLUE
 Rush led by piano
RICHMAL CROMPTON
 Control imp charm
RIDICULOUS
 Ludicrous, I
RINGED PLOVER
 Proven glider
ROALD AMUNDSEN
 Laud'd Norseman
ROBIN GOODFELLOW
 Wood elf or goblin
ROBINSON CRUSOE BY DANIEL DEFOE
 Friday – one boon on becursed isle
A ROLLING STONE GATHERS NO MOSS
 Stroller, on go, amasses nothing
ROMEO AND JULIET
 Ole! Junior mated
ROME WAS NOT BUILT IN A DAY
 Any labour I do wants time
RONALD REAGAN
 (i) A darn long era   (ii) An oral danger

RUSSIANS
    As in USSR
SADAM HUSSEIN
    (i) Had assumed sin   (ii) Has sudden aims
SAINT ELMO'S FIRE
    Is lit for seamen
SAINT GEORGE AND THE DRAGON
    Aha! Strong giant ended ogre
SAINTLINESS
    Least in sins
SALMAN RUSHDIE
    (i) Read, shun Islam   (ii) Rue Islam's hand
SANDWICH TERN
    Wind-snatcher
SATISFACTION
    An act is so fit
SAUCINESS
    Causes sin
SAY IT WITH FLOWERS
    We flirt so this way
SCHOOLMASTER
    The classroom
SCOTTISH NATIONAL PARTY
    Oh! nasty tartan politics
SEA VIEW
    i.e. waves
SECLUSION
    Closes us in
SEMAPHORE
    See arm hop
SEMOLINA
    Is no meal
SENECA
    Scenae
A SENTENCE OF DEATH
    Faces one at the end
SEPARATION
    One is apart
SHEENA EASTON
    She's a neat one

SHIRLEY WILLIAMS
    I whirl aimlessly
A SHOPLIFTER
    Has to pilfer
THE SIGN OF THE CROSS
    He's right to confess
SILVER AND GOLD
    Grand old evils
A SILVER MINE
    I've minerals
A SIREN
    I snare
SIR PATRICK MAYHEW
    Make wry Irish pact
SKIN CARE
    Risk acne
SLANDEROUS
    Done as slur
SLITHERED
    Slid there
SLOT MACHINES
    Cash lost in 'em
SNOOZED
    Dozes on
SOFTHEARTEDNESS
    Often sheds tears
SOUTHEND-ON-SEA
    See thou on sand
SOUTHERN CALIFORNIA
    Hot sun or life in a car
SPRING, SUMMER, AUTUMN, WINTER
    "Time's running past" we murmur
STAGHOUNDS
    A hunt's dogs
STATUE OF LIBERTY
    Built to stay free
STEALTHY
    At the sly
STEAMINESS
    Seen as mist

STIPEND
    Spend it
A STITCH IN TIME SAVES NINE
    This is meant as incentive
STOCKHAUSEN
    A tune shocks
STONE DEAF
    Tones fade
STRAIT-LACED
    A deal strict
SUGGESTION
    It eggs us on
SUNSHINE AND SHADOW
    Show in sun and shade
SURGEON
    Go, nurse
SUSPENDED ANIMATION
    Supine man is not dead
THE TAMING OF THE SHREW
    Her mate won the fights
TANTRUMS
    Must rant
TAX COLLECTION
    Exact coin toll
TED HEATH
    (i) Had teeth   (ii) The death
A TELEPHONE GIRL
    Repeating "Hello"
TEMPESTUOUS
    Seems put out
TEMPORISED
    Or time sped
TEN COMMANDMENTS
    Can't mend most men
THEODORE ROOSEVELT
    Hero told to oversee
THERAPEUTICS
    The cure is apt
THIS EAR
    It hears

THUNDERSTORM
  Thor must rend
TIMOTHY WEST
  Most witty, he
TIN CANS
  Stannic
TO CAST PEARLS BEFORE SWINE
  One's labor is perfect waste
TONY BLAIR
  Tory in Lab.
TONY BLAIR M.P.
  I'm Tory plan B
TONY BLAIR'S LABOUR PARTY
  Or playboy's brutal train
TORTOISE-SHELL BUTTERFLY
  O, it'll flutter by the roses
TOTAL ABSTAINER
  Is not late at bar
THE TOWERING INFERNO
  Not worth fire engine
TOWER OF LONDON
  One old fort now
TRAGEDIAN
  Egad, I rant
TRAIN
  It ran
TREACHEROUS
  Ruse or cheat
TREASURE ISLAND
  (i) A sail returned
  (ii) Set insular read
  (iii) Sure is darn tale
TREPAN
  Entrap
TRIBULATIONS
  Is but on trial
A TRIP AROUND THE WORLD
  Hard to plan wider tour
TRUSTWORTHINESS
  I now stress truth
T.S. ELIOT
  Litotes

TWENTY THOUSAND LEAGUES UNDER THE SEA
 Huge water tale stuns – end had you tense
TWINGES
 We sting
UNDER MILK WOOD
 Rum do now liked
UNDIPLOMATIC
 Mad, unpolitic
UNIFORMITY
 I form unity
UNITED
 In duet
THE UNITED STATES BUREAU OF FISHERIES
 I raise the bass to feed us in the future
THE UNITED STATES OF AMERICA
 Attaineth its cause, freedom
UNRIGHTEOUSNESS
 Guess then our sin
UPHOLSTERERS
 Restore plush
THE US LIBRARY OF CONGRESS
 It's only for research bugs
VACATION TIMES
 I'm not as active
VALETUDINARIAN
 A nature invalid
VERSATILITY
 Variety list
VICTORIA, ENGLAND'S QUEEN
 Governs a nice quiet land
VIETNAMESE
 Seem native
VILLAINOUSNESS
 An evil soul's sin
VIRGINIA BOTTOMLEY
 I'm an evil Tory bigot
VOCIFERATIONS
 Strain of voice
A VOLCANIC MOUNTAIN
 Lava in a conic mount

THE WAGES OF SIN IS DEATH
  It's owed Satan high fees
WAITRESS
  A stew, sir?
THE WATER BABIES
  Bathers a bit wee
WESTERN UNION
  No wire unsent
WHITHERSOEVER
  Oh, wherever 'tis
WILDCAT
  It claw'd
WILLIAM CLINTON
  I'm it, an ill clown
WILLIAM EWART GLADSTONE
  (i) Wild agitator means well
  (ii) We want a mild legislator
  (iii) Wit so great will lead men
WILLIAM SHAKESPEARE
  (i) We all make his praise
  (ii) I am a weakish speller
WILLIAM SHATNER
  Well, I am in trash
WILLIAM WALDEGRAVE
  Will wage dim veal war
WISE MEN
  Misween
WOODY ALLEN
  A lewd loony
YELLOW FEVER
  Feel very low
YORKSHIRE PUDDING
  Hungry, risk odd pie

21st Century Synonym and Antonym Finder

Barbara Ann Kipfer Ph.D.

This extensive modern word finder combines the thoroughness of the classic thesaurus with the rapid-access format of synonym and antonym sources. Students, professionals and business people will find a wide variety of appropriate contemporary synonyms and antonyms to help them create documents that convey instructions and ideas with power and precision. Today having the right word for the right occasion is more important than ever, and the *21st Century Synonym and Antonym Finder* offers more features and more word choices than any other paperback word finder.

- Created by a leading expert in linguistics and lexicography
- The only synonym and antonym finder that includes definitions and parts of speech for each main entry
- Alphabetical listing of over 200,000 synonyms and antonyms
- Plentiful selections accompany thousands of main entries
- Modern preferred usages – no useless archaic or obsolete words
- Pocket-size for use at home, school or office

Roget's 21st Century Thesaurus
Barbara Ann Kipfer Ph.D.

'. . . outstanding value . . . *Roget's 21st Century Thesaurus* usefully combines the functions of both dictionary *and* thesaurus, with brief definitions of the words introducing the lists of their synonyms. Here, the synonym count is as high as one could well conceive – no fewer than 48 for 'brave'.
Times Educational Supplement

'Undoubtedly a more efficient system . . . a fine reference book.'
Scotsman

'Exceptional . . . unique words and groupings . . . This resource is a gem!'
Booklist

'Outstanding!'
American Bookseller

'User-friendly . . . great value for money.'
Middlesbrough Evening Gazette

Combining scholarly authority with a new awareness of today's communication demands, *Roget's 21st Century Thesaurus* is the simple, reliable way to find the perfect words for your needs. It features an easy-to-use dictionary format plus a revolutionary concept index that arranges words by idea, thus enhancing the user's process of association, and leading to scores of additional selections. The inclusion of a wide spectrum of words and phrases with each new entry – from sophisticated choices to completely new vocabulary in the language – brings users an exceptional number of alternatives to fit any variation of style and tone.